Henry Havard

Picturesque Holland

a journey in the provinces of Friesland, Groningen, Drenthe, Overyssel, Guelders and

Limbourg

Henry Havard

Picturesque Holland
a journey in the provinces of Friesland, Groningen, Drenthe, Overyssel, Guelders and Limbourg

ISBN/EAN: 9783743438149

Printed in Europe, USA, Canada, Australia, Japan

Cover: Foto ©Andreas Hilbeck / pixelio.de

Manufactured and distributed by brebook publishing software (www.brebook.com)

Henry Havard

Picturesque Holland

PICTURESQUE HOLLAND

LONDON: PRINTED BY
SPOTTISWOODE AND CO., NEW-STREET SQUARE
AND PARLIAMENT STREET

DEVENTER.

PICTURESQUE HOLLAND

A JOURNEY IN THE PROVINCES OF FRIESLAND,
GRONINGEN, DRENTHE, OVERYSSEL,
GUELDERS AND LIMBOURG

BY

HENRY HAVARD

AUTHOR OF 'A VISIT TO THE DEAD CITIES OF THE ZUYDER ZEE'

ILLUSTRATED BY 10 ENGRAVINGS ON WOOD AND A MAP OF THE NETHERLANDS

LONDON
RICHARD BENTLEY & SON, NEW BURLINGTON STREET
Publishers in Ordinary to Her Majesty the Queen
1876

All rights reserved

CONTENTS.

CHAPTER I.

A word of explanation—A geographical annexation—Ethnological discussion—Preparations 1

CHAPTER II.

The departure—'Aurora'—Love of the old-fashioned—Sneek goes forth to the wars—Great men and little women . 9

CHAPTER III.

Bolsward—A genealogical difficulty—St. Martin—The 'Stadhuis' and its riches 23

CHAPTER IV.

Sneek Lake—Joure—The peat bogs of Schoterland—Heerenveen and the 'Oranjewoud' 33

CHAPTER V.

Leeuwarden—Its prisons—An improvised play—The Chancellerie—The château of Cammingha—History of the Saint Eelko Liaukama 45

CHAPTER VI.

The 'Schier-Stins'—The wood of the murder—Dockum—The miraculous spring—The 'Harmonie' . . . 56

CHAPTER VII.

North Friesland—Schiermonnikoog—A hot reception—A model Burgomaster—Saint Willibrord and the Downs—Awkward beds 66

CHAPTER VIII.

Zoutkamp — Grijpskerk — Groningen — Military and commercial history — The churches—Architecture — Two heavy law actions—Riperda—The Academy—The Deaf and Dumb Institute 77

CHAPTER IX.

The Midwolde tomb—Delfzijl and Farmsum—Appingedam—The Harddraverij—Female barge towers . . . 105

CHAPTER X.

Winschoten—The monument of Heiligerlee—Nieuwe Beerta—The 'Beklemming'—The 'Boerderijen'—A model school . 121

CHAPTER XI.

Drenthe—The country and the peasants—The 'Hunnebedden'—Zuidlaren and Tijnaarloo—Assen and its ethnological museum—The history of a chignon 136

CHAPTER XII.

Steenwijk—A heroic siege—Meppel—The penitentiary colony of Veenhuizen 154

CHAPTER XIII.

The villages of Drenthe, Rolde, Eext, Gieten, Borger, and Exlo —A rural printing-office—Lost!—The pastor of Zweelo—Koevorden 169

CHAPTER XIV.

The old Salian country—Deventer—Its military history—Edward Stanley and Colonel Taxis—Saint Lievin and the Bergkerk—A painting by Terburg—The 'Donat' of the Athenæum and the 'Reynardus Vulpes'—Kijkindepot . 188

CHAPTER XV.

Apeldoorn — The Loo — An abdication — Zutphen—Pillage — Hollandsche Tuin—A letter from Louvois—Archives—The museum—Saint Walburgus and Notre Dame . . 213

CHAPTER XVI.

Nederlandsch Mettray—Hengelo—Euschede conflagration—Almelo — Oldenzaal — Saint Plechelme — The Hunnebed of Oldenzaal 238

CHAPTER XVII.

Doesburg—Doetinchem—The Kruisberg—The Koloniaal Militair invalidenhuis — Dutch Switzerland — Rosendaal—Zonsbeek and Biljoen 257

CHAPTER XVIII.

Arnhem—'Vir Bonus'—The Arnhemse fabrique—Saint Eusebius and Saint Walburgus—The Devil's House—Carnival of 1525—Pleasures and amusements — 'Gelre! Gelre!'—The Rhine and the Waal 275

CHAPTER XIX.

Nymegen—The Valckh of Charlemagne's Chapel—Insurrections—Town hall and museum—The peace of Nymegen—The Houtenrokken—Saint Stephen—'Sic vos non vobis' . 296

CHAPTER XX.

Grave—Duke Arnold—The defence of Grave by Chamilly—Carnot's maxim—The Church of Saint Elizabeth—The charnel house 324

CHAPTER XXI.

The Mookerheide—Venlo—Saint Martin—Vanitas vanitatum—
An ambitious inscription—The celebrated sons of Venlo . 340

CHAPTER XXII.

Roermond—Flemish Catholicism—Small chapels—A work of
ingenuity and patience—The Munster—Saint Christopher—
Patriotic poetry—Introduction of the pipe . . . 353

CHAPTER XXIII.

Maëstricht—Ancient souvenirs—The outskirts of Wijck—
History of a chapel-master—The Gate of Hell—Notre Dame
—Saint Servais—The Chapel of Charlemagne—The fair of
relics—The Treasury and the archives—Purgatory—The
miraculous stone 370

CHAPTER XXIV.

Maëstricht (conclusion)—The Town Hall—The Library—The
promenades—*Pietersberg* and the Bohemians . . . 399

CHAPTER XXV.

Conclusion 411

ILLUSTRATIONS.

DEVENTER	*Frontispiece*	
THE WATER-GATE OF SNEEK . . .	*to face page*	15
THE TOWN HALL OF BOLSWARD	,,	30
LEEUWARDEN (THE CHANCELLERIE) . .	,,	46
THE *COLLECTHUIS* AT GRONINGEN . . .	,,	80
THE *HUNNEBEDDEN* OF TIJNAARLOO . . .	,,	147
THE CHURCH OF KOEVORDEN . . .	,,	183
ZUTPHEN (BANKS OF THE BERKEL) . . .	,,	219
NYMEGEN (THE GREAT MARKET-PLACE) . . .	,,	319
MAËSTRICHT (ANCIENT RAMPARTS) . . .	,,	371
MAP OF THE NETHERLANDS	*to face page*	1

ILLUSTRATIONS.

DEVENTER	*Frontispiece*
THE WATER-GATE OF SNEEK . . .	*to face page* 15
THE TOWN HALL OF BOLSWARD	,, 30
LEEUWARDEN (THE CHANCELLERIE) . .	,, 46
THE *COLLECTHUIS* AT GRONINGEN . . .	,, 89
THE *HUNNEBEDDEN* OF TIJNAARLOO . . .	,, 147
THE CHURCH OF KOEVORDEN . . .	,, 183
ZUTPHEN (BÀNKS OF THE BERKEL) . . .	,, 219
NYMEGEN (THE GREAT MARKET-PLACE) . . .	,, 319
MAËSTRICHT (ANCIENT RAMPARTS) . . .	,, 371
MAP OF THE NETHERLANDS	*to face page* 1

PICTURESQUE HOLLAND.

CHAPTER I.

A WORD OF EXPLANATION—A GEOGRAPHICAL ANNEXATION—
ETHNOLOGICAL DISCUSSION—PREPARATIONS.

THE time is not far removed, when to cross the frontiers of France was sufficient in the eyes of the public of that country, to constitute a hardy explorer. Thirty years ago the excursions of Théophile Gautier in Spain, of Paul de Musset in Italy, and of Victor Hugo on the banks of the Rhine, attained the proportions of voyages of discovery. Sterne's 'Sentimental Journey' was exhumed, and Töpffer's 'Zigzags' again found admiring readers.

Since that time a revolutionary change has taken place. Steam, in traversing the ocean and covering continents with a network of iron roads, has diminished and nearly dissolved distances ; and, the telegraph, in revealing each evening the course of the events of the day in the four corners of the world, has brought the ends of the earth together. So true is this, that nothing short of a voyage round the world, or the discovery of some new kingdom, excites public interest and arrests public attention.

There is no exaggeration in this. Travels, which of old would have been accounted fantastic, seem now-a-days to be natural and commonplace.

Yesterday Australia, Java, Jeddo, and San Francisco were unveiled by the Count de Beauvoir.

It was Indo-China that we ran through with the lamented Francis Garnier, China that we visited with Messieurs Cernuschi and Duret, or the two continents that we traversed in the genial society of Count Gabriac.

To-day the Marquis of Compiègne takes us for a walk across the deserts of Equatorial Africa. To-morrow Stanley, or our valiant countrymen De Brazza and Marche, will relate their daring explorations of an unknown continent, if they chance to return to tell what they saw in such dreary, deadly solitudes.

In these circumstances it needs great audacity or very special reasons to venture again to talk of a quiet, commonplace, loyal, and hospitable country distant twelve hours from Paris, where cruel carnivora and highway robbers are conspicuous by their absence.

Although it is easy to defend the proposition that the nearest countries are neither the best known nor the easiest to make acquaintance with, I must conscientiously avow that my audacity would have failed me if I had not strong reasons first to undertake and then to relate the travels which I now publish. I feel bound to account to my readers for the motives which are at once, the explanation and apology of my book.

When I prepared the second edition of my journeyings to the Dead Cities of the Zuyder Zee, I had the curiosity to hunt up all that had been published in Germany regarding the countries of which I had revived the history.

Among these books was one entitled 'Leitfaden für den Unterricht in der Geographie.' I glanced over it at first with little interest, but my indifference was short-lived.

On two occasions this little book made mention of the kingdom of the Low Countries, and each time the Netherlands were swallowed up in Germany.

The first mention was when speaking of the States of Central Europe (p. 90). The Netherlands were classed under the head of 'Germany' ('Deutschland'), in a numerous and comely company, however—to wit, Denmark, Belgium, Luxemburg, Switzerland, and the Grand Duchy of Lichtenstein. The second occasion (p. 173) placed it again in the same category, but under a more specific designation—'Deutsche Aussenländer' (Trans-Germania, or Outlying Germany), and this time the author gives his reasons for it.

'The six states above mentioned are regarded

as an appendage of Germany, (*a*) firstly, because they are in a great measure situated within the natural limits of Germany; and (*b*) secondly, because, with trifling exceptions, they belonged to the ancient German Empire; and in part because, until 1866, they were included in the Germanic Confederation.' Thus it will be seen, that this is a particularly cool geographical and historical annexation of six foreign countries.

I had scarcely recovered from the profound astonishment caused by this strange discovery, when the course of my studies brought me into contact with a learned German, who had come into the country to pursue certain investigations.

I thought myself the more entitled to call his attention to these scholastic eccentricities, because the book in question was not one of those commonplace publications, of which the exact meaning of the words used is of no importance. Written by Dr. Daniel, a learned professor of Halle, it has been revised and edited by Dr. Kirchhoff, professor of geography in the same university, and it has now run to a seventh edition, which is exhausted annually.

'Such errors,' I observed to my interlocutor, 'are a real danger. When thirty millions of square heads have admitted such things as truths from their cradles, it is difficult to convince them afterwards that they have been mistaken. You ought to hold it a point of honour to correct such dangerous and absurd errors.'

'I see nothing absurd or erroneous in it,' said my savant. 'Denmark, Switzerland, the Low Countries, and the other States which you have mentioned, are the natural completion of the Empire of Germany. Their manners, their language, their history, and their traditions all bind them to ancient Germany.'

'It is no business of mine,' said I, 'to answer for the other States. I know nothing of the Grand Duchy of Lichtenstein, and I have but a tourist's acquaintance with Switzerland, Luxemburg, and Denmark. I have only dwelt casually in Belgium; but the Netherlands are quite another matter. I have spent five years on this hospitable soil, and I can certify, for I am thoroughly aware—'

'Well, you know them ill. You have only seen the centre of the country, the sole part which has an autochthonous character. If you had traversed and studied the eastern provinces with the care you have bestowed upon those of the west, if you had dwelt, even for a few days, in the part bordering on Hanover and Westphalia, you would have seen the disappearance of differences, and the blending of the shades of diversity.'

'You will never persuade me,' I replied, 'that these provinces have an overweening affection for you. Your own writers, too, frankly avow the contrary. Heinrich von Treitschke complains somewhat bitterly of the Lowland antipathy, and your novelist Gutzkow loudly cries "Treason."

'I agree to that. But we have other proofs of the community of origin. You know our patriotic song or saying, "Where is the country of Germany? As far as the German tongue is heard."'

'It would be a strange misapprehension to confound the language of Vondel, and Hooft, and Bilderdyk, and Da Costa with that of Goethe and Schiller. But even admitting your theory you would have to eliminate from your States North Slesvig, where nothing but Danish is spoken; Lorraine, which has never spoken German; and Alsace, where it was little known. Still further you would have to exclude, on the authority even of your infallible Chancellor,[1] all countries annexed for more than a century. You see that your song is discordant. What more have you?'

'Religion. . . . The two countries are Protestant.'

'Yes; but you are Lutherans, and the Dutch are Calvinists—a wide difference, unless you reckon the third of the nation which has remained Catholic; but this, I think, would be a false calculation.'

'In short, we have community of origin, similarity of race, the same blood, the same ethnical characteristics.'

---

[1] 'It is above all necessary that the study of the German language should be made on a wider and surer basis, not only in the province of Posen, but even in Upper Silesia and in Western Prussia' (Speech of Prince Bismarck in the Chamber of Peers, March 6, 1872). That was a sufficient recognition of the fact that German was scarcely used in the different provinces. On February 13 of the same year the same Minister said, in the Chamber of Deputies, 'The evangelical Pole, who will perhaps acknowledge a German as a minister of his faith, will never forget his nationality so far as to favour, from confessional zeal, the study of the German language.' It is difficult to be more explicit.

'This,' I rejoined, 'would have to be proved, but you surely must know that M. Quatrefages declares "all political arrangements founded on ethnology to be absurd," and that Prof. Virchow assents to this view. Moreover, it seems to me to be difficult enough to make a Dutchman avow himself to be a *mof*.[1]

'All I can tell you,' replied my impatient interlocutor, 'is that our learned men do not write carelessly, and that men like Daniel and Kirchhoff are never mistaken.'

There our confab ended; but, from that moment I made up my mind to traverse those frontier provinces, to explore them thoroughly, to ransack their traditions, and to learn their history at the fountain-head.

However easy this journey to the *threatened frontiers* appeared, it was in reality hedged round with all sorts of difficulties, and I needed above all a devoted companion, willing to dawdle with me in the tangled web of old parchments and the dusty monuments, which, among archæologists bring people who have passed away, to life again. Friendship furnished the companion. Baron de Constant-Rebecque offered to share my studies and my peregrinations. He was just the comrade I desired. A gentleman grafted on an artist, a cultivated, energetic, robust

[1] May not this be the origin of our English *muff*? It is a term without definite meaning, but is an expression of contempt, by which, in certain parts of Holland, the German people are designated.—*Translator's Note*.

individual, whose never-failing good humour charmed away all fatigue.

Our next need was to secure a sympathetic reception. It was absolutely necessary to visit libraries, ransack old archives, and find our way into fortresses. To accomplish this I applied to the highest authority in the country. M. Heemskerk, Minister of the Interior and President of the Council, received me with a refined courtesy, which demands my warmest acknowledgments. By his kind intervention, I obtained from his colleagues in the War Office and Department of Justice, all the introductions necessary.

'You are undertaking an unusual journey,' said the Minister when I took leave of him, 'in the course of which you will meet with difficulties; but I will take care to smooth your way for you as much as possible, in recommending you warmly to the governors of the provinces you are about to visit.'

And relying with good reason upon this kindly promise, we set out on June the 22nd, 1875.

CHAPTER II.

THE DEPARTURE—'AURORA'—LOVE OF THE OLD-FASHIONED—SNEEK GOES FORTH TO THE WARS—GREAT MEN AND LITTLE WOMEN.

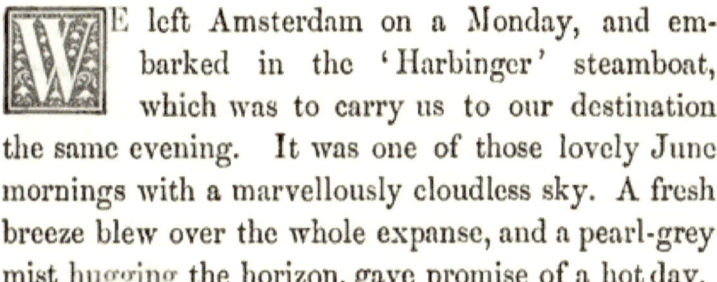E left Amsterdam on a Monday, and embarked in the 'Harbinger' steamboat, which was to carry us to our destination the same evening. It was one of those lovely June mornings with a marvellously cloudless sky. A fresh breeze blew over the whole expanse, and a pearl-grey mist hugging the horizon, gave promise of a hot day.

It was not without a certain emotion that we saw our boat shake herself, pass the river Y, and clear the sluices of Schellingwonde. We found ourselves once more in the midst of the Zuyder Zee, which we had so thoroughly explored two years before. This immense gulf greeted us, as a friend whom we met again. We passed the same banks and picturesque islands, traversing in a day as much as had taken a month to run through, leading us almost to fear that we should not again experience the pleasurable feelings which had left so charming a memory behind.

Marken, with its grassy slopes and wooden houses, Enkhuizen and its *hump*, Hindelopen and Stavoren, were they still in the land of the living? How surprising it would have been to have seen those dying cities regain a touch of youth—a little animation and fresh charms! And at the same time what fears of not seeing them all! Alas! if our apprehensions were groundless, so were our hopes. In the distance we saw those royal cities file past one by one, asleep on the shore of the grand gulf. As we saw them two years since so were they now—silent, impassive, awaiting in funereal solemnity, for old Time to complete his customary work.

That evening, at the appointed hour, we reached Harlingen. The little Friesland city had not changed its aspect. The harbour alone differed, the great basin at which they were working during our former visit, having been completed. A crowd assembled to witness the arrival of the steamboat. They greeted us cheerily, the porters took possession of our luggage, and we directed our steps to the hotel, the 'Heerenlogement.'

At daybreak the next morning we set out again. We traversed the still sleeping town to embark on board the Sneek boat, and here was the real commencement of our journey. We were, in the first instance, about to traverse Friesland, to travel southward to visit Sneek and Bolsward, and then turning our steps to the north-west, to touch at Leeuwarden in the north-east, then reach Dockum, cross the sea, and thus land at Schiermonnikoog.

The little screw-steamer in which we had taken

our passage was appropriately named the 'Aurora.' At six in the morning we set out, and after skirting the ramparts of the city, we boldly entered the Leeuwardervaart.

This is a long and tedious canal, bordered by those never-ending meadows which constitute the wealth of Friesland. Everywhere around us, to the boundary of our horizon, it was impossible to detect an undulation in the land. Grassy plains stretching their blue outlines on the grey morning sky, dark steeples, a few red roofs, an occasional hamlet, a large village, a small town with its gables and chimneys, formed the sky-line of the landscape. Nearer at hand those immense plains were dotted with cattle, with here and there a cottage, or one of those rich, substantial farm-houses, where everything indicated order and plenty.

This country is called the 'Paradise of Cows,' and never was name better bestowed. White and black, resplendent with health, buried up to their middle in this clean and rich herbage, the female inhabitants of those vast pasturages appeared to be surrounded by perfect happiness. From morn to eve, and from eve to morn, they enjoyed their quiet occupation. With sleepy eyes silently grazing, they selected their tufts, and gathered full-tongued their delicious repasts. Their dreams could not realise greater fortune, for they slept and ruminated.

Then there were brick-kilns, with their immense black roofs and strange balconies, and lime furnaces, with rounded, white, dome-shaped cupolas resembling mosques.

On the right were seen the spires of Hitsum, on the left those of Franeker, with its shady ramparts, and the country was enlivened by the belfries of Tjum, Winsum, and Spannum. The villages followed with their tidy houses and their yellow and blue blinds, where their thrifty housewives, in golden casques, thronged the thresholds, and exhibited their bright, great, copper jugs glistening in the sun.

Along the whole route we passed boats, and were saluted by the boatmen. They all wore red shirts, short blue and white breeches gripped at the knee, with thick, brown, woollen stockings. Their ruddy countenances, hair of infantine fairness, earrings, and bright, joyous smiles complete the picture. Behind them, peeping out of the open hatchways, were usually visible four or five curious heads struggling to see the steamboat pass, with staring eyes and mouths agape. Even to return their greeting caused joyful peals of laughter, which reverberated within the sides of the boats.

Above our heads flew the storks, traversing the canal with great beating of wings; also the *wulpen*, and flights of lapwings. Right and left the sea-gulls were our faithful companions, uttering plaintive cries, skimming the undulations caused by the boat, and constantly diving beneath the foam, to bring up little fishes in their long, slender beaks.

But Sneek appears in the distance, protected by

a rampart of verdure. Another turn ahead, the boat stops, and there we are.

Nothing is more charming than the approaches of these little Friesland towns. Old fortifications have made way for shady walks. Behind is left the green country, redolent of the sweet smell of new-mown hay. In front stretch lines of houses, shining and pretty, with white wood-work and spotless windows. The good folks flock to the doors to see us pass, the gossips whisper, and the playing children raise their heads—all uniting in a greeting compounded of friendliness and curiosity.

Sneek, more than any other place, presents this aspect of hospitality and kindness. The principal streets are reached by a line of inns, and are themselves winding, not too broad, and exquisitely clean. They are bordered by low houses, which would seem to be in a Dutch town, were it not for the names ending in *a* over most of the doors. These first streets lead by a turning into the Grand Place, which is an elongated parallelogram of no great extent, and which can never be particularly lively, since two great girls were lying down lazily removing the grass between the stones with the points of their knives. Here, nevertheless, are the chief public buildings—the public 'Poids' or weigh-house, a large, ugly, commonplace shed; and the High Court, a very simple building of fair proportions, surmounted by an appropriate device.

The Town Hall, near at hand, is more than a

century older, and was finished in 1736. Its style is not particularly chaste, but the façade is curious, eccentric, and almost extravagant. In it the contortions of the rococo of the eighteenth century, are mixed up with the fluted wood carvings of Louis XIV. It is a two-storied building, with a raised courtyard, reached by a flight of steps. The roof is surmounted by an open belfry, and has corbels supported by the strangest brackets imaginable—children turned topsy-turvy, and grotesquely contortioned—while the flight of steps, surcharged with wood carvings, distinctive decorations, and vases, carries proudly the arms of the city. These arms are on a plate above the gate, in a tangle of ornaments, of palms and of foliage, overhanging a small stone lantern, gilded and painted red, which is the bright spot of this strange frontage.

In all this there is nothing very imposing or masterly. The old Town Hall, of which a drawing has been preserved by Blaeu, had a more severe and appropriate exterior. It was a large, noble structure, with three gables, crowned by two battlemented towers. Alongside of it was an old castle, the *Gruitersma Stins*, with projecting galleries, giving it the repulsive look of the fortifications of olden times. It had an imposing appearance, but when the rococo fever prevailed, the ancient structures were removed, and the existing coquettish *Stadhuis* was built.

The destructive effects of this fever did not stop there. It transformed to the taste of that time an old gate of the town, which now has the strangest

possible appearance. Picture to yourself two fine, brick-built, octagonal towers, with alternate ridges of stone, each crowned by an enormous pointed roof, loopholed for musketry, and with a decidedly warlike aspect.

To unite these fine towers is a heavy masonry foundation divided by two large openings, one over the other. These are surmounted by a gable, ornamented with three huge windows, bordered with carved foliage, over which is a balustraded belfry—all in the purest Louis XV. style.

Never has so singular a juxtaposition produced so strange an effect. At a distance the amalgam has a Chinese and Japanese look, and removes one some five thousand leagues from Sneek and Friesland.

This singularly restored gate rejoices in the name of *Hoogendster-pijp*, which means a water gate, because it surmounted the canal, of which it commanded the access. The lower part was large enough to allow boats to pass through, and the bridge over this bay is one of the highest points of the town, one of the rare spots never reached by inundation. The floods nevertheless often flowed along the streets of this pretty little Friesland town. In 1750, and in 1825 in particular, they caused great and irreparable destruction.

Of the tendency of this last disaster, as threatening the destruction of the whole of Friesland, mention has been made in my former work on the Zuyder Zee.

The waters had covered the country for several

days, when the neighbouring peasants, driven from their farms and villages, encamped with their cattle on the quays and streets, and sought an asylum from the generous little town.

In this way passed All Saints' Day, when in the evening, in spite of wind and rain, an attempt was made to light fires. Suddenly a terrible grinding noise was heard—the dikes of Sneek had burst, and in a few moments there were five feet of water in the town. The open spaces, streets, and quays all disappeared under this sudden flood. Wild with fear, the cattle burst their bonds, and the disorder was at its height. Carried away by the torrents which rushed in every direction, men, women, children, and cattle were cast into the canal and pitilessly drowned. For several hours the groans and cries of the victims mingled with the howling of the hurricane. Then there was silence, icy and terrible, for inexorable Death had closed for ever, the lips frozen by fear and cold.

Notwithstanding, several peasants found refuge on the bridge of the Old Gate, where, on this shaky shelter, they passed a fearful night, trying in vain to rescue some of the victims carried away by the current.

At daybreak a sad sight was unfolded. The carcases of cattle and their human companions, carried along by the current, were engulfed under their feet, to continue their cadaveric career far away. The green fields, covered by the floods, looked like floating cemeteries. Suddenly on the horizon, in the grey dawn, appeared a pale blue form, from which shrill and strange cries proceeded. As the phantom approached, the cries became more piercing, when a daring fisher hooked a cradle, in which were an infant and a cat. The cat, by its cries of terror, had attracted attention. The dear little cherub was asleep. Who was he? Whence came he? He was considered an orphan—which doubtless he was—was adopted by the city, and grew into a good citizen.

And the cat?

The cat! The writers of the sixteenth century took no note of cats, and so we know nothing more about it.

If floods were unfriendly to our little Friesland friend, fire was nearly as inexorable, for on a hundred occasions it carried its destruction across her streets and along her canals. The two most memorable visitations, were those of 1294 and 1456. In the first of these disastrous years the whole town was destroyed, with the exception of two houses almost miraculously preserved. In 1456 twenty-six houses perished in a single day from this destroying curse. Happily, these melancholy dates are now far removed, and Sneek has had time to heal her wounds. To see her to-day, smart and coquettish, with her shady canals and her dainty places, no one could realise the trials she has undergone.

Here and there good old houses with arabesqued gables or attics, alternate with wooden habitations, all, whether ancient or modern, being scrupulously clean and sedulously cared for. Add to this several good shops, particularly jewellers' and pastry-cooks',[1] and Sneek's pretension to be the capital of Friesland is easily explained, for the ambitious little town is not afraid of disputing with big Leeuwarden for the provincial sceptre—a quarrel of old standing. In the fifteenth century, when the turbulent towns of Friesland were skirmishing for the general emancipation of the province, each of them essayed to subdue the other; they waged internecine war with varying fortune, and Sneek in 1486 possessed the honour, if it be one, of vanquishing her rival. Their citizens were already marching to the siege of the distant capital, having fraternised with Franeker, when they fell in with two ladies, and then occurred one of those gallant adventures that occasionally cropped up in the Italian partisan campaigns. 'Whither are you bound?' enquired the two charmers. 'To the war,' responded our citizen heroes—'to the war of brave soldiers.' In the words of the old Venetian ballad—

> 'My gentle lord, whither away?'
> 'To the war I go, my pretty maid,
>   With soldiers brave to share the fray.'

'And with whom are we at war?' 'With Leeuwarden, to abate her pride.' But our fair travellers were honest maidens of Leeuwarden, and so they entreated

---

[1] All the small Dutch and Friesland towns possessed good jewellers' shops and pastrycooks, especially those surrounded by rich and fertile country. Like most other towns, Sneek has a cake of its own called *drabbelkoeken*.

with such tender prayers that all hearts were softened, the Sneekers halted, and after holding counsel, sent the gentle wayfarers with an ultimatum to their rival. It proved a fruitless mission, for the town was taken and sacked, and many of the most notable citizens were carried prisoners to Sneek. And it was thus in the fifteenth century, that Sneek fought for her supremacy.

But, to sustain her pretensions to a leading position, our little town is neither very ancient nor particularly well peopled. Her first appearance in the history of the province was in 1268, and in 1294, at the time of the great fire, her houses were all of wood, and she had scarcely a surrounding wall. Her population, which now numbers 8,000 or 9,000 souls, was probably never much in excess of the latter figure. Her industries, confined to a few textile factories, mills, and timber-yards, did not justify her lofty pretensions. The surrounding meadows are beautiful and productive, but so are those of Leeuwarden, and at the time of the war above referred to Sneek was actually inferior to her rival in those respects—for her chief wealth consisted in eels, which abounded in the vicinity, while that of Leeuwarden was made up of the fat of the land, the produce of her meadows and rich kine. The name of eel-merchants (*schieringers*) was applied to the Sneekers in the time of Blaeu, who mentioned that the eel-fishery was the chief source of their wealth.

But pride of pedigree, courage, and audacity

justified such pretensions in those days. Mention was made just now of the *condottieri*, and there is, in truth, much analogy between the contests of the small Italian Republics and those which caused bloodshed in the Friesland cities, and between the chiefs engaged in those little adventurous exploits, which scarcely attained the dignity of war.

The Church of St. Martin at Sneek contains the remains of one of the most renowned of these partisans—Peter van Heemstra, born no one knows exactly when or where—a bold chieftain on sea and land; feared everywhere—who breathed his last at Sneek on the 18th of October, 1520. This fiery fighter had some of the quaint characteristics of his time. He was nicknamed 'Lange Pier' ('Long Stone'), from his great height, and under this *nom de guerre* (the epithet is appropriate) he became renowned in Holland, Friesland, and Guelderland.

Lange Pier was not the only giant reared in Sneek, which boasted, with a better title than that of receiving the last breath of the big admiral, of having given the first breath to 'Grand Jakob,' who was authorised to add the name of his native town to his title of 'Lange Jakob,' to distinguish him from all other Jakobs, past, present, and to come.

Lange Jakob was over eight feet high, and stout in proportion; and, to verify the ancient adage that married couples should be well matched, the giant married a dwarf of scarcely forty-eight inches. She was known as 'Korte Jannitje' ('Little Jenny'). This pretty couple at the beginning of the last century were a source of endless fun to the good people of Sneek. They were invited everywhere, and even artists made capital out of them. A great engraver printed the giant's portrait, and a poet illustrated it with a couple of versicles, which may be thus interpreted: 'I am great externally,' said Lange Jakob, 'and have an equally capacious interior. I can lick the whole world in eating and drinking.' 'And I,' said his little spouse, 'am Little Jenny. If a woman is a plague abroad, and a pest at home, I am the smallest plague you can find.' Thus it will be seen that courtesy and gallantry had decreased in Sneek since the time when the two 'honest damsels' had softened all hearts with their tears and prayers.

The great Church of St. Martin, where Lange Pier and Lange Jakob lie together, is a vast structure dating from the second half of the fifteenth century, repaired in 1503, nearly reconstructed in 1682, and so transmuted as not to merit much attention. Besides, something may be said about it when we speak of the church of Bolsward, built on the same plan, and probably by the same architect.

Of late years another church, equally large and in good style, has been erected. It belongs to the semi-Byzantine, semi-Gothic fashion, which M. de Cuypers, a contemporary architect, has introduced into Holland. Its grand outlines are exhibited in the midst of the centennial trees ornamenting the old ramparts.

These ancient bastions are now a charming promenade, fashioned like an English garden, and form one of the most agreeable features of Sneek. Not that the inhabitants are destitute of others, for the love of Sneek is engraven on the heart of every good Dutchman, and the Frieslanders cherish it still more.

A young magistrate, who received us as an old friend, detailed to us with affectionate emotion the tranquil charms and thousand hidden beauties discoverable on more intimate acquaintance with these kindly little towns. 'Although not born here, I hope yet to pass long years in Sneek, where I have always been happy and contented.' Reflecting on this a little later on, I perceived that my friend was treated with well-merited distinction everywhere; had an agreeable house, a good cellar, a charming wife, and fine children.

With such adjuncts could not one be happy anywhere?

CHAPTER III.

BOLSWARD—A GENEALOGICAL DIFFICULTY—ST. MARTIN—THE 'STADHUIS AND ITS RICHES.

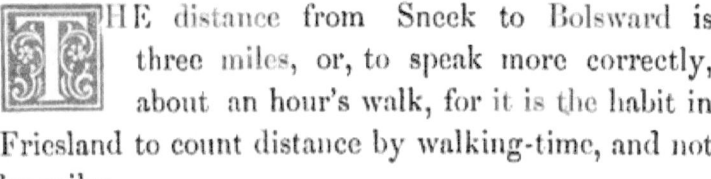HE distance from Sneek to Bolsward is three miles, or, to speak more correctly, about an hour's walk, for it is the habit in Friesland to count distance by walking-time, and not by miles.

The road to Bolsward is charming—shady, delightfully winding, and running through green meadows dotted here and there with pretty little cottages. One passes the villages of Ijsbrechtum and Nijland, and enters Bolsward through a grand, fine old avenue, though it is as well to mention that the little city loses its imposing appearance the moment the ancient ramparts are traversed. One is much more inclined to believe oneself in the centre of a large village than in the middle of a very ancient and formerly a very powerful town. And yet it ranks amongst the oldest towns in Friesland, and its origin dates so far back that it is difficult to know when it was founded.

In fact, no three of its genealogists agree on the same point. The old chronicler Andréas Kempius, whose opinion is endorsed by Occo van Scharl, a scholar of the sixteenth century, says that the town was founded about the year 713 by Princess Bolswina, a daughter of Radbod. On the other hand, Blaeu and Schotanus assert that it derives its name from the old Frison word *bodel* (signifying depth, and applicable to the canals surrounding the town), from which came Bodelsward, and, in course of time, Bolsward. But Ubbo Emmius affirms that this much-disputed name took its origin from one Bolone or Bodelone, who, according to a somewhat vague tradition, was the founder of the town, if not the lord of the whole province.

Hence, there is no certainty on the point, and no one would be unreasonable enough to expect a foreigner, like myself, to know better than the people of the country.

The inhabitants themselves appeared to me to be very doubtful about the exact origin of the name of their town. The money coined at Bolsward in the eleventh century bears the name of *Bodtiswe* or *Bodtiswer*; a will relative to the Convent of the Frères-Mineurs speaks of it as 'fratrum minorum conventus *Boldiswerdiensis*;' a chart in 1423 writes *Bodelswert*; the seal of the Commune for the year 1496 bears the inscription 'Sekretum civitatis *Bodelswardia*;' and the great seal for the year 1640, that of 'Magnum sigillum *Bolswerdianum*,' from which date the name is written indifferently *Bolswerdt*, *Bolswerd*, or *Bolsward*, and I think we will adhere to the last named.

However difficult the etymology of Bolsward may

be, there is one fact about the town which is indisputable—its ancient power and wealth. We referred just now to the coinage of the eleventh century. Bolsward was one of the four Friesland towns which, under the reign of Bruno III., Count of Brunswick, Stavoren, and Westergo, and that of the Emperor Henry III., received the privilege of coining money between the years 1039 and 1047. The other three were Dockum, Leeuwarden, and Stavoren. Bolsward had also the honour of becoming, at the same time with Stavoren, one of the Hanseatic towns, an honour all the more remarkable because no other Frison city enjoyed the same privilege. Added to which Bolsward was not situated, like Stavoren, on the borders of the Zuyder Zee, but a good mile and a half farther inland, and could only be reached by means of a long canal, which traversed the *Koudemeer* and wound its way in a circuitous route to the gates of the little city: hence the privilege was a very special distinction.

The old commercial activity has long since disappeared, and the only proofs of its ancient splendour consist of two or three old monuments, and they even, are not, relatively speaking, of such very ancient date. Two churches of Gothic architecture and a neat-looking town-hall are about all Bolsward has to offer in the way of interest or curiosity.

The oldest of these two churches, called now the 'little church,' was built, according to Van der Aa, in 1270, and according to Blaeu in 1281. It is constructed of huge bricks, which rain and sunshine have turned into a glorious colour. It was formerly dependent on a convent of Franciscans, destroyed about the date of the Reformation.

The large church is still more modern, dating from the middle of the fifteenth century. It was begun in 1446 and finished in 1463, and dedicated to St. Martin, Bishop of Tours. Similar to the other churches of Friesland and the province of Groningen, it is built entirely of brick, without ornament of any description, and has a heavy, massive appearance, in consequence of the materials used for its construction. It is supported by four enormous columns, the capitals of which are formed of very simple mouldings supporting the beadings of the vaults. Above the arches one perceives large mullioned niches, which have the same effect as windows hidden behind brickwork. At the top of each of these false openings there is a small aperture through which a dim, faint light penetrates and casts its rays on the nave below. The nave has no transept, and the choir, which has no circumference, terminates in a semi-decagon. The same simplicity and massiveness regulate the exterior. The tower topping the church has a heavy form and appearance, and finishes, like all the Frison steeples, in a tiled roof, that does not add to the elegance of the building. On the whole, although the dimensions of the structure are immense, the architecture is poor, and has very many faults that no one should tolerate in a Gothic monument.

However, one is forced into believing that this

church, such as it is, must have pleased the Frisons of the sixteenth century, for we are told that when the inhabitants of Sneek and Dockum resolved to build two temples worthy of St. Martin of Tours, they found no better model to copy, than the Church of St. Martin of Bolsward.

Poor from an architectural point of view, St. Martin is not much better off in regard to its interior decoration. There is some tolerably good carving about the choir, and two or three rows of stalls of the same date as the construction—that is to say, about the end of the fifteenth century. Although the work was somewhat hastily executed, the style in general is good—some few of the scenes sculptured on the divisions being really worthy of note. But, alas! it is all in such a terrible state of dilapidation, that it has not even a picturesque look. Below this carving there are several tombstones sculptured in demi-relief in blue granite, of a very grand character. I will describe one referring to an old burgomaster of the town, M. de Heerma, who died in 1611, and lies by the side of his wife, the 'honestissima matrona Sithia de Cammingha.' These two people are represented as lying in a very natural position, their feet resting against their arms, supported by cherubim, while above their heads is the following inscription, not very exact as to rule, but very energetic in expression:—

QUI VOS ESTIS NOS FUIMUS, QUI NOS SUMUS
VOS ERIS.

Both figures are draped in the most sumptuous

toilettes—he with his long beard, his collar, and his cuirass; she with her plaited frill, Medici head-dress, and a long embroidered corsage and farthingale.

Many of these beautiful tombstones are knocking about the church, half destroyed by neglect, time, and by the shameful manner they are trampled on by the worshippers. It would take a dozen pages to enumerate and describe them all; but two others must be mentioned, because, from an artistic point of view, they are of special importance. The first refers to the Binkes family, and has an elegant bas-relief, representing Christ healing the sick; the other belongs to the Monsma family, and is of graceful form in the Italian style, and contains several niches holding emblematic figures, somewhat similar to those designed by Goltzius.

These remarkable works of art evince the fact that several sculptors of considerable merit must have existed at that period in the town. It would be an interesting study too to find out their names and histories and what attracted them to Bolsward; if they were Huguenots expelled from France or the Spanish Low Countries, or if they were the same sculptors who were employed on the decoration of the Town Hall, being erected about that same date (1614). In any case, the archæologists of the country would have an interesting problem to solve if they cared to trace their origin. While inspecting all the ancient tombstones, covered with portraits, inscriptions, arms, and even allegorical compositions, we came across a mausoleum of more modern date, but nevertheless worthy of our attention. It belonged to Gijsbert Iapiks, the last of the Frison poets, according to date.

Like many another of his compatriots, like the great Vondel himself, Iapiks had to wait a long time before his countrymen signalised their appreciation, of the glory of his merits, by raising a monument to his honour. Indeed, it was not till the year 1823—more than half a century after the death of the author of '*Friesche Rymelerye*'—that his country honoured itself, by honouring the memory of one of its greatest sons.

But perhaps it is as well to mention, in justification of this neglect, that the poet was guilty of a great crime in their eyes—the crime of being poor. In a country where money is thought much of, a fault of this grave nature is rarely condoned. What would become of the prestige of wealth if a statue were raised to the memory of a poor author? Now if Vondel, according to a strange remark of one in authority, was an 'ingenious stocking merchant,' Iapiks was not of much more importance. In his native town he was only a poor schoolmaster. Certainly a fine profession for a public statue! But we will leave the dead in peace, and turning to the living, give a look at the building where marriages are celebrated and births registered. But before arriving at this Town Hall we will take a peep to our left, on our road from the church, and examine the place where formerly existed a chapel, called the Chapel of the Miracles of Our Lady. Inside this building a little statue of the Virgin used to stand, which had the virtue, so it is said, of curing sickness and infirmity, by a touch. When the Reformation took place, the Virgin miraculously disappeared, and somewhat later on the chapel itself. But the miracles did not cease, but instead of the Virgin, it was men who undertook to perform them—railroads, electric telegraphs, photography, and other marvels of modern science, that the pious of olden time would have regarded as diabolical discoveries. A couple of centuries ago presentiments of the revolution these new things would accomplish, began to make themselves felt.

But here we are at the Town Hall. It is a fine building, brightly coloured, built in alternate brick and stone, and has a goodly aspect. It is two stories high in front, and has a huge black roof, surmounted by a curious-looking bell-tower of a mixture of rococo and Japanese style. A sort of fore-building, the stories of which do not join on to the front, is divided into two unequal parts, which adds considerably to the odd appearance of the building. A pinnacle, studded all over with projections and juttings, surmounts this fore-building, in front of which is a flight of steps, with a double balustrade supporting two lions holding in their paws the arms of the town—a golden eagle with two sable heads. This flight of steps leads to the public entrance,

THE TOWN HALL OF BOLSWARD.

which is framed in by fluted columns and caryatides so excessively ornamented as to be heavy in appearance. A statue of Justice stands in a niche above the entrance, and several allegorical figures, placed above to the right and left, complete the decoration of this very curious façade, which is at once the most irregular and the most pleasing I ever saw.

Unfortunately, the interior of this Town Hall is very disappointing. There is only one chamber worth mentioning at all. It is an immense whitewashed room, with the ceiling ornamented with large brown beams, the monumental fire-place supported by caryatides in blackened stone, and the doors framed in by a portico of sculptured wood, the whole topped by pyramids and pinnacles. The corbels supporting the beams of the ceiling are very cleverly carved, representing a series of allegorical designs.

The only furniture in the room consists of the large traditional table, covered with a green cloth, on which are placed several pewter inkstands, and a number of high-backed armchairs. A long white pipe filled with tobacco, and ready for use, lies by the side of each place. It would not do for me to affirm that each of these pipes awaits a councillor, because I once made a similar remark in reference to the Town Hall at Leeuwarden, and I got into trouble through it. It appears that the magistracy of the Frison capital are not addicted to smoking a pipe—in fact, only a cigar. Those whom I saw smoking pipes were simple *zetters*, whose business it was to adjust imposts on patents. I was informed of this in such a peremptory fashion when I returned to Leeuwarden that I was not likely to expose myself to a similar rebuff again. Besides the high-backed chairs, table inkstands, and pipes, there are several old pictures of mediocre quality in this room, and a large press containing the archives of the old city. These archives, arranged in order by M. Eekhof, are sadly incomplete. The most important only date from the sixteenth century, a date singularly modern in proportion to the antiquity of the town. After glancing over the chief charts, a few letters from the Duke of Alba, certain privileges granted by Charles Quint, and a few other documents of value, and looking at the large pewter pots kept in remembrance of the banquets of olden times, we took our leave of the guardian of these municipal riches.

And as we had seen all that Bolsward contained worth looking at, there was nothing else for us to do but to return to Sneek, if we wished to continue our journey towards the south-east.

CHAPTER IV.

SNEEK LAKE—JOURE—THE PEAT BOGS OF SCHOTERLAND—
HEERENVEEN AND THE '*ORANJEWOUD.*'

OUR intention on leaving Sneek was to cross the great lake known to the Frieslanders as Lake Sneek (*Sneekermeer*), to proceed past the Goingarijp marshes, and thus reach the large village of Joure; thence on foot to Heerenveen, to visit that celebrated retreat called the *Oranjewoud*; and, lastly, make direct for Leeuwarden, thus covering the entire eastern portion of the province.

We went on board early in the morning. Our little vessel, in company with the usual gulls and sea magpies, sailed in the direction of the *Sneekermeer*, and, after following for fully half an hour the various bends of a broad canal, we suddenly came into the middle of this great lake—an immense extent of water, the limits of which were scarcely visible.

That which gives to these inland seas of Friesland an appearance almost unique, is the uniform flatness of the shores, also the nature of the soil which constitutes the bottom. This, in fact, formed by inexhaustible peat-bogs, gives to the water a dark violet

D

colour, just like that of copying-ink, the smallest ray of sun on the ripples, producing a golden tint, positively magical. Near land, this curious shade becomes more intense; in contrast with the tender green of the fields and the reed beds, it becomes almost black.

As soon, however, as you leave the shore, the land, being so low, becomes almost imperceptible. One would imagine it a green cloak eternally floating on the face of the deep dark waters, without fixity or solidity. The clumps of trees perceptible in the distance, the houses which lose themselves in the grey mist, the church steeples, with their varnished tiles shining in the morning fog, seem to rise up from the water and to float on its surface. Even those extensive plains covered with reeds, always moving and bending to the softest breeze, only add to the fantastical appearance of the watery shores. Pliny's astonishment is easily understood when seeing, for the first time, these curious landscapes, and his comparing their inhabitants to eternal navigators, 'navigantibus similes.'

To obtain an idea of this singular spectacle, imagine an endless plain everlastingly inundated, on which floats, in all directions, a large fleet of round, bulging, flat-bottomed vessels, employed in distributing to the four corners of this aquatic district, the produce of the earth and man's industry. Were only one of those large craft on the horizon, it might well be taken for Noah's Ark, and one could imagine to oneself the Deluge, when the dove left never to return. But there are too many of them; besides, they are too gay with their large, red-brick or saffron-coloured sails, reflecting on the violet-coloured waters, and the silver background of the sky, to create any but pleasant and happy thoughts.

Amongst these heavy and massive craft some are noticeable by their more finely-cut bows, carefully varnished, delicately carved, and glaringly coloured and gilded on the poop. Their masts bend to the wind, and the dark red sails appear manufactured of delicate, fine material. They look like so many gentlemen lost amongst navvies. These elegant vessels are known as '*boeiers*.' They are the yachts of these inland seas, and the necessary equipment of the wealthy families of Friesland. They are provisioned with every delicacy, especially French wines, and friends often form a party from four to six, and go cruising about the country. It frequently happens they are not alone. Three or four *boeiers* start together, with noisy, happy crews. Cruising well together, a constant exchange of visits, dinner parties, &c., is kept up during five or six days, when visits are made at the *châteaux* of mutual friends, thus keeping the ball of gaiety continually rolling, and laying in a rich store of amusing anecdotes for winter evenings.

After Sneek Lake we cross the '*Goingarijpsterpoelen*.' Here the water is darker still, the reed-beds are closer together, and the wind, which nothing stops, raises a host of little waves around us. Then suddenly the wind drops, the water resumes its natural colour; we have entered a wide canal bordered with rustic dwellings. The large thatched roofs succeed one another, almost touching the ground. Behind the window-panes appear beautiful blue blinds, and artistically attached to the outside walls, a regular arsenal of copper buckets, shining like gold. These proclaim the labours of the farm and the wonderful cleanliness of the establishment.

Sometimes, before one of these country dwellings, will be seen a *tjalk* loaded with pottery, tissues, or groceries. It is the merchant in his boat calling on his clients. For in this strange country it is not the buyer who has to inconvenience himself by going shopping—the shop comes to him, bringing with its modest stock, the outside news and the scandal of the neighbouring village. The houses now become more numerous—the sound of hammers is heard —and we find ourselves amongst a swarm of boats, large trees, and overhanging houses. It is Joure. We have reached our destination.

Nothing can be more lively and picturesque than the entrance to this important village. On the right stands a strongly-built *château*, with high windows and an elegant veranda. It is an ancient building, at the same time rich, roomy, and simple. It is surrounded by a large, finely timbered park. We knew that the proprietor of this lovely retreat had a fine collection of pictures, so we hastened to pay our respects to him first. The owner was from home; we were nevertheless admitted, and allowed to visit the gallery. It is not a bad collection, comprising about forty pictures, most of which are remarkable, and some very good. No great names, but a selection from those small Dutch masters, who are in their right place, in Dutch houses. If I remember rightly, there were 'Fêtes Galantes,' by Dirk Hals; 'Swans and Ducks,' by Hondecœter; 'Village Music,' by Miense Molenaer; 'The Interior of an Inn,' by Teniers; 'An Effect of Snow,' by Avercamp. To these masters we, at any rate, attributed these fine, fresh-looking works; but, being hung rather high, we had, owing to the absence of the owner, to content ourselves with a summary inspection.

Our curiosity satisfied, and thanks tendered, we next visited Joure. It is a large village, consisting of one interminable street, wide in proportion, on either side of which, are houses having the pretension to belong to the middle classes. A few side alleys, turning off to the left, lead down to a narrow canal, crossed by a drawbridge, and bordered by cottages, with pretty gardens, and shaded by trees, where large boats seem to be entangled between the almost touching banks. Houses, trees, and boats, with their various colours, form a most pretty picture.

Seated all along the quay, with dangling legs and attentive eyes, is a band of boys enjoying the pleasures of fishing. Their tackle is not very complicated—the stem of a tree, a piece of twine, and a bent pin, being the extent of their stock—but somehow they manage to land a few victims.

Certainly these Friesland fish must be very self-sacrificing. I firmly believe them to be veritable philosophers, caring nothing for life, and that it does not matter to them if they are swallowed by pike, struck by gulls, gobbled up by storks, or fished up by man. The latter death seems to me to be preferable, as by this means they do get the chance of a breakfast off the hook.

The canal led us back to the large street, and the large street to the inn, and then we required a guide to take us to Heerenveen. 'I have noticed,' wrote somewhere M. de Gabriac,[1] 'that in all foreign ports, such as Pernambuco, Bahia, Callao, Beyreuth, &c., one finds an inn, bereft of all comforts, but furnished with a billiard table.' As much may be said of the Friesland inns and taverns. I never remember seeing one without the triumphant notice, 'BILLARD ROIJAL.' Why royal? I cannot tell, and nothing justifies the proud title.

It was to the happy possessor of one of these royal tables that we spoke. A stout man with a red nose, and a corporation too large for his waistcoat—in fact, everything to invite confidence. He at once procured us a little dried-up old man, but a good walker, and after agreeing as to terms, we buckled on our knapsacks and started for Heerenveen.

There is no better means of knowing and seeing a country than to tramp it. What with having to ask one's way, and ascertain the best road, &c., one

[1] The Count de Gabriac, his humorous 'Travels Round the World.'

learns more in a few hours, than would be possible in as many months, in travelling either by coach or boat. Your forced companion—i.e. guide—soon becomes an acquaintance. All inequality of rank ceases for the time being; he forgets his reserve, and soon initiates you into the petty sorrows of his life and the history of his neighbours. Although the Frieslander is far from communicative, he obeys the common law of nature, and a good walk soon loosens his tongue.

We had, therefore, no reason to be dissatisfied with our resolution, more especially as the road to Heerenveen is very good, being large, well kept, and almost free from dust. Like all Friesland roads, it is bordered with immense meadows, which would be somewhat monotonous but for a clump of trees here and there, a modest-looking farm, or a small, pretty village lending animation to the scene. Sometimes, on either side, are large marshes, worked for their valuable peat, mountains of which can be seen drying in the fields. Men loading carts and vessels, indicate that we are approaching the '*Schoterland*,' one of the districts most famed for peat. In these bogs the manufacture is carried on somewhat curiously. The peat is fished up with a species of dredge, called *beugel*, fastened to the end of a long pole. The peasant in his boat floats over the marsh, dips in his dredge, and empties the contents into the craft, where he leaves it to drain. He then carries it to land, and after the fashion of three centuries ago, he treads it with his feet, then spreads it out to a thickness of about two feet, which he divides into small cubes of equal size, and then carefully dries it. The marshes thus worked are comprised in the official statistics under the name 'low' peat bogs, and are not subject to any regulation.

Besides this kind of peat bog the official classification includes two others—the 'high' peat deposits (*hooge veenen*) and the *polders* of peat (*veenpolders*). The first are so called because the layers are above water. The working is therefore easier and less costly. It is but necessary to clear the surface, and the material is at hand. This is divided into numberless cubes, and then dried. Labour easily and cheaply performed. But the peat, thus easily obtained and manufactured, is of poor quality. Being neither crushed nor pressed, it is less dense than the kinds that undergo the double operation. Moreover, it contains a certain quantity of fibre and sand, which depreciate its use and value.[1]

The peat *polders* are rich prairies, situated below the level of the sea, containing a stratum of peat more or less thick. To work this necessitates

---

[1] It is on account of its easy extraction and defective quality that its market price is so low, and the labour so badly remunerated. As in the high peat deposits the price of labour per ton varies from 10 to 40 cents, and by the day from 1 florin to 1 florin 5 cents, in the peat *polders* it reaches 30 to 65 cents per ton, and 1 florin 20 cents to 2 florins 60 cents by the day.

In the lower peat works the price is still higher, being at the rate of 44 to 75 cents per ton, and 2 florins 75 cents by the day—figures which are considered high for the country. It must be remembered that the cent is the hundredth part of the florin, equal to 2 francs 10 centimes French money, or 1*s*. 9¼*d*. English money.

the destruction of the green plains, which are thus converted into ponds or small lakes—if not unproductive, very nearly so. Hence it can be understood, why the Government reserves to itself the supervision and the regulation of these particular bogs. Public interest would give way to the private greed of the landowners, who, but for the aforesaid supervision, would soon convert one of the most beautiful provinces of the Netherlands, into an inextricable marsh.

No one, therefore, can work a *polder* without authority, and the payment of certain dues—the amount of which is placed to the credit of a fund, to be used by the Government for irrigation, and the drying up of worked-out *polders*, by which means fresh ones are constituted.

The total production of peat throughout the Netherlands is very large. In Friesland alone it amounts to five and a half millions of tons, and employs seven thousand workmen. Strangely enough, all the men are mostly natives of the country, whereas the reapers and many of the agricultural labourers are imported from Germany.

Naturally the *polders* furnish the largest quantities, and employ the most labour. They employ, in fact, four thousand five hundred hands, and annually produce three and a half millions of tons. Next come the 'high' peat bogs, employing twelve hundred men, and producing fifteen hundred thousand tons. Lastly, the 'low' peat bogs, whilst employing about one thousand labourers, only produce about half a million tons. Thus, it will be seen that the extraction of peat is one of the chief industries of Friesland, besides being the oldest in this curious land. As far back as antiquity takes us, the natives have used it for fuel. When the Romans entered the country, the use of it was generally known; and Pliny shows us the inhabitants 'burning the earth' to cook their victuals. '*Terra cibos rigentia septentrione viscera urunt.*'

It is from the peat bogs that the pretty little city of Heerenveen, which we are about to reach, takes its name. It means 'The Lords' Peat Deposits.' The name was really much longer, being '*De Heerencompagnonsveenen* ('The Lords' Peat Bog Company'). Whether it was a limited company and paid a dividend history does not state. It was, however, formed in 1551, by M. Pieter van Dekema, knight and counsellor at the Court of Friesland, and had for its objects the opening up and working of the peat bogs in the neighbourhood. It was this company who raised the first houses on the present site, which were soon followed by a host of others for workmen and tradesmen. But Heerenveen never attained its full development until the Princess Albertine, daughter of Frederic Henry, and widow of William Frederic of Nassau, Stadtholder of Friesland, took up her residence in the neighbourhood and built the '*Oranjewoud.*'

This amiable princess had taken a great dislike to Leeuwarden in consequence of the death of her husband, who was accidentally killed. Whilst visiting his armoury and examining a pistol the weapon exploded, smashed his jaw, and the wound proved fatal.

The unfortunate Albertina Agnes, in order to avoid a spot so pregnant with sorrow to herself, determined to retire into absolute solitude. She went to Heerenveen; the site pleased her and she built a country-house close by, and began the magnificent plantations which afterwards gave to the residence the name of Orange Wood (*Oranjewoud*), which it has retained ever since. Her son, Henri Casimir, often visited her there, and later on he, in his turn, dwelt in this magnificent retreat, and greatly improved it. His successors, Jean Guillaume Frison and Guillaume Charles Henri, made it a sort of little Versailles. It was then that Heerenveen became the rendezvous of the Friesland aristocracy. Roads were made and old ones newly surveyed, houses built, avenues traced, parks and gardens planted; and the wretched peat bog, thus transformed, took the surname of 'Friesche Haagje,' which means a little Friesland hedge, in allusion to the Hague, the residence of the Stadtholders of Holland.

To this day the '*Oranjewoud*' remains celebrated; standing as it does in the midst of endless bogs and marshes, it appears like an Eden in a desert. Its magnificent avenues of fine trees remind one of those at Versailles; besides, the number of canals around shaded with verdure, give it a stamp of princely grandeur.

This magnificent estate, however, is no longer the privileged residence of the family of Orange. At the beginning of the present century it was confiscated by the Batavian Republic, and in 1812 was portioned off and turned into private dwellings. But the new owners have respected the fine trees, and the '*Oranjewoud*' forms an aristocratic community, the smallest houses of which are elegant villas, and the cottages small *châteaux*.

CHAPTER V.

LEEUWARDEN—ITS PRISONS—AN IMPROVISED PLAY—THE CHANCELLERIE —THE CHÂTEAU OF CAMMINGHA—HISTORY OF THE SAINT EELKO LIAUKAMA.

ON leaving Heerenveen we started direct for Leeuwarden, where we purposed staying but a few days. Our intention was not to explore this large and noble town again—I having done so two years ago, and fully described it in my other work, 'The Dead Cities of the Zuyder Zee'—but only to pay our respects to the governor of the province, and to visit the penal establishments of the Friesland capital, which are very celebrated, and which we were unable to see before, for want of necessary introductions.

Baron van Panhuys, commissary to the King, gave us a most affable reception, placed himself entirely at our disposal, and offered us letters of introduction to the burgomasters of the different towns through which we might pass; and I am all the more anxious to thank him again through the medium of these pages, as it was due to his courtesy that we were enabled to visit the lordly mansion of Cammingha, access to which, is most difficult, as well as to cross the sea on a Sunday to reach Schiermonnikoog.

For the prisons we had a golden key, in the shape of a letter from the Minister of Justice, an enviable favour not always to be obtained. If, therefore, the sound of iron-barred gates turning on their hinges, the drawing of bolts and rattling of keys, are not disagreeable to my readers, I will take advantage of my passport to visit the inside.

There are two penitentiary establishments in Leeuwarden, one situated in that delicious palace known as the Chancellerie; the other is a fine newly-built prison, both elegant and strong in appearance. The architect seems to have done his best to make it so ornamental that, instead of calling up dismal thoughts, it goes far to add to the embellishment of the town, and when finished will be a model of its kind.

The interior of this fine building justifies the excellent impression formed outside. It is completely built of stone, bricks, and iron, consequently fire-proof; staircases, halls, and workshops are built with mathematical precision, and in such manner as to permit of constant surveillance, so necessary in such places. Throughout, the yards are large and spacious, the rooms whitewashed from top to bottom and well ventilated, the inner and outer walls even bearing witness to the proverbial Dutch cleanliness.

The steps and passages are equally clean; you

LEEUWARDEN (THE CHANCELLERIE).

would look in vain for a soiled spot or grain of dust. I doubt whether a cracked or tarnished pane of glass could be found. Everything is washed, brushed, and waxed with a care we might well envy in our own homes.

The dormitories are also carefully looked to— scrubbed every day, and well ventilated. There is none of that close smell so noticeable in barracks and prisons. Their aspect, however, is sufficiently curious to be worthy of description. Each consists of a large whitewashed, asphalt-floored room, in the centre of which is an immense iron-trellised cage, armed on the inside with spikes. This cage is divided into above one hundred cells, each separated by sheet-iron walls; each has its bed, with the absolute accessories—viz. a thin mattress, an apology for a pillow, a pair of coarse sheets, and two coverlets. Each night the prisoners are locked in these narrow cells, and thus repose perfectly isolated from each other.

All round the dormitory run iron water-pipes, with taps fixed at intervals, at which the convicts are supposed to perform their ablutions. Water, I may add, is general throughout the place, and is to be met with on each story. Baths, which the prisoners are compelled to make use of at certain times, are on the ground floor. This must have been a novelty to many of them, as they are recruited, as a rule, from the agricultural classes, who, if I am rightly informed, shun the limpid liquid.

We were able to see most of these wretched persons either in the workshops or taking their mechanical 'constitutional' in the yards. Many of them are deformed, and the majority have a repulsive appearance, which in a great measure, maybe, is due to the prison garb, their shaved faces, and closely-cut hair.

Although the prison can contain 575 prisoners, there were only 412 at the time of our visit. These unfortunate beings have three meals per diem. In the morning, luke-warm milk and water and a piece of dry bread; at midday, a soup composed of vegetables; in the evening, coffee and brown bread. Sometimes they are allowed a small quantity of meat, but more often bacon; but, as a rule, it is vegetables and barley which form the basis of this primitive cookery. It is but a poor diet, especially as the bread is black, damp, and thick, and reminds one of that eaten during the siege of Paris.

The prisoners, however, can improve upon this food by the money they earn. They have, in fact, a small interest in their work, four-sixths of which is at their disposal, the balance being very properly capitalised and handed to them on their dismissal.

The work is varied according to their ability. They do a little of all kinds; either they carry on their own particular trade or, if they have none, are taught one. One finds in Leeuwarden prison wooden shoe makers, tailors, carpenters, and boot-makers, but chiefly mat-makers and weavers.

As far as possible the labour is turned to naval, military, or prison purposes. Each particular branch of manufacture occupies one or more workshops, under the supervision of a chief, and the inspection of several subordinates. Everything is conducted with military discipline, which allows neither of ill-will nor question. The dungeons, a kind of subterraneous cells, are for the unruly, and irons for the mutinous. The punishment is severe, but then it is not often had recourse to.

During working hours silence is imperative, and yet the prisoners manage easily enough to carry on a conversation between them which is difficult to be detected by the warders. This has been proved time after time. On one occasion these miserable creatures undertook to perform a play, and, without its being known, completed all the dresses and other accessories, even to the bell that was to announce the rise of the curtain.

There was a king in the piece, whose crown (and what king has not a crown?) had been made out of gilt cardboard, ornamented with precious stones in the shape of bits of broken looking-glass; all this without its ever being known where they procured the cardboard and the glass. Unfortunately, so much ingenuity did not reap its reward. At the last moment all was found out, the stupefaction of the authorities only being equalled by the disappointment of the performers.

But this is nothing compared to some of the acts

of insubordination. As I said before, they are of rare occurrence—as rare as attempts to escape, of which latter only one has succeeded, since the prison existed.

One day six of the prisoners broke through the roof, and escaped by sliding down a wall and swimming the moat surrounding the prison. All but one were recaptured the following day, and he was drowned while crossing the moat.

To complete our description we have only to mention the school, the master of which has anything but a sinecure. The convicts generally are totally uneducated, and their dormant intelligence rebels against being wakened. Some, better taught, assist the master, but the proportion of ignorance is too great not to leave room for grave consideration as to this want of education being conducive to crime. I should be sorry to assert that compulsory education (which all well-meaning Dutchmen are anxious to see carried out) would prevent crimes, and reform evil-disposed persons; but I think it would materially diminish the number of those who are led away to do wrong on the spur of the moment.

As we said at first, Leeuwarden contains another prison, viz. the Chancellerie, which is a far less important establishment than the one we have described. It is, as its name implies, an old provincial building turned into a prison. As such, the interior presents nothing interesting. At the time of our visit it contained but sixty-six prisoners, mostly thieves condemned to short sentences, besides eleven women, nearly all of whom were hardened beggars whom the law tried to correct by imprisonment.

Here we miss that strict military discipline observable in the other establishment. The prisoners toil in the large rooms without supervision. The beds, narrow frames, with the coverlets rolled up at the head, have none of that hard, severe appearance we saw elsewhere. The rules are not strict, but then the prisoners have not that dull, wretched appearance visible in the others.

What chiefly took us to the Chancellerie was the hope of finding in the interior traces of its ancient architecture, but we were disappointed. The staircase, however, formed an exception, and was certainly remarkable, as also a dozen charmingly sculptured consoles supporting the pillars of the infirmary, and the room of the military prisoners.

I have already remarked that, thanks to the courtesy of Baron van Panhuys, we had the good fortune to visit the Castle of Wiardastate, belonging to M. Cammingha. It is very certain that without his kind introduction this pleasure would have been denied us. The Château of Cammingha is not one of those places the doors of which are open to all visitors. It is an enclosed castle and difficult of access except to the friends of the owner, who asserts that a gentleman is master in his own house. Hence, he only receives those friends, he has long known and likes. All titles fall to the ground at his threshold, and

E 2

recently a most august personage was unable to make him depart from what he considers his right.

Is it not a curious proof of the independence of character and liberty so dear to the Frieslander that a private gentleman should refuse a king the inspection of his mansion? Hence the Château of Cammingha is a sort of torture of Tantalus to the lovers of antiquities. This curiosity is quite excusable from the fact that both family and castle are the most ancient in the country. As far back as the ninth century the annals of that date refer to the Villa of Cammingha. A chart, contemporary with the death of Charlemagne (814), mentions the property as belonging to a gentleman named Gerulf. In 1481 the house of Cammingha underwent a regular siege. This is how it occurred. That year the brewers had obtained a charter by which it was agreed that no beer but theirs should be drunk in the town. One market day, however, the peasants introduced Haarlem beer, and began drinking it in the public places. The brewers tried to prevent it, and the result was a free fight. But as the poor villagers had all the townspeople against them, they had to take refuge in the house of Pierre de Cammingha, who afforded them protection. Since then historians have often mentioned this hospitable dwelling, without however, clearly determining its importance or its whereabouts.

It was rebuilt at various periods, and the house we now see only dates back to the fifteenth century, probably not so far. It is, however, none the less an architectural curiosity, as there are probably but two or three similar castles in the country. For during the fifteenth and sixteenth centuries the parties who divided the land made a regular sacrifice of these feudal castles. First came the 'grease merchants,' then the 'eel merchants,' who pillaged the manors of their noble enemies. In less than fifteen years they burnt and generally destroyed the Castle of Wilko Ringia, that of G. Iuusma, and those of Wibo Jaricx, Igo Galama, Thierry Valta, and ten others of equal importance. Then came the Guelders with Lange Pier and their enemies the Saxons, followed by the Spaniards under Gaspar de Robles, and then finally the Reformation. What escaped the former became a prey to the latter, and in the end nothing was left.

These castles were in reality not very strong, being merely useful as a refuge in a moment of danger, but quite unable to withstand anything like a regular siege. The one we have in view is a large, fine building constructed in brick and stone, with an immense roof surmounted by a belfry, and with ten oblong windows in front, so narrow as to look like gigantic loopholes.

The interior is composed of several fine apartments, each furnished in the olden style, and having the haughty appearance of those of the Dutch Renaissance. Two especially are comparatively intact, one completely covered in Cordova leather, the other with Flemish tapestry, tables, chairs, &c., being in keeping with the fashion of the period. The castle contains besides a theatre and chapel. The latter has a fine collection of relics, &c., preserved from the wholesale destruction of the Reformers, and amongst several good pictures one of the venerable Eelko Liaukama.

This Eelko is a saintly personage of the country, whose history is but little known beyond the limits of Friesland. In his lifetime he was a monk of the Order of 'Prémontoré,' whose dissolute ways he purposed reforming. To carry out this task he undertook to visit the different convents and monasteries throughout the kingdom, and by the example of his spotless life to carry conviction with his counsel. But the very first he stopped at, his brethren, who little relished this fresh innovation in their daily pursuits, took the opportunity of making the reverend gentleman tipsy. The poor man, feeling very sick, began to give unmistakable signs of being about to scatter on the floor what he had imbibed from his glass. Instead of depositing, amidst general laughter, what all expected, nothing but roses dropped from his mouth. The cry of miracle went forth, but that was insufficient to convert these perverted Gentiles. Some time afterwards poor Eelko Liaukama was found near a wall with his skull fractured. He was thus got rid of to avoid further remonstrance on his part.

This veracious story was told us in front of the portrait of the pious and energetic reformer by M.

Dirks, a distinguished archæologist who accompanied us during our visit.

This picture of Eelko is not the only one of note in M. Cammingha's mansion. Besides a magnificent collection of his ancestors, this gentleman possesses several historical portraits which it is needless to mention here, as they have been fully described elsewhere by a friend of the family.[1]

The castle containing all these beautiful things is surrounded by a lovely garden, itself surrounded by a moat. A small bridge effects communication with the outer world. At the entrance is a fine ornamental porch, fixed in massive walls perforated with loopholes. All this goes far to increase the feudal appearance of the place.

M. Cammingha did personally the honours of the place, and conducted us to the edge of the moat, where we took leave of our host, terrible to the outside world, but at home a really charming man.

[1] 'Het slot Wiardate met de Schilderyen oudheden enz,' door G. A. Six. Utrecht, 1869.

CHAPTER VI.

THE '*SCHIER-STINS*'— THE WOOD OF THE MURDER — DOCKUM — THE MIRACULOUS SPRING—THE '*HARMONIE.*'

FROM Leeuwarden we proceeded to Veenwouden, a pretty village buried in trees. That which attracted us to this part of the country was another ancient castle, called 'Schier-Stins.'[1]

This mansion belongs to my personal friend M. van Heemstra, who, although absent, had doubtless advised his steward of our intended visit, for we received a hearty welcome. To tell the truth, *Schier-Stins* is less of a feudal castle than a fragment of one, for of the original edifice nothing remains but the tower, a kind of square belfry, the walls of which are thick enough to attest its former strength.

During the past century a new modern wing has been added to this grand relic, doubtless very comfortable and convenient, but somewhat of an eyesore

---

[1] The word *stins* in Frison signifies 'stone,' and was the old name for castles built of this material, because all other buildings were constructed of wood. Although houses generally are now built with brick, the word *stins* has not lost its signification.

when contrasted with the grandeur of the fine old ruin, and very out of place by the side of the tower, which is full of old curiosities most interesting to those making researches in the country.

The old belfry is divided into three stories. The ground floor, with its arched ceiling giving it the appearance of a chapel, contains the heaviest objects. We noticed, amongst others, figures of monks supporting a bench, copper lanthorns curiously embossed, arms, banners, and one of those large stone coffins in which the inhabitants of Oostergoo placed their dead to protect them from the wolves. It is of sandstone, roughly hewn, and of a size which proves the gigantic stature of the ancient Frieslanders.

The upper stories contain objects more or less curious and valuable—furniture, books, glass, cloth, and arms, amongst the latter an old sword said to have belonged to Albert of Saxony, but which, I strongly suspect, is only that of an executioner of the seventeenth century, as its simplicity of manufacture and the German inscription on the blade, prove the impossibility of its princely antecedents.

Our inspection finished, we had to return to Dockum before evening; and although the paint-box was not very heavy, we enquired for some one to carry it and show us our road. A lad was brought to us in a long coat, smoking a cigar as large as his head. We at once saw he was not the kind of person we wanted, as it seemed more than probable that we should not only have to relieve him of his burden, but also carry him on our shoulders. He, however, after weighing the box and taking a few whiffs at his cigar, consented to accompany us. We therefore started; but what we foresaw soon happened, at least partly, for we had scarcely accomplished a quarter of the journey when we were obliged to take the box from the poor boy, who was done up. Luckily we were not obliged to carry him—only to drag him as far as Murmerwoude (otherwise known as the 'Wood of the Murder').

Murmerwoude is a pretty hamlet, about half an hour's walk from Dockum, and although standing on either side of the road, and of pleasant appearance, yet it cannot but recall gloomy recollections. For on the 5th of June, 853, St. Boniface and his fifty-two followers were mercilessly massacred by the inhabitants. They had come from the southern provinces to reform the unbelievers, but found those of Dockum mere barbarians, who, instead of listening to their exhortations, fell upon and murdered them. Such a crime could not be left unpunished. At the news of the martyrdom of St. Boniface, King Pepin sent an army across the Lauwer and took Dockum, killed those he could catch, and burnt the village, those that escaped having to remain in exile. These, however, it would appear, could not escape the vengeance of God. They were condemned thenceforth to carry a stigma on their persons: the men were born with a tuft of white hair on the head, which has reproduced itself from generation to generation; and the women have a bald patch on the head, which is a cause of laughter throughout the country. To speak of a *Friesche-kaalkop* (a bald head of Friesland) is to designate a girl of Dockum.

On the spot where the murders took place Pepin's soldiers raised a hermitage; later on it became a chapel of wood, then one of brick. It still exists, although three-parts reconstructed. Since then Protestantism has made over its walls to whitewashers, and broken its windows. The pulpit alone is curious; it is sculptured and coloured, but the work is anything but delicate.

After resting a short time in the little churchyard which surrounds the chapel, we continued our journey. Soon afterwards we sighted the town of Dockum, built on a slight eminence in the midst of trees, and overlooking the neighbouring country. This accidental position gives to the place quite a coquettish appearance, which is borne out by its undulating streets, slanting squares, vast canal—which divides it into two unequal portions—clean and large quays, and pretty houses; all conducing to make it a most charming little town, which, notwithstanding its uncommon antiquity, does not seek to vie with, or ape, the air or manners of larger cities.

It is, however, one of the oldest in Friesland, its origin being traced as far back as the year 240. That year Prince Urbo built on its chief site a castle, which he called Dockenburg. As usual in those days, the vassals by degrees came and grouped themselves round their lord. In 700 the houses were already sufficiently numerous to be entitled to be called a large village. In 739 Gondebald fortified it and surrounded it with a wall; we, however, know how in 853 it was taken by King Pepin's army. It was not very long however before it righted itself, for in the eleventh century we find it figuring as one of the four cities of Friesland having the right to coin money.

Its comparative strength and commerce did not protect it against its enemies. The factions that divided the country, came and besieged it in turn. In 1308, 1399, and 1414 it was taken by assault and partly burnt. Again in 1498, the Friday before Easter, the Saxons also took, pillaged, and burnt it. Then came the Guelders, Dutch, Spaniards, and finally the Reformation. Each conqueror left traces of his passage in the shape of ruins. At length came peace; Dockum healed its wounds, recouped its losses, and is now flourishing. With a good inland harbour well filled with ships, a few breweries, potteries, workshops, and a gin distillery, but chiefly on account of its agricultural produce and its flax, it has become one of the principal European markets.

A wide canal of two leagues in extent, called *Dockumer Diep*, places the town in communication with the gulf known as Lauwers-Zee. It is by this route that the export of textile goods to England, France, and Germany is made, in all of which countries the large Dockum firms have agents.

Close to the harbour is the Town Hall, large, but on the exterior, of insignificant appearance. Built in the seventeenth it has been almost entirely rebuilt during the last century. In the interior two fine rooms of the former period have been retained, viz. the council room and antechamber, which are the most curious specimens that can be seen of the architecture of the time of Louis XV. applied to municipal purposes.

The anteroom, entirely covered with Cordova leather, has a fine chimney-piece. As to the council room, it is wainscotted with curiously carved wood, representing scenes of that pastoral period. The mantel-piece and door panels are likewise embellished, whilst four allegorical figures, of municipal life of Dockum, ornament the wall facing the windows. That which, however, stamps this handsome room is the fine old furniture. 'Many times,' said M. van Vries, the amiable burgomaster, whilst doing us the honours of his municipal residence, 'many times have I been offered heavy sums for these tables and chairs, but I have always declined, for I should look on a sale of the kind as a profanation.'

We complimented the worthy man on such sentiments, whilst regretting that so many others in his position had shown themselves wanting in that respect.

Unfortunately, all the monuments of Dockum have not been so religiously respected. St. Martin's Church, the oldest, is a proof; for, although not very ancient, the large church of Dockum was deserving of better treatment. Formerly it possessed some famous and valuable relics.[1] Besides the bones of St. Boniface and some other saints, it possessed the gold chalice and 'missal' entirely written by the hand of the pious bishop, with which he was wont to celebrate mass, and which were exhibited every seven years to the people, as also the pastoral rod of the glorious martyr, a relic doubly precious, as it was to its presence amongst them that the inhabitants of Dockum were indebted for the salubrious state of their town.

Close to it—in fact, about five minutes south-west of the Woudpoort—there is a spring rising in the middle of a field, forming a large pond of clear water, running thence in a stream to the canal. This water is the best in the country, and on being analysed during the last epidemic of cholera it was proved to be of the purest kind. To its use is attributed the small number of victims to the different epidemics which have raged in Dockum at various times, and the ancient chroniclers aver that it had the reputation of curing fevers, preventing hydrophobia, and restoring health to the infirm.

Ask any child of the country the origin of this famous spring, and he or she will tell you that St.

---

[1] In 1667 its wealth had already disappeared. Hegenitus mentions it in his 'Itinéraire,' in referring to Cornelius, from whom he took the description. He adds: 'Ego tamen quia nullum ex illis vidi; nihil etiam de re vetusta ac incerta heic adfirmare ausim.'

Boniface riding near the spot, and his horse becoming thirsty, he stretched forth his hand, and the animal struck the ground with its hoof, and immediately water sprang forth. This is the common legend. That of historians is more impressionable. It is not a horse that thirsted—it was the people; no longer an unconscious beast striking the earth, but a priest, a man of God, who desires to quench the thirst of his faithful flock. 'Wonderful and merciful spring, always full when the country was laid waste with drought. God, your Architect, through the saintly martyr striking the ground with his pastoral staff, made you rise in this miraculous manner.'

It is in these terms that C. Kempius, a serious historian, expresses himself on the subject. He is the author of one of the best works that the sixteenth century gave to Friesland. He was born at Dockum, therefore well acquainted with all that related to his well-loved city, of which he never speaks without emotion. (The title of the chapter in which Kempius refers to his 'beloved country' shows sufficiently the affection the old Frieslander bore to Dockum: 'Hic jam de situ civitatis Doccomanæ aliquid dicere amor dulcissimæ patriæ meæ me cogit.') It is him, therefore, and his version that we should believe.

The fountain still runs, but the rod has disappeared, as also a church erected by the invocation of the saintly man, as also the cloister that surrounded it and bore the name of St. Boniface. All passeth away in this world, but the gratitude of nations does so even sooner. However, during many years the name of the saint shone like a halo, and afforded his masters, the lords or aristocracy, numerous privileges. Moreover, the cloister we mentioned was indebted to him for its immense wealth. Its spiritual power extended to the islands of the North Sea. There now remains nothing of it except a few dependencies, out of which an orphanage has been made. The other buildings have disappeared, and nothing but a large, barren, deserted space, called *Kerkhof*, now remains to show what were once the avenues and garden of the cloister.

But let us leave this deserted spot, and the sad memories it recalls, and turn to another spring close by, which will give a different current to our thoughts. It is surmounted by a beautiful vase of white marble of the Medicis form, the base covered by foliage and ornaments interlaced. What is it? where does it come from—this antiquated vase, with its suggestive love scenes inscribed at the foot of it? It would be interesting to discover its origin; yet no one seems to know it, and cares less. Yet it is one of the two æsthetical curiosities of the town, the other being the little entrance-gate to the Asylum for Old Men. It stands between two rustic pillars, surmounted by a portico bearing a coloured coat of arms. The house of which this is the entrance is cold, cheerless, and falling into decay. The yard into which it leads is equally so: moss and rank grass grow in the crevices between the slabs, and cover the walls. Add to that poorly-clad old men, a few shreds of linen hanging on a line, an old woman washing the steps, and you have before you a complete picture of aged poverty without family ties, without means, without support of any kind, having to ask of public charity the care of providing the bread for their declining years.

But let us go to the 'Harmonie,' for the burgomaster waits us there. The 'Harmonie' is the town club, where people smoke, drink, play, and talk. In the summer time it is a pleasant garden resort; in winter it is used as a concert-room and occasional theatre. Thorbecke's bust ornaments the whitewashed walls, showing plainly the political feelings of the country. Wine flows into large glasses, and the evening is pleasantly spent. Even a Frenchman might find something there to remind him of his far-off country.

'Yes, sir,' remarked a dignified-looking magistrate with a long white beard—'yes, sir, last year I spent a fortnight in Paris, and you may believe me when I tell you that it is a town well worth visiting!'

I need scarcely mention that I was quite of his opinion.

CHAPTER VII.

NORTH FRIESLAND—SCHIERMONNIKOOG—A HOT RECEPTION—A MODEL BURGOMASTER—SAINT WILLIBRORD AND THE DOWNS—AWKWARD BEDS.

E were anxious to visit the island of Schiermonnikoog on a Sunday. We had been told of the picturesque costumes and other usages; this was enough to rouse our curiosity. Unfortunately, the Saturday evening on which we purposed starting we were told it was too late, the communications between *terra firma* and the island being few and far between—being, in fact, but a small sailing-boat running once a day from Oostmahorn to Schiermonnikoog and back, carrying the mails and a few passengers. This means of conveyance is even interrupted on the Sunday, the owner's respect of the Sabbath being greater than his cupidity. To cross, as we proposed, on this Saturday was out of the question, as it would take us at least two hours to reach Oostmahorn alone, when the boat would have long since left.

The excellent burgomaster of Dockum, who gave us this somewhat tardy information, seeing how great

was our disappointment, took a heroic resolution.
'Sometimes,' said he, 'in urgent cases the vessel
comes over on the Sunday. I am now going to
telegraph my colleague at Schiermonnikoog that two
strangers are here, recommended by the Minister of
the Interior, and are anxious to cross to the island.
I will beg him to despatch the boat, and possibly he
may be in a position to do so.'

Thanking the ingenious magistrate, we left, and
the next morning started in good time, wondering
whether we should cross the *Friesche Gat* that day.

Cornelius Kemp, as an ardent lover of his country,
worshipping it as Montaigne did Paris, even to its
alleys, describes the free portion of Friesland that
stretches from Dockum to the sea as the most lovely,
the most fertile, and the most populated country in the
world: '*pulcherrima, populosa, et totius mundi fertilis-
sima.*' Although this eulogium is somewhat hyper-
bolic, yet we must admit it to be partly justified.
Certainly if riches constitute the beauty of a country,
then there are few countries that can vie with North
Friesland. Everywhere one meets with fields covered
with golden harvest, colza, flax, and oats; immense
luxuriant meadows, stocked with glossy-coated cows
and magnificent black horses; and, further, in the
midst of this abundance, wealthy farms, surrounded
by orchards, the trees of which bend beneath the
weight of their still green fruit. On the horizon can
be seen the pointed spires of ten churches, indicating
as many villages, and the wide twisting road stretches

like a gigantic serpent through this carpet of verdure. All along the road can be seen peasants, dressed in black, with large Bibles under their arms and long pipes in their mouths, gravely walking along, whilst their female companions, with their head-plates glistening in the sun, chatter by their side.

This road, without tree or shade of any kind, seemed to us interminable. At length, after two hours' fast walking, meanwhile cursing the curves in the road and passing through Metslawier, Morra, and Anjum, we reached our point of embarkation in a profuse perspiration and covered with dust.

We scarcely thought of either studying or inspecting Oostmahorn, which is but a hamlet of little or no importance, but hastened to the quay to see if the boat had arrived, as it would have been anything but pleasant to spend our Sunday in this comparative desert with the promised land in sight. Our hopes, however, were not deceived, for the craft was waiting; but those of the owner certainly were, for on the strength of the telegram he evidently expected to have the carrying of persons of distinction, our sunburnt faces and dusty attire going far to damp his expectations. As it was, however, there could be no mistake; he had come to carry us across, so he took us on board. The journey was somewhat long, for as there was no wind it took us three hours to cover the two leagues that separated us from Schiermonnikoog.

As we neared the land our attention was attracted

by the extensive breakwater that protects the central portion of the shore of the island. This appeared crowded with people; many men, more women, and more children than adults. They appeared to be waiting for something or somebody. As, however, we neared the shore, most of the grown-up persons seemed to retire, and the number of children to increase. This somewhat surprised us, but we were still more surprised before we had finished. Arrived within about 400 yards of the shore, the boat stopped, when several small boats put out and made towards us, followed by a peasant's cart with two horses, which without hesitation took to the water. It was in this vehicle that we had to complete our journey and reach the land. When one goes to Venice one gets out of the train into a boat, which to a newcomer is somewhat surprising. At Schiermonnikoog it is the contrary. You get out of the vessel into a cart, which goes rumbling and stumbling through the different holes in the sand, threatening to swamp us or for us to be carried out to sea by the waves, but usually arriving safely to shore, the boats confining themselves to acting as convoy and giving passengers a hearty welcome.

This reception was very gratifying to us, but it was nothing compared to the one we received on reaching the parade. We could doubt no longer that the 200 or 300 children and people assembled, were there to see us, and us only. The cheers, laughter, and jokes were unceasing; but they, like the owner of the craft, were evidently disappointed in our appearance, and would have wished us more majestic and better dressed. As for myself, I felt so keenly their being undeceived, that I would have given much for a general's cocked hat and uniform.

At the entrance of the village we perceived massed together the whole female population of the place. Doubtless from modesty or delicacy they had retired from the pier, but their curiosity was none the less lively, for they inspected us with a closeness approaching to rudeness. Happily a good angel in the shape of one of the authorities was watching over us, for a stentorian voice called out: 'Now that you have had a good stare at them, perhaps you will let them pass, and leave them alone.' The speaker was the Government gamekeeper; the words were followed by a graceful sign with his stick as an invitation to disperse, which was at once complied with. Thus we were enabled to gain our quarters at the inn.

Our first visit was to the burgomaster, as we wished to thank the worthy magistrate for his kindness in sending for us. We therefore traced our steps to his residence, the prettiest in the island, and found him in the midst of a charming family, who appeared to do their utmost to welcome us. This cordiality never ceased during the whole of our stay, and I may add it is a well-known characteristic of the burgomaster of Schiermonnikoog.

Never was magistrate more in his proper place. M. van der Worm is an old sea wolf, one of those charming wolves with a courteous word and kind smile on the lip—one who would never injure the Florian flock. Originally captain of a vessel, he has not changed his profession, he has only exchanged from his ship, for Schiermonnikoog is after all but an enormous raft of shells and sand, wrecked on the Friesland coast. Its population are all sailors. This tiny spot of earth, lost in the North Sea—deriving its name[1] from its compressed form—fits and sends out to sea no less than seventy 'long-voyaged' ships. All the year round, the male population of the island live on the vessels, and of the 500 men it contains there are seldom more than thirty residing in the place. All the others are away either in the tropics, Pacific, or Mediterranean Sea—everywhere, in fact, except at home. Imagine, therefore, the peace of mind of these good people, having at their head a man initiated in all the secrets and dangers inseparable from such long journeys, and the terrible consequences they may entail. M. van der Worm

[1] 'Oog,' means eye, which is the shape of the island. Schiermonnikoog means the Monk's Eye of the sect of 'Schieringers.' The island in fact was originally inhabited by monks, who placed it under cultivation. The convent was under the jurisdiction of Dockum, and when the Chapel was raised by the Bishop of Utrecht to the rank of Church he left it in the dependency of the Monastery of St. Boniface at Dockum.

Previous to that period Count Albert van Beijeren had, by a Charter, the tenor of which has been retained by E. Verwijs in his work called 'De Oorlogen van Hertog Albrecht van Beijeren met de Friesen,' given to Herman Howenpe an island called Moenkelangenœ, situated near the Lauwers (7th December 1400). But in 1440, according to M. W. W. Buma, in his work entitled 'Schiermonnikoog de Lauwers de Scholbaey,' the island had returned into the hands of Philip of Burgundy.

appears born to his judicial functions, for he is a sailor by taste, and a burgomaster by his ancestors. He is, in fact, the last descendant of van der Werf, the gallant and immortal defender of the town of Leyden.

The burgomaster of Schiermonnikoog retains, as a precious treasure, the gold medal that shone on the breast of his glorious ancestor, as commemorative of this memorable siege. He showed it to us. It bears the date of 1574, and the device, 'Godt belooede Leyden' (God protects Leyden). He keeps it in a casket, but he has also retained in his heart the virtues of his illustrious ancestor. Ten times, in fact, this intrepid mayor has not hesitated to resume his profession of sailor, and to start off with others to the rescue of vessels wrecked or ashore on the sand banks surrounding the island, casualties which occur on an average three times each year.

In 1863, in less than a month, five vessels were wrecked on these fatal banks; amongst them was one of the English navy. That night, notwithstanding the most fearful gale—'amidst a sky of sobs and a sea of tears'—the lifeboat was launched, and succeeded, after innumerable dangers, in rescuing the crew. As a reward for his gallantry, Her Britannic Majesty made to the sailor mayor a present of a magnificent chronometer. At the same time these good acts brought him a still greater reward, in the veneration and love of those he ruled.

He is, at once their ready counsellor and friend;

in fact, a sort of venerated master, and each time he walks through the village all come out to salute him. His island is a little realm, over which he reigns paternally. We went over it with him. It is less a large village than a double street, lined with pretty, simple, modest, clean, well-kept cottages, each fronted by a small garden. Trees, lately planted, have only to grow, to form a pretty and shady park.

The rest of the island is composed chiefly of large meadows, somewhat sun-burnt, and a few fields, cultivated by the farmers of the owner, for Shiermonnikoog belongs solely to a wealthy inhabitant of the Hague. Beyond these fields, and protecting them on three sides, rise sand-hills, forming an immovable rampart to the waves.

Such is this Eldorado, the remembrance of which follows those brave sailors beyond the tropics; who, born there, wish to die there. This is the paradise, full of childish recollections, which they have forsaken to see the world, and which they dream of returning to some day.

To look at it in its entirety it is necessary to mount one of the lighthouses. From there one can see not only the whole island, but also the grey or green girdle of sea that surrounds it, and, to the south, the coast of Friesland, swarming with pleasant church spires. To the right, in the distance, appear large yellow spots, which seem to float on the surface of the waters: one of them is Ameland, the other the island of Rottum, like two sentinels watching the fatherland. Then before one is the calm open sea; not a wave disturbing its horizon, which after undergoing a process of various colours as the day advances, seems to blend itself with the sky.

The immensity that surrounds one on all sides is a moving spectacle to behold. At this height the island appears isolated from the rest of the world, and the cottages below appear sunk in the ground, so narrow and small do they look. The sand-hills have the appearance of a small chain of mountains of uneven, parched, and dried-up summits, with not a tree or blade of grass to vary their monotony. You know their legend : like that of the Dockum spring, they are the result of a pastoral rod.

The rod was that of a saintly man named Willibrord, the first apostle of the new faith in this rude country. The waters were continually encroaching, and spreading havoc and desolation around. Saint Willibrord took his staff and drew a line along the shore, when, following his steps, up rose the mountains of sand, against which beat continually the waters of the ocean, but stopped in their wild career, by this immovable barrier, as if the Almighty had spoken, saying, 'Thus far shall ye go, and no further.' This is the legend : science tells us differently. But this is not the time for explanations. Since we are on the subject of science, let us visit the Schiermonnikoog school which will be more quickly disposed of than the origin of the sand-hills.

This school is also very clean, well kept, and well

ventilated. It is under the direction of a young but well-educated man, well up to his work, and fully aware of the responsibility of his post. It is not a merely superficial education that is required for the children of the island ; all must be sailors, and all wish to become captains. Not only, therefore, must they have a fair knowledge of general subjects, but are moreover expected to learn three or four languages, have a thorough acquaintance with geography, and as much knowledge of mathematics as to be enabled, with the assistance of the compass and the sextant, to find their way across the solitude of the ocean. Add to this, book-keeping, history, philosophy, and a smattering of medicine, and you have a fair idea of what is taught at Schiermonnikoog school.

Each year the wealth of this little school is increased, either in money or by scientific instruments, by old scholars, who by this means try to show their gratitude to the establishment that educated them.

It was with the burgomaster's family, the director of the school, and one of the magistrates that we spent the day and evening, during which pastry and Rhine wine were freely partaken of, and so pleasantly did the time pass that it was one o'clock before we separated. Our friends accompanied us as far as the modest inn, where something very like hard labour awaited us in the shape of a gymnastic performance to reach our beds. These were, after the fashion of the country, imbedded in the wall, resembling cupboards, but placed at such a height from the floor as to be almost beyond scaling. If it is difficult to get into these narrow boxes, it is more so to get out, for the bedding being composed of five trusses of straw and a feather mattress, you find yourself on awaking at the bottom of a sort of precipice, from which, to say the least, it is awkward to get out.

CHAPTER VIII.

ZOUTKAMP — GRIJPSKERK — GRONINGEN — MILITARY AND COMMERCIAL HISTORY — THE CHURCHES — ARCHITECTURE — TWO HEAVY LAW ACTIONS — RIPERDA — THE ACADEMY — THE DEAF AND DUMB INSTITUTE.

IT had taken us two hours to go from Oostmahorn to Schiermonnikoog; it took us six from the latter to Zoutkamp—I mean by sea, for having started at day-break, and it being low water, we had to 'do' an hour in the 'cart' to reach our craft—besides, there was still less wind than when we crossed on the Sunday. However, the tide gradually rose and did for us what the wind refused, and finally carried us to the landing stage at Zoutkamp. Here we climbed the ladder and hastened to the inn, taking care on our way not to trample on some dozen lazy fellows lying stretched on the ground with fixed eyes and immovable countenances.

Zoutkamp is an average sized village of about 600 inhabitants, and is of no great importance beyond being the harbour, or seaport of Groningen. Situated at the mouth of the Reitdiep, which is the obligatory channel of all vessels going to or coming from Groningen, it is usually filled with foreign seamen, who somewhat enliven it. Such a place has neither character nor history. We did not care to stay there long, but hastened to reach the capital of the province. At the tavern we found it difficult to find anyone to speak to. The master was one of the lazy party we met on the quay, and did not seem the least inclined to disturb himself to receive his customers. He at length came, hat over eyes, pipe in mouth, and an uncivil tongue. It was with regret he appeared to serve us with some bread, ham, and beer, and with a snarl informed us of the best means to reach Groningen, namely, to walk to Grijpskerk—two good leagues—where we would find the railway.

Notwithstanding the ill-favoured countenance of this strange inn-keeper, we could do nothing but take his advice; we, however, took the precaution to ask for a guide to show us the road and relieve us of part of our luggage. An old man was brought to us, who in his turn fetched a child, and we all four crossed the Lauwers in a boat and landed in a field from whence we cut across country, during which sundry ditches had to be jumped and numerous gates climbed, both of which were difficult and unpleasant with forty pounds weight on one's back. At length, after these most fatiguing performances, we found ourselves in a narrow, dirty road, stretching out of sight; we thought our troubles o'er, but they were but commencing.

Our guide, in fact, had only taken a companion so as to be able to talk more at his ease. A fine speaker, he measured his steps by his sentences, and so as not to interfere with the harmony of his discourse, would slacken his pace at a ' comma' and stop altogether at a 'full stop.' To give expression to the notes of 'interrogation' and 'exclamation,' he would put down his load and gesticulate with his hands and arms. We were, however, in too great a hurry to appreciate the beauties of his eloquence. Many times we had to stop that they might overtake us, *strong* expressions had no other result than to call forth disdainful looks and a shrugging of shoulders. At length we got angry, and having to explain himself, the good man informed us that his light load was irksome, and wanted us to relieve him of it. As to his walking pace, he said it was the right one, and as he was our guide we ought to follow his example.

Had it not been for his arrogant appearance and impertinent looks we should have laughed the matter off, but they were too palpable to be overlooked. In a minute we had repossessed ourselves of the small trunk he carried, and having paid him just half the amount agreed upon, requested he would 'make himself scarce.' He protested, but seeing that we were determined, and that all his eloquence was in vain, he retraced his steps with his companion, showering on our heads innumerable maledictions.

We now found ourselves in an unknown country, scarcely knowing where we were, but we lost no time in discussion; having divided the luggage, we started afresh. Directed by an agent of the police, who evidently took us for deserters, and by some girls, who by their smiles thought we were pedlars and expected us to display our goods in the shape of silks and sham jewellery, we at length arrived, covered with dust and in a profuse perspiration, at Grijpskerk just in time to see the train leave the station.

The mischief, however, was not so great as we imagined; there was another train in the evening, and we waited for it whilst wandering about the village, which is simply an interminable street, bordered with small houses with four or five taverns. In one we found bad beer, but splendid girls, who certainly were not from Dockum, for their chignons threatened to reach to heaven. In another, an ill-favoured old hag, but a first-class dinner, which we scarcely hoped for. We next visited the church, from which the name of the village is derived, being that of its noble founder Nicholas Grijp, who in 1476 also erected a chapel of brick.

Repaired at various periods, the church is the sole monument in the place; we therefore quitted it without regret and hastened to the capital.

Groningen is not only a fine large town, populous, rich, and flourishing, but is moreover the most ancient in the country. It is generally agreed that Holland has no history. Never was greater mistake made. On the contrary, she possesses one of the most moving and interesting kind imaginable. To understand it thoroughly it is not only necessary to study the facts, but also how and when these facts were brought about, and be able, as the saying goes, ' to read between the lines,' for the political reactions, at first so incomprehensible, and which are the foundation of its history, are easily understood when the independent spirit, which characterises the Groningeners, is taken into account.

In early times, Groningen, if not emancipated in appearance, was so far so in reality as to be able to retain her right of government. She was constantly changing rulers, and never retained any single one long enough to imperil her liberty.

The ancient chronicles date it as founded 500 years B.C., some by a person called Grunus, who gave it his name; according to others by a German race, the Gruines, mentioned by Tacitus. But neighbouring towns, jealous of its pedigree, affirm that the name is derived from the Dutch adjective ' Groen ' (green), and from the substantive ' inigen,' which in the Drenthe and Overyssel patois means ' field ' or ' meadow,' and that really she takes her name from the green pasturages with which she is surrounded.

This, however, signifies but little, for from whatever source the name is derived, one thing is certain, that in the year 48 of the present era, Corbulon found the town thriving and the position good, whereupon he endowed it with sundry institutes, and better still with fortifications, which were more in keeping with the age. A century later its importance was such that the geographer, Ptolemy, thought it worth mentioning in his works. In 398

G

the Normans, finding it easy of access, paid it a visit. An old chronicler, who refers to it as 'Grins,' mentions it as defended by a palisade. Cornelius Kempius tells us that in 1110 the Emperor Henry IV. pulled down the palisade and substituted a rampart of bricks surmounted by forts. In 1570 the Spaniards surrounded it with double fortifications, that of the interior of brick, and outwardly with earthworks. Finally the great Coehoorn, the Vauban of Holland, turned it into a fortification of first rank.

Take a plan of Groningen, and you can easily trace these three last transformations. First is the larger circular street which envelopes the tower bearing the suggestive name of 'Achter den Murr' (behind the wall). Then the also circular canal, which forms a second girdle, known successively as the 'Loopende diep,' 'Katten diep,' 'Zuider diep,' 'Noorder and Zuider Haven.' Lastly the actual fortifications which encircle the place with a third enclosure.

If the military history is easy to follow, the commercial history is equally so. It was in 1116 that Groningen obtained its most important privileges, and in 1220, with Lubeck and Bremen, organised a fleet that took part in the Crusades. In 1220 its sailors were in constant communication with the people on the Baltic, and besides signing a treaty with the inhabitants of the Island of Gottenburg, in 1257 it contracted a commercial alliance with the King of England. In 1284 it figured amongst the

Hanseatic towns. In 1285 it signed a treaty of commerce with the King of Sweden, and in 1298 with the Counts of Holland. So much for the thirteenth century. The fourteenth is none the less prolific, and gives us an insight into its outside commerce. The fifteenth deals with the formation of markets; that for fish in 1446; for provisions generally in 1447; then come those for cattle and horses; and, finally, that for corn—all of which exist to the present day; the latter being one of the most important of the Low Countries. Since then its agricultural importance has so far increased that the neighbouring provinces allow its cattle to pass through free of duty; and, as early as 1469, twelve Groningen farmers were seen driving one thousand head of cattle to the fair at Bois-le-Duc.

Amidst such agricultural prosperity the manufactures of a town could scarcely remain idle. In 1436 the different trades formed themselves into the 'guilds' (gilden), so influential in the Low Countries, first to the number of eighteen, but later on to thirty; and these constituted a real power, for their individual numbers and resources are, to say the least, considerable.

The situation of Groningen is, however, exceptional. It not only provisions the neighbouring towns, where it has no rivals, but, lying between two rivers, the Hunse and the Aa, it is in communication, by the Damsterdiep, with 'Eems,' and by the *Reitdiep* with the North Sea; besides which it joins Leeuwarden and the Zuider-Zee by its canals, and by means of the 'Winschoterdiep' holds communication with the German provinces.

Naturally this flourishing state of business tends to the happy temperament of the inhabitants. Groningen is mentioned by old chroniclers as a kind of 'Eldorado.' The festivities, according to Rabelais, were specially esteemed by the inhabitants. As early as the fourteenth century it was famous for its good living; and we find a young Danish prince speculating on its 'failing,' to avenge the death of his father and the glory of its king. He arrived at the mouth of the Eems with a shipload of provisions and wines, well knowing he would not remain long without visits from the heads of the community. He was not deceived. Before long, officers and magistrates vied with each other for invitations to the navigator, who, it is needless to say, received them in the most affable manner, and invited them to dinner. Others who came on board, but could not find room, got tipsy, and laid down to sleep. Whereupon the prince raised anchor and carried off those rebel magistrates who, having assassinated the governor, had overthrown the yoke of the kings of Denmark.[1]

The lesson does not appear to have been lost on the inhabitants; for, from that date, they have become more steady and sober. In the seventeenth century they went so far as to publish prohibitions

---

[1] See *Chronicle of Holland and Zeelande.*

against certain marriages and festivities. A citizen, when giving a ball, had to curtail his orchestra to two fifes and three string instruments, and was further forbidden to allow the performers more than two bottles of wine apiece.

In the fifteenth century we find the inhabitants boasting of the quiet and steady habits of the town, which is corroborated by Guicciardini, C. Kempius, and Blaeu. The gates were shut at twilight, and no one could enter the town, not even the burgomaster, unless he was known to be absent on business relating to the city. At night no one could walk the streets without a lantern. A watchman was on every fort to give notice of fires or riot, besides sentinels, who sounded a bugle every half-hour. To this day these precautions continue partly to be taken; for watchmen still sound the bugle from the church-tower of St. Martin. Nevertheless, the heads of the community are worthy of their ancestors; and no better proof can be had than in the club known as the 'Harmonie,' the most celebrated and best known throughout the Low Countries. It is a magnificent building, containing concert, reading, and dining-rooms. It is ornamented by a magnificent and well-kept garden or pleasure-grounds, frequented by the fashionable society of Groningen, who, more liberal than their neighbours of the adjoining provinces, do not banish their wives and daughters from their personal resorts, where lively conversations and pleasant music are enjoyed.

The inhabitants of Groningen have, however, much taste for music, of which we had a proof. Struck by the beauty of the morning we got up early, and, attracted by the chants coming from the Catholic Church, we went in and assisted at the mass. Seldom had I assisted at one performed with such taste and devotion. The 'Hosanna' was simply splendid; and the pronunciation of the Latin by the priests was most curious to French ears.

This church, belonging to the Roman Catholic faith, was originally very fine, but having undergone numerous repairs, has nothing of interest left. Groningen, however, has two larger and finer ones of the Calvinistic creed, namely that of *Aakerk*, and the celebrated edifice of Saint Martin.

Aakerk, the true name of which is 'Onze Lieve Vrouwekerk ter Aa,' that is to say, Our Lady of 'Aa,' was erected on the site of a chapel dedicated to Saint Nicholas, and afterwards to all the Saints. In 1246 the Bishop of Utrecht conferred on it the title of a parish church, but being struck by lightning in 1465 and burnt in 1671, and partly rebuilt in 1710, it has lost much of its primitive character. The nave has, however, retained its magnificent elevation; it has, moreover, some fine organs and a curiously sculptured pulpit.

As regards Saint Martin's Church, we know that it was built in the twelfth century. In the fifteenth it was almost entirely rebuilt; the lower portion and the gallery were demolished, so as to extend the aisles. Like all churches in the country, it was constructed in brick, and of the most simple architecture. The steeple is of stone, and rather more ornamented. It was erected between 1469 and 1482, and is composed of five stories, the two first of which are square, and the three others octagonal, resting on a square base pierced with a lofty vault which serves as a passage.

This tower, whose top story is 94 metres above the ground, is celebrated throughout the country. Even in the sixteenth century it was looked upon as a wonder, and C. Kempius, who liked to dwell on its merits, states that, looking down from the top, the people walking below appeared no larger than children a year old. I confess that, either from confidence in this faithful historian or from some other motive, we did not trouble ourselves to verify the fact.

As may be supposed, the churches are not the only monuments the town contains. At the foot of St. Martin's Church, in the great market-place — which, by the way, is one of the largest and best-regulated in the Netherlands—stands a very curious house, which goes back to the fourteenth century. M. Acker Stratingh has published a work on this curious house, entitled, 'Het aloude raad en regthuis thans de hoofdwacht te Groningen.' It really dates from 1338, and was for some time made use of as the court of justice, *Raad en Regthuis*. Beneath its windows stood the pillory and gallows, for the Groningen judges had the power to pass all kinds of sentences, against which there was no appeal. Later on the building became a guard-house.

If we are to credit M. Diest Lorgion, in 1852 it was one of only two houses left of that early period. The fact, however, is not surprising, for all those built during the fourteenth and part of the fifteenth century were of wood, but the latter has left some few of interest. They are large buildings with projecting eaves, and a high arched window. They are sprinkled throughout the town, but the best specimens are to be seen in the *Brugstraat*.

The sixteenth century was still more prolific, and to this period we are inclined to attribute the erection of the house in the market-place, which at one time also served as a residence for the Duke of Alba; also many others, with their curious fronts and narrow windows, more like the loop-holes noticed on the *groote Spilsluizen*, and on the *Ossenmarkt*, near the Deaf and Dumb Institute; and also that noble construction the Court House, with its pleasant front, which, although it bears the date of 1612, appears to me to be at least thirty years older.[1]

But the most classical piece of architecture of that period is a pretty little house, built entirely of stone, standing close to the 'Harmonie' Club, and occupied

---

[1] This charming edifice bears two dates, that of 1612 and 1779; the latter applies to the repairs, and more especially to a small gate of curious style, which notwithstanding its anachronism has not a bad effect. The former appears also to refer to a restoration, the great entrance door for instance with its fine arched ceiling and decorations. But the windows and the building generally are certainly anterior to the seventeenth century.

THE COLLECTHUIS AT GRONINGEN.

by M. Cardinaal, a banker. It has three stories of different styles of architecture, the ground floor being Tuscan, the first floor Ionic, and the second Corinthian. The latter has but one window, whereas the two former have three each.

Fluted columns of exquisite taste run up to about one-third of its height. Beautifully delicate and elegant friezes divide the first two stories, and the second has two buttresses bearing medallions in demi-relief, surmounted by an attic which worthily completes this attractive *façade*.

This graceful little building dates from 1559. It was not, however, until the seventeenth century that the Groningen architecture adopted any original style, of which only a few specimens remain in good condition. Three or four still stand on the great market-place, the most notable being that of the collector (*collecethius*) which is a genuine gem.

With the passing away of the seventeenth century this charmingly original style disappeared also, and the style generally adopted throughout Holland took its place. The fashion was set by the Hague. A few fine large houses, and the one inhabited by Count von Heiden, governor of the province, are the only exceptions to this general rule. Then came the period, still more to be deplored, which terminated the last century and began the present.

The Town Hall belongs to this unfortunate period; an immense building of grey stone and brick, with large columns and Corinthian pilasters. On the front it bears the grievously eloquent date, M.D.C.C.C.X.[1] It was the year of its inauguration. In the interior it has the same cold common-place, but pretentious appearance. The old *Raad en Wijnkins*, as represented to us in pictures, was infinitely superior. But wings surmounted by pinnacles and historical weather-cocks were out of keeping with the style adopted in 1800.

At that period the antique was the rage, the models being supplied by Greece, and thus bringing about those inopportune reminiscences.

Fortunately, although the walls are bare and the rooms and passages gloomy, the archives contain many precious treasures.

Thanks to the archæologist, M. H. O. Feith, who is one of the most learned and kind of the Groningen palæographers, we had a most instructive and pleasant visit. Everything was in perfect order, methodically classed, and without any important blank or gap. The charters, carefully labelled and dated, are stored in large cupboards full of small drawers. Each drawer corresponds with a period of ten years, beginning at the year 1250 and ending with the last century. After the charters come the town registers, then those of the guilds, precious in their information, and precious also in their valuable bindings. The registers of the jewellers, brewers, and victuallers, with their silver coverings, are of great value. I may say the same of the *Stadbock*, which, with its corners

---

[1] The first stone was laid April 29, 1793.

of embossed silver, is, as a work of art, worthy of Goltsius. Its contents date from 1424 to the end of the sixteenth century.

In this municipal treasury are still kept the silver maces of the presidents of the corporation and the burgomasters' sceptres, which are curious and interesting specimens of old jewellery. Then comes the emblematical hat in green velvet, with the town arms and the following grand device: *Summum libertatis est testimonium moribus et legibus suis uti.* It dates from 1685, but was also copied on the former one, which also served to hold the famous beans. These latter number twenty-four, five black and nineteen white, all of silver, and have heretofore played their part in the policy of this powerful city.

The corporation was composed of eight burgomasters and sixteen 'life' councillors; four of the former, and eight of the latter really exercising their functions. At the end of each year, the burgomaster in power used to place the beans in the hat, and present it to the councillors and their colleagues, those drawing the black ones having to enter on active duty for the ensuing year. (See Leclerc's *History of the United Provinces.*)

As we have seen, the authority of the magistrate was boundless. He had the power to pass both heavy and light sentences, rectify the duties or taxation, and dispose of the public funds. It was he who represented the town at the councils of the province, and as all the territory surrounding Groningen—known as the Ommelandes—had but one vote, the town in itself, therefore, was as powerful as the whole of the province. As their interests were seldom similar, it is easy to understand the difficulties to which this unequal division of suffrage gave rise. Groningen, more ambitious than the Ommelandes, was constantly encroaching on the rights and privileges of its neighbours. Hence innumerable squabbles, often ending in open warfare. On ten occasions they led to war. In 1577, on the 1st of November, 'the prelates and nobles of the Ommelandes in the province of Groningen, having been called upon to meet in the town, to discuss certain differences existing between the two, were seized by the authorities and put in prison.'

In vain did William the Taciturn grieve over these dissensions in such serious times, and send Marnix de Sainte Aldegonde and the pensioner of Sille to arrange matters—they could do nothing; their intervention being looked upon as misplaced and uncalled for.

Two years later (1579) Groningen, who had never forgiven this interference by the States, declined to adhere to the Union of Utrecht. To obtain its consent it became necessary to send Count de Renneberg to besiege it. Vanquished, it was compelled to comply; but its spirit of indiscipline became contagious, for Renneberg, having been named governor, was the first to raise the standard of rebellion. The 3rd of

March, at 4 A.M., he assembled to the sound of the drum, in the market-place, the gendarmes and citizens of his party. Seated on his horse with drawn sword, he addressed them as follows: 'Children, help me to do that which is necessary for His Majesty's service and our own protection;' whereupon doors were forced open and the partisans of the Union made prisoners. In the meantime the Count's cavalry scoured the streets, and no one could appear at a window without being shot.

The States, to punish this fresh act of rebellion, sent against the town Count William of Nassau, but without success; and it was only fourteen years later that it re-entered the Union, and this only after a lengthened siege, during which 18,000 cannon shots were fired against it, after which it was carried by assault. It was then, and then only, that the inhabitants entertained a compromise. Even then they allowed no peace to the States, for in 1599 we find the Government reinforcing the garrison, disarming the population, and threatening to rebuild the citadel to keep them in subjection.[1]

What about the Ommelandes? it will be asked. During all this period the quarrelling continued between them, and it was only in 1640 that the complaints, being brought before the States General, were judicially settled. They must have been some-

---

[1] See Guicciardini's 'Description of the Low Countries'; Le Petit's 'Chronicles of Holland and Zeelande'; and Meteren's 'History of the Low Countries.'

what complicated, for the judgment alone forms a large volume, the report of the case generally comprising twenty-seven volumes of 1,200 pages each. They can be consulted at leisure in the archives of Groningen.

This is not the only heavy law action the town had to undergo. Two centuries previously it had to fight the terrible tribunal of ' *Vehme.*' The origin of this redoutable Areopagus, whose jurisdiction extended to Westphalia and its provinces, has been lost in the darkness of time. The learned Henry Bruman, whom Dom Pitra calls, not without reason, the Tacitus of Overyssel, states it to have been instituted by Charlemagne. The Saxons, rebels, perjurers, thieves, and murderers so often vanquished by this great emperor, had deserved for their crimes an unique punishment. The illustrious monarch had, therefore, this secret tribunal, which hung like the sword of Damocles over the heads of these evil doers. It had branches throughout the country; would move about unnoticed, inspecting everything, and meeting at night in conference.[1]

Each member was at the same time witness, prosecutor, judge, and executioner. No exception could be taken by any member of the family of the accused, to the ruling of the court. A hatchet placed on the door of the residence of the culprit was a sign of condemnation. No one was exempt from its juris-

---

[1] In the 5th act of his play, Goetz de Berlichingetn produces a moving scene in which these free judges appear.

diction, not even the powerful lord of Berg, Ulric de Passau, Chancellor of the Empire, who with the Emperor Frederick III. himself, had to appear before it. Whole towns and provinces came under its curse. The *Vehme* was never so terrible as when resisted by numbers. Zutphen, Ootmarsum, and Groningen had in turn to appear at its bar, the latter being summoned on a purely civil question. It unlawfully retained the sum of 5,000 florins belonging to a party of the name of Dirck, and for this sum it was placed outside the pale of the law and held up to execration. This took place in 1456. A century earlier the sentence would have carried its full weight, but in the fifteenth century the terrible tribunal had lost much of its power, and Groningen was in itself too powerful. It rebelled, therefore, against the decree, and formed a league which was joined by Deventer, Kampen, and Zutphen. The Emperor was called upon to take notice of the case; the Archbishop of Cologne intervened, and many other theologians took part in the debates. Finally a learned prelate, who had travelled throughout those countries, and could testify to the dreadful consequences of this anonymous Areopagus, and who was no other than Æneas Sylvius, ascended the pontifical throne as Pius II., and launched forth a bull[1] in 1483 which struck a death blow to this tribunal.

The archives of Groningen still retain the copy

---

[1] This bull was addressed to the Chapters of St. Martin (Groningen), St. Libium (Deventer), and St. Nicholas (Kampen).

of the famous *Vehme* judgment as hurled against the valiant city. It is probably the only trace to be found of its relations with Germany. There are, besides, some large glasses or tankards of a size sufficient to frighten the drinkers of the present day, whose appearance is certainly more lively than the musty-smelling papers. Add to these, three ancient carved and painted coffers, and a picture representing the planting the 'tree of liberty' in the great market on the 14th February 1793, and you have a complete list of the curiosities and treasures the Town-Hall contains.

Those to be seen at the Government Palace are of a different order. They form a small pre-historic museum, which, although still in its infancy, already contains many interesting specimens of the antiquities of the country, chiefly polished and cut stones, bone skates, and a few bronze and iron articles of the same period. On the ground floor of this large palace, built in 1602 and rebuilt in our time, is a vast fine chamber bearing the impress of the seventeenth century. It is the States room; at the end there is a memorial chimney-piece, and a very fair allegorical painting signed Collenius, and dated 1712.

The building overlooks a triangular place, well planted with trees, beneath which children play. It is close to this spot that John William de Riperda was born, one of the greatest impostors or adventurers the eighteenth century has produced.

Born in 1690 of a noble and rich family, Riperda,

at the age of twenty-two, commanded a regiment of infantry; his intelligence obtained for him a diplomatic mission to Madrid.

Spain doubtless pleased him well, for he stayed there altogether, and having renounced his religion, managed to ingratiate himself amongst the courtiers of Philip V. Soon he captivated the King himself, and in 1725 succeeded, in the name of his new master, in concluding that famous treaty of alliance with the Emperor Charles IV., of which Voltaire said: 'This is the strangest compact. Two opposition houses uniting, whilst distrusting one another. It was the English, who, having done their best to dethrone Philip V., acted as mediators to this treaty, and a Dutchman, having become an all-powerful duke, who signed it.'

From this time Riperda's fortune was at its climax. At one time he was ambassador to the Court of Vienna, and later director of the King's cabinet, and holder of three portfolios, viz., that of Minister of the Interior, Finance, and War. He was, in fact, everything and everybody; but the old Spanish aristocracy became jealous of his good fortune at last, and conspired to ruin him. One fine day this spoilt child of fortune and brilliant minister, awoke to find himself a prisoner in the Tower of Segovia. There he remained two years, seduced his jailer's daughter, and ultimately escaped and returned to his country, where he re-entered the Calvinistic faith. But Groningen was not to his liking. Its area was too limited for a

H

man of such ambitious views. He therefore started for Morocco, turned Mussulman, gained the confidence of Muley-Abdallah, became a general under the name of Osman Pacha, and induced his new master to declare war against Spain. Less successful in the field than in the cabinet, he was defeated at Ceuta and exiled to Tetuan, where he founded a new religion of which he was the head; but scarcely had he began to obtain proselytes, than death overtook him, and thus saved the world from fresh fanaticism.[1]

It is difficult to meet with a more diversified career, and when one looks upon the prosaic habitation with its humble surroundings, it is difficult to imagine that such a man could have been born there.

His biography, however, was published throughout the country in French, English, Spanish, and Dutch. The latter contains some interesting details on the conversion of our hero to Islamism.

Curiously enough, this adventurer is about the only inhabitant of Groningen whose name has obtained an European celebrity. It is not that the city has not produced great and noble men, but somehow their names have died out. Who now remembers Wessel Gansfort (born 1419, and died 1489)? Yet he was Luther's predecessor, and his contemporaries had surnamed him the 'Light of the World.' Who knows Rudolphus Agricola? Yet in his day he was

---

[1] Chenier denies this last conversion; he says: 'People who knew him assert that he ended his life at Tetuan without having either changed his dress or religion.'

looked upon as a kind of phœnix. He was the Picus de Mirandole of North Europe.¹

Ubbo Emmius himself would be unknown had he not written the history of his country,² and been the chief rector of the Groningen University.

This University was founded in 1614, that is to say, twenty-two years before the one in Utrecht, and thirty-nine years after that of Leyden. Long before its institution, however, it was celebrated throughout the literary world, and as early as the sixteenth century its school attracted students from all parts of Europe especially whilst under the direction of the rector Reynerus Prædinius, who died in 1559. On its opening, the academy had a fair number of pupils. Afterwards in certain years there were as many as 6,000 at one time, 2,500 of whom were foreigners. They came from Germany, Hungary, Switzerland, and France; and it was no more than the University deserved, for it spared no expense or trouble in obtaining the best masters.

Amongst the number were Antoine Dusing the learned Eastern scholar, Maresius (Maretz, the lord of Feret) the brilliant theologian and antagonist of Coccejus, and Gomar, the adversary of the redoubtable precepts of Arminius, whose eloquence echoed through

---

[1] His epitaph was as follows:
'Invida clauserunt hoc marmore fata Rudolphum,
Agricolum, Frisii spem decusque soli.
Scilicet hoc vivo meruit Germania laudis
Quicquid habet Latium, Græcia quicquid habet.'
[2] Hegenitus proclaims him the most learned historian of Friesland.

the halls of the academy. Unfortunately the success was of short duration. Theological discussions took the place of serious studies. The dispute emanating in the sanctuary of study, spread to the streets, and turned into a battle. The religious parties fought with such bitterness for the different chairs, that in order to stay the conflict, the authorities declined to allow the re-occupation of those becoming vacant. From this date the academy began daily to decay— and when its centenary came round there was nobody to celebrate it.

It required no less than the support of the Princes of the House of Orange to raise it from its ruins, and it was thanks to them that it ultimately saw better days; but it never regained its former glory, although it still possessed several illustrious teachers. Amongst others John Bernouilli, who, after Newton and Leibnitz, was the greatest mathematician of the time; also Babeyrac, exiled from France by the revocation of the edict of Nantes; Petrus Camper, the emulator of Boerhaave; Schroeder the orientalist, and Muntinghe the theologian, still attracted a considerable number of foreigners. But the exciting events that occurred at the end of the eighteenth century were as fatal to the unfortunate university as the theological discussions of the preceding century, and in 1812 it was proposed to suppress it altogether.

It was, however, once more preserved from destruction. Reorganised in 1815, it became from a provincial, a State University. Its new title, however, did not restore the prosperity of former days. Education was fast spreading throughout the neighbouring provinces, and these were no longer dependent on Groningen for the teaching of their children: besides increased facilities of communication enabled students to go either to Leyden or Utrecht to complete their studies. At present the unfortunate university is on its 'last legs,' and the professors esteem themselves fortunate if they get an audience of five or six students, for they are frequently compelled to be satisfied with the attendance of a solitary individual. The number of 'freshmen' steadily declines—the average for the last ten years being twenty-seven, and for the present, 1875–6, being but fourteen. The Student's Almanack, gleaned from all sources, counts but 188.

The professors especially suffer by this state of things, and are compelled to seek outside employment in order to preserve their social standing and bring up their families. The most eminent, however, have left Groningen. M. de Vries is at Leyden; M. Jonckbloet has entered the political world, and many others are on the point of leaving.

It will be unfortunate if this desertion continues. The past of the Groningen Academy is too illustrious for it to disappear without regret. Until lately its instruction has been carefully watched by all learned men in Europe. Independently of the celebrated names before mentioned, Groningen possessed, twenty years since, a theological school of great renown. Under the inspiration of Messieurs Pareau, Hofstede de Groote and Muurling, it proclaimed that the Bible, although containing the word of God, was not His word, and not in keeping with the sentiments of the present day. It moreover refused to identify Christ with God, preferring to allow Him a celestial pre-existence and a miraculous origin. It is easy to imagine the tempests of controversy raised by such teaching.

Now M. Hofstede de Groote is the apostle of other doctrines, and the learned societies trouble themselves no further about the Groningen Academy. But the ancient city has not abandoned the hope of restoring to its University its flourishing state during the seventeenth century. It is not for want of trouble or expense, for only a few years since it had the buildings reconstructed, giving them almost a majestic appearance. The rooms are spacious, and the passages wide and lofty. It moreover contains a justly celebrated cabinet of Natural History and a valuable library, containing, amongst other treasures, two hundred incunabula, of which the 'Gemmula vocabularum cum addito diligenter revisa et emendata' is supposed to be unique.[1]

---

[1] Studying at the Hague with Mr. Campbell, the director of the Royal Library, it was proved that this *Gemmula* is no other than that described on page 116 of the *Annales de la Typographie Néerlandaise*, one of which was put up at the 'Inglis' sale, in 1871. The work, therefore, cannot be unique, for two are now known to exist, viz. that of Groningen, and that of the Inglis sale.

Amongst other rarities must be mentioned a 'book of hours,' printed on vellum, by a Frenchman, Simon Vostre; also a Bible filled with notes, and said to have belonged to Luther. Of manuscripts there are but few, but we must not forget to mention an interesting chronicle dated 1237, and a Propertius, which, although not very old, is none the less celebrated.

The Academy is not the only establishment deserving attention. There is another well worth visiting, namely, the Deaf and Dumb Institute. It ranks third in importance to similar establishments in Europe. It follows, in fact, immediately after that of St. Petersburg, which is only surpassed by the Paris Institute, the largest of all. At the time we visited it it contained 173 inmates—ninety boys and eighty-three girls, who only met together for study. They are first taught to talk on their fingers, in which they (the girls chiefly) are most proficient; then by moving the lips. It is curious to see these unfortunate creatures holding a conversation with strangers. The guttural sounds, uncontrolled by the ear, are often screeches and very disagreeable; but this is of little account compared to the advantage they derive from being able to converse with their relatives and friends and fellow-sufferers.

It is to Henry Daniel Guyot, a clergyman of the Reformed French Church, that Groningen is indebted for this institute. To this good man the corporation have raised a modest monument, which consists of a large square pillar, surmounted by a lamp, standing in the shade of the lofty trees, and near the small place where the institute stands.

The old capital of the Ommelandes has many other charitable institutions ; for, notwithstanding its turbulent spirit and dreams of independence, it always took care of its sick and infirm, as also those otherwise afflicted by nature. In the sixteenth century it had already ten hospitals and five monasteries. At the Reformation the latter were naturally abolished, but without ill-treatment or violence to the inmates; for Groningen was always tolerant as regards religion, and Guicciardini tells us that the laws on religion were never enforced, everyone being allowed to follow the dictates of his or her conscience. The convents abolished were replaced by orphanages and other establishments of the kind, and Groningen now counts twenty-five orphanages, hospitals and refuges for the infirm.

CHAPTER IX.

THE MIDWOLDE TOMB—DELFZIJL AND FARMSUM—APPINGEDAM—
THE *HARDDRAVERIJ*—FEMALE BARGE TOWERS.

TO the west of Groningen, on the frontier of the Drenthe, there is a hamlet called Midwolde, where can be seen the burial place of the Lords of Inhausen and Kniphausen. To this spot we directed our steps on leaving the great town.

At the gates of Groningen the country is rich and fertile, and wonderfully diversified. The winding canals, the houses lost in foliage dominated by windmills with their many-coloured sails, pleasantly blend their various shades. But on nearing Midwolde the neighbourhood of the Drenthe makes itself felt. The foliage becomes gloomy and the earth darker. The oak takes the place of plane trees, and high hedges rise up on all sides. The soil becomes sandy, and the dwellings poorer in appearance. Midwolde is a modest hamlet, and its celebrated church is of the plainest architecture. A square tower of medium height, a concrete roof, covering a low narrow nave, the entire edifice is built of large bricks mellowed by time. Such is this rural temple standing across and in the middle of the traditional *Kerkhof*.

The escutcheons and armorial bearings on the white-washed walls, the carved pulpit and baronial pew, lend to this little sanctuary an air of antiquity quite refreshing. At the further end, where originally stood the altar, now stands the famous mausoleum. It is a large monument of black and white marble on which repose two statues. The first is that of Charles Jerome. The noble seigneur is stretched on a rush mat and enveloped in a mortuary robe. His hands emaciated by suffering, drooping eyelids, and parted lips, have a strikingly truthful appearance. His long hair is thrown back, thus exposing the forehead, and his noble and likewise handsome figure is not unlike that magnificent bust, by Rotrou, we all so admired in the 'lounge' of the Comédie Française.[1]

At his side, reclining on her left arm, is the baroness his wife, seemingly watching him she so dearly loved. In the background is an enormous scroll supported by little angels, half cupids and half cherubs, containing a long, proud epitaph, enumerating the titles of the deceased, whilst a wreath of escutcheons tells of their illustrious alliances. Possibly so much glory had softened the widow's regrets, for her look is more that of reflection than sorrow, more

---

[1] This statue, and that of the baroness, are by R. Verhulst, born at Mechlin in 1624. The statue of the Baron d'Inhausen is the masterpiece of this artist.

calm than despairing. In her hands, however, she holds an hour-glass, which seems to attest that time shall not assuage her grief. So doubtless she thought when raising to the memory of this beloved husband, too soon taken from her by inflexible death, this superb mausoleum. 'But foolish they who believe in eternal sorrows.' This the lovely Anna of Ewsum soon learnt by experience, for before long she was untrue to the memory of her first husband, and married her brother-in-law, whose statue in full armour stands at the foot of the monument.

At about 500 yards from the church is the château originally inhabited by this illustrious family. It had been mentioned to us as curious and interesting, we therefore took the trouble to visit it.

Although the word 'château' or castle appears a somewhat proud title in a country where the Queen's palace is known as the 'wooden house,' and that of the King's uncle as the 'peacock house,' we scarcely expected to meet with much magnificence.

Thanks to the courtesy of M. Ter Horst, an editor of Groningen, I had a large old map of the country showing the different castles throughout the land, none of which I can safely say deserve the title. They are, as a rule, modest houses surmounted by a pigeon-house and surrounded by a muddy moat. Although more or less prepared, we could not help feeling disappointed, as we had expected the dwelling of the living to be in keeping with that of the dead.

It would be scarcely worth mentioning if it was

not for a kind of stone portico at its entrance, pretentiously covered with absurd allegories, and rising like a triumphal arch. Behind this gate is a miry moat covered by a drawbridge, on either side of which are loop-holed watch towers, shelters which would appear menacing but are in reality ridiculous. This abuts on a weedy courtyard, in which are two old culverins peaceably resting on their rotten carriages. Then comes the 'château,' a modest one-storied building, with a farm and its appurtenances. This completes this ambitious but unimposing dwelling, which certainly gives some little animation to this comparative desolation. Nature alone, with its lofty trees, shady groves, and emerald green lawn, lends something noble and grand to this spot by enveloping it in verdure.

Our visit ended, we returned to Groningen by way of Enumatil, Den Horn, and Hoogkerk.

The following morning at daybreak we were once more on the road, but this time taking an eastward course, as we wished to visit Appingedam and Delfzijl and see the mouth of the Eems and the Bay of Dollard.

Delfzijl, the most distant of these places, is eight leagues from Groningen, at the mouth of the *Damsterdiep*, placing the ancient capital in communication with Eems and its German shores. It therefore possesses a strategical position opposite its powerful neighbour, of such importance that at various periods it has been enlarged and fortified by those who were desirous of lessening the power of the ancient city.

Twice Delfzijl was on the point of becoming as rich and powerful as her rival. The first time was in 1568. The Duke of Alva, according to Meteren, seeing the fine situation of the spot and its good harbour, determined to unite to it the village of Farmsum, which is on the opposite shore of the *Damsterdiep*, and thus form one large town. Paccioto, the most intelligent engineer of the day, was entrusted with the work of erecting the fortifications, and the bishop Jan Knijff was ordered from Groningen to bless the foundations. But by petitions and the influence brought to bear on the Duke and the Count de Megen by their secretary Albuccos, the Groningeners persuaded him to renounce his plans.

The second time was in 1591. Groningen was in open rebellion against the States. Prince Maurice held the country, and had just captured Delfzijl without striking a blow. Masters of this important position, the States again thought of carrying out the Duke of Alva's project of making of it a powerful city, and by this means punishing the capital for its everlasting rebellion.

To avert this the Groningeners endeavoured to ward off the blow by suppressing or destroying their rival. On the 12th of February, 1593, it took advantage of the river being completely frozen to send a small army to surprise Delfzijl. They started by night, sliding in all directions, and came in sight of the fortifications without having been observed. Crossing the moat, breaking through the palisade and scaling the ramparts, they succeeded in surprising the garrison. But a man-of-war lying off broke the ice with cannon shots, and, taking up a position in the rear of the assailants, 'raked' them with its sixteen guns, and compelled them to retreat. Their rout was complete. They carried away thirty-seven sleighs full of dead and wounded, leaving besides seven of the former on the field.

What once more saved Groningen from having a formidable rival in Delfzijl was her own subjection. Masters of the great city, the States no longer thought of ruining her; on the contrary they enriched and made her yet stronger.

Let us hasten to add that the attempt by the Groningeners of the 12th of February failed, owing to Delfzijl's position and strongholds. In 1499 the mouth of the river had been fortified by Odsard, Count of Friesland, with special care. Again in 1568 the Duke of Alva had increased the fortifications, and if in 1578 they were partly destroyed, care had been taken to restore them the following year; so well, in fact, that in 1591 'its ramparts were large and wide, and its moat about 110 feet wide.'[1]

Notwithstanding the good state of its old fortifications, they were increased in 1696, when the great Coehoorn surrounded it with the girdle of bastions which we see to-day.

[1] De Meteren, 'History of the Low Countries.'

At the present time the fortress has become a pleasant simple little town, without monuments; its modest houses seem to conceal themselves behind the green banks of the ramparts, shaded by lofty trees. The streets are wide, but the houses are low, and often but one story high. Sometimes they are below the level of the road; and viewed from above, with their red tiled roofs and flower gardens, have a very pretty appearance.

To the east the ramparts overlook the Eems and the Bay of Dollard, stretching like an immense lake to the foot of the green bastions. On the horizon can be seen the German coast sharply defined against the clear sky. To the west is the river with its ships and sluices, which give animation to the scene, for Delfzijl is both a fort and a port. In the distance Farmsum rises against the blue sky out of massive clusters of tall trees. Further still, endless meadows streaked with silver canals, and stocked with cattle, cut here and there by avenues of lofty trees, amongst which appear pretty cottages, all this forming together a most charming picture, which one could contemplate for hours. This is what we should have done had we not been disturbed by the sound of bells.

It was the town-crier. He made his announcements surrounded by a troop of boys. We mechanically followed him at a distance about the town, seeking by this means to discover any similarity between the people of this extreme end of Holland

and their German neighbours, but our research was vain. People, houses, types, language, and dress are purely Dutch. The cleanliness alone is an irrefutable proof of their nationality. In all this town we found but one slight trace of the German; it was in the offer for sale, in a Jew's shop window, of some small statuettes, representing Bavarian gallants and Prussian soldiers making love to fair-haired servant girls. But little proud of this discovery, we left Delfzijl and crossed the sluices to reach Farmsum.

Farmsum is a little village situated on the breakwater that stretches along the Dollard. In the distance it has a Swedish or Muscovite appearance—I might almost say Chinese, were it not that those two words, China and Holland, coupled together, are disagreeable to Dutch ears. This strange aspect is due to its bulging church steeple, low and many-coloured houses, varnished tiles, broad square chimneys covered with large cowls; to this add little wooden bridges, with their white rails, which stand out clearly against the dark green of the fields, and the likeness is complete.

In the interior, Farmsum has the look of a Groningen village, not too well kept, with twisting streets, and houses sufficiently old without being ancient. The oldest construction is a little bridge that bears the date of 1712. The church bears that of 1869. Nothing you see could be more modern. None the less it has a pleasant and elegant appearance.

This lack of ancient buildings is remarkable, as

Farmsum is far from being of modern origin; for, as we have seen, it was already in existence in the time of the Duke of Alva. This cheerful hamlet had, to begin with, a château belonging to the Riperda family. Fortified in 1401 by the Schieringers, this mansion was taken by the Spaniards in 1536, who failed to repair the breaches made in the walls. Since this date it remained a majestic ruin; it was the sole *souvenir* of old times, its demolition was completed in 1812.

After a saunter through the streets of Farmsum, we took the road for Appingedam, which we were in a hurry to reach, as the horse races were to take place there that day. We regarded these races as a piece of good fortune, for they afforded us an opportunity of seeing a small Groningen town on a gala day, and also to make more intimate acquaintance with the rural population of this curious country.

You have no doubt remarked, dear reader, that our first impressions of these people were not very favourable. Upon entering the province by Zoulkamp and Grijpskerk, we met with a rudeness and roughness for which our experience in the other provinces had not at all prepared us. Our reception was almost malevolent, so little are these good people hospitable by nature. This impression was dissipated at Groningen. There, on the contrary, everyone was polite and eager to please, with agreeable manners and a bearing full of tact. Everyone with whom we were brought in contact, from Count Heiden Reinestein, governor of the province, who is the very type of an

I

accomplished gentleman, down to the meanest *employé*, comported themselves with the most perfect politeness, and gave every proof of the strongest desire to please. We were received by professors, savants, and merchants with a charming courtesy. We insensibly came to the conclusion that our first impressions were wrong, and to think that those whom we first met, and to whom our unfavourable impressions were due, constituted but an exception to the rule. Unfortunately it was not so.

There are, in fact, two very distinct populations in the province of Groningen, which it is important not to confound one with the other: the population of the capital which is amiable and polite, and that of the country which is quite the reverse. In days gone by, this same difference existed in all the other provinces between the country and town's people. 'As regards the populace,' said an author of the last century, 'they are coarse almost to excess, and it is said that the low people and the citizens are two different nations.'[1]

I would not suggest that the 'populace' of the other provinces are altogether better, or that they constitute to-day a model of urbanity, but certainly the countries of Groningen have, on this subject of rudeness, a sad superiority which no one will dispute.

It must be concluded that this rudeness is somewhat contagious, for people in easy circumstances,

---

[1] 'Defence of the Dutch nation against the calumnies written in the letters on the Dutch.' The Hague, 1736.

public functionaries, and magistrates even, have not succeeded in divesting themselves completely of this external roughness. With them, it is true, the absence of ceremony does not extend to outrageous familiarities; but it is turned into a cold and haughty reception, which would be most painful if it were not ridiculous.

These reflections recurred to me in consequence of the scenes witnessed during the day, especially at our reception by the burgomaster of Appingedam. 'It is often more difficult to get access to the burgomaster of a village, than to the Prime Minister or the King himself;' said to me one day one of the most prolific novelists of the Young Netherlands, my friend, Jan Ten Brink.

I took this for a joke, little thinking the very birth-place of my friend would furnish the opportunity for verifying the truth of the remark.

I was received with the greatest kindness by the President of the Council of Ministers, without any other claim upon his good-will than the nature of my studies, and my works. I was introduced by him to the governor of the province, who was most solicitous on my behalf, and who gave me a warm recommendation to the burgomaster of Appingedam. Under shield of this double presentation, I thought we were sure of at least a cordial reception; and our first care upon arriving in the little city was to present ourselves to the burgomaster.

Alas! we laboured under a mistake. Our reception was cold, haughty, and so patronising, as to border upon the unpolite. It was municipal arrogance carried to excess. I must admit that we were somewhat dusty; but the toilette of the honourable magistrate, also, was not exactly perfect, for he received us in his shirt sleeves! We were tired, but was that a reason for forgetting to offer us a seat?

The worthy burgomaster, no doubt, desired to appear important and imposing: he might have saved himself the trouble.

> Spectatum admissi risum teneatis amici.

We took leave of him, having the greatest difficulty imaginable to retain a serious countenance.

Having gained the street we laughed to our hearts' content, and profiting by the earliness of the hour, proceeded to visit the town.

Appingedam is a picturesque little town, through which runs a narrow river without quays, on each side of which are decaying houses and small gardens invaded by rank weeds. Add to this the great high pitched bridges, some large gaudily-painted boats, in the distance a few old trees through the foliage of which the houses may be seen, and the white painted barriers, and one may form some idea of the beautiful blending of colour and outline which this pretty little river presents.

The streets are parallel or at right angles to the course of the stream, and are pleasantly laid out, giving one the impression that the town is prosperous, and the country rich.

The principal monuments of Appingedam are found on a large irregular square or place extending to the right. First there is the church which, begun in 1254 and finished in 1327, has been so often restored that it offers but mediocre interest. By its side stands the Town Hall with an out-building in brick and stone after the fashion of the houses of Groningen. Its *façade* is decorated with a bas-relief set off in colour, representing Justice, and bearing the date of 1631.

The interior of the Town Hall contains one immense chamber devoid of all character, but furnished with large presses enclosing a few *souvenirs* of past grandeur. We inspected them hastily, as we were anxious to get out of this unsympathising municipal atmosphere.

The great square or place referred to above, attracted us by its noise and bustle.

On the occasion of the races it was invaded by manufacturers of *poffertjes* (a kind of small fritter, insipid in taste but of savoury odour, made in the open air), with merry-go-rounds and booths of every description.

It was a sort of improvised fair, extending from the neighbouring streets as far as the ancient cemetery surrounding the church.

These itinerant players and groups of drinkers, gaily installed in the resting-place of the dead, had a very singular effect, and produced a still more singular contrast.

On the bastions of the ancient rampart, behind the cemetery, several acrobats and gipsies had established themselves. This rampart, which is now planted with trees, was demolished in 1539. In 1536 it had been scaled by the troops of Charles V., who were obliged to take the town by assault to bring it to subjection.

The town has since remained dismantled; nevertheless it did not lose its ancient importance, for it was still the capital of one quarter of the Ommelandes, the Fivelingo, and had forty-five villages subject to its jurisprudence. It had also the right to coin money, which right it retained till the end of the sixteenth century. Although troops have defiled through its streets, from the army of Prince Maurice to the Cosaques in 1813, Appingedam still remains important and rich.

But this importance does not rest now, as heretofore, on privileges more or less dearly acquired. Appingedam is the centre of the agricultural population, and the cattle markets periodically held within its walls make the town a focus of business, and preserve to it the character of the capital of the district.

This horse-fair, above all, has a wide-spread reputation; people travel from far and near to attend it.

Indeed, it is owing to this market that the races are so important. The high-class stallions to be had here are much sought by vendors, who pay dearly for them.

The *Harddraverij*,[1] as these sports are somewhat pompously called in the country, take place on a road in the middle of a large plain. The preparations consist in the erection of two ornamented poles with a strong cord extended the length of the course. The poles designate the starting point and winning post, and the stout cord marks the reserved places. At two o'clock the municipal council appeared, preceded by a discordant band of music, of which each musician played in his own time and key. I am not even sure if they all played the same tune. Surrounded by a halo of municipal glory, distributing right and left their patronising glances, urbane and smiling, the burgomaster and his colleagues appeared quite to enjoy this atrocious noise.

After the bustle occasioned by such a pompous arrival had somewhat subsided, each settled into his place, and the races commenced. Enormous horses, ridden by big lusty men, began to trot vigorously down the macadamised road.

This should have lasted about three hours, but it was a great deal longer, as the jockeys were constantly obliged to stop to allow some carriage or cart to pass.

Our Groningen friends had strongly advised us to stay till the end of the day. These *fêtes*, it would appear, usually end in characteristic excesses. The gin, beer, and wine fermented by enthusiasm and the

---

[1] *Harddraver* corresponds with race-horse. It is a term seldom used with reference to cart-horses.

heat of the sun, are conducive to strange sounds and friendly familiarities.

As to the concerts, we had had enough of the municipal band. What we had already observed of the familiarities, was more than sufficient to lead us to believe they would end in the wild excesses, usually to be seen at the great fairs in Holland.

We, therefore, decided to withdraw from these family scenes, which are all very well if the people are handsome, and the costumes original; but on this occasion we had met no less than twenty-three hunchbacks, and the attire of the people of Appingedam has nothing very attractive about it.

We returned to Groningen by boat, following the *Damsterdiep* which had taken us to Delfijl. Our journey was performed without trouble, but we felt rather sad at the sight of the poor women who, with drawn haggard features, and covered in dust and perspiration, their bodies bent double, tow enormous 'tjalks' or barges loaded to the water's edge, the owner of the craft lying, smoking carelessly, at the helm.

This terribly hard work was, originally, partly carried on by dogs. But the Society for the Prevention of Cruelty to Animals interfered and put a stop to the abuse. Since then, women and children are harnessed in their stead. The dog, I admit, is man's best friend. But then what is woman? Before thinking of the animals would it not be better to do the same of the people, and stay that protection of the former which is at the cost of the latter.

CHAPTER X.

WINSCHOTEN—THE MONUMENT OF HEILIGERLEE—NIEUWE BEERTA—
THE '*BEKLEMMING*'—THE '*BOERDERIJEN*'—A MODEL SCHOOL.

To understand thoroughly the province of Groningen, it remained for us to visit the southern portion, which extends below the Bay of Dollard, and lies between the Drenthe and the German frontier. The most important town in that part is Winschoten, situated about five hours' walk south-east of Appingedam. It is a bright and clean little town; the houses are low but well kept, and the winding streets are carefully swept. It is full of hotels, jewellers, and confectioners. On the other hand, it has scarcely any ancient monuments, but has some good perspectives, especially the one on the great canal, called *Binnenveeu*.

The Town Hall is both modern and modest-looking, useful and clean, but of no architectural character. Here, however, we first directed our steps, as we hoped to find the Burgomaster there.

Count de Heiden, with his usual courtesy, had informed us that he had advised this magistrate of our proposed visit, and that he would conduct us as far as Heiligerlee. We naturally depended upon a warm reception ; but it was a warm deception that awaited us. But coldly received at Appingedam, we were not received at all at Winschoten. The secretary at the Town Hall informed us, in the most natural manner, that the Burgomaster had left for Groningen by the train corresponding with our arrival here.

We easily consoled ourselves for this slight mishap. None the less it seemed to us to reflect the inhospitable manners of the country, which feeling proves how little it requires to influence travellers for or against a place. Never for one instant doubting that business of importance had taken the chief magistrate of Winschoten to Groningen, his absence appeared as a kind of corollary of the unfriendly spirit we had noticed both at Zoutkamp and Appingedam. Happily it was reserved to a peasant of Beerta, and a village schoolmaster, to overthrow these hastily-formed impressions, and bring us back to more charitable sentiments. But we are anticipating.

If the Town Hall of Winschoten is modern, the same cannot be said of its church, which goes back, at the very least, to the fifteenth century. Although much renovated, it still retains a proud appearance. It consists of one sole nave of medium height, pierced by a number of long narrow windows resembling large loop-holes. They, in fact, served this purpose; for the little edifice had formerly to undergo a regular siege. In 1593, when the town was surprised by the Spaniards, a sergeant named Moda took refuge, with a portion of his regiment, in this sacred asylum, which he held against the enemy during a whole day. Towards evening, finding that, owing to the losses sustained, he was unable to defend such a large area, he withdrew to the belfry, overlooking another portion of the same street. There he held out some time longer, but at length had to give in from lack of provisions and ammunition.

We should like to have seen the interior of the church, but the '*Koster*' was also absent from Winschoten, and had taken the keys with him; but they did not tell us if he had gone to Groningen. Unable to enter the only monument of interest in the place, we took the road to Heiligerlee to visit the glorious battle-field where, on the 24th of May, 1568, the first engagement, for the independence of the United Provinces, took place. It is reached by a shady twisting road, bordered by fertile fields and rustic houses. On nearing the eventful spot the ground becomes slightly uneven. It was, it appears, the knowledge of these undulations that decided the day. Thanks to them, Count Louis Nassau, brother to William the Taciturn, was enabled so to dispose his forces as to surround the three thousand five hundred Spaniards, under the command of Counts d'Aranberg and de Meghern and Colonel Braccamonte. The shock was terrific. Count of Adolphe Nassau perceiving Count d'Aranberg, rushed upon him, when a hand-to-hand fight took place, which ended by their rolling over in the dust, to rise no more. The death of their principal chief led to the total defeat of the Spaniards, who in that day lost twelve hundred men, all their baggage, and six guns.[1] The army of Nassau could not altogether rejoice over this brilliant victory, for it also had lost one of its most intrepid chiefs, a young hero of the greatest promise. Count Adolphe had fallen amidst the triumph of his party, and three centuries later, the grateful Netherlands raised a monument to his memory, on the spot where he so gloriously fell.

This monument stands on the top of a slight eminence. It is composed of an octagonal pedestal in Belgian bluestone, surmounted by a group representing the death of the young Count. Struck down, the generous soldier, still clad in his armour, grasps his sword broken in the fray. Behind him a figure, representative of the Netherlands, armed with a sword and shield, stops fighting to cast a look of sorrow on the dying hero, whilst the Dutch lion, roaring with rage, approaches to protect the body and avenge his death.

In the midst of this plain, surrounded by a girdle of foliage, under a grey sky which seems to associate

---

[1] De Meteren's 'Histoire des Pays Bas'; Leclerc's 'Histoire des Provinces Unies,' &c. &c.

itself with sorrowful memories, the monument appeared perfectly majestic. Nevertheless one cannot help feeling a little dissatisfied with the two artists, Messrs. Egenberger and Josef Geefs, who, it appears to me, have — from a purely æsthetic point of view—made some slight mistakes. In the first place, it is a little too round, and the figure of the Lowlander appears to me altogether too melodramatic. It would have been better had it been more simple. The Count, on the other hand, is not sufficiently excited by the struggle. The artists, I imagine, have never seen war or a battle-field, or they would have observed that almost all corpses have the eyes open and the mouth contracted, and that after death they retain the expression of the passions and emotions engendered by the struggle. It was a further fault not to have left out the helmet, which scarcely permits the features of the hero to be seen. The desirability of following historical truth will perhaps be suggested, but it is not done here; and I cannot think that the figures of the Lowlander and of the Dutch lion can be anything but emblematical. Lastly, I don't like the lion with his paw on the parchment. Once the sword is drawn, treaties are of little value. Then, again, what charters are these? Are they those titles of Philip II. which the young Count tore up, and were the artists ignorant of the fact that the struggle of the Nassaus against Spain, was that of the rights of the people against an ancient feudality?

Our pilgrimage finished, we took the road for Beerta and Nieuwe Beerta, perhaps the two richest agricultural villages in the whole province. They are situated two miles from Winschoten, just below Dollard Bay, in the midst of alluvial plains of marvellous fertility.

Notwithstanding the distinction of Old and New Beerta, these two villages date almost from the same period. Old Beerta does not date back beyond the early years of the seventeenth century, while the first houses of New Beerta were built in 1636, and its church in 1665. From a distance, they both appear as if enveloped in large trees, overlooking and watching, so to speak, the luxuriant harvest, the rich meadows, and the fields of colza which surround them. They both stretch along the road in an interminable range of farm-houses. There are no cottages, and no tiny retreats; the village scarcely seems to contain small houses such as tradespeople and shopkeepers would occupy.

The houses of the peasants, *boerderijen*, as they are called, are four stories high, and are broad in proportion, shaded by a great roof which juts out over the angle of the gable.

A beautiful lawn, strewed with baskets of flowers, a moat full of water and crossed by a pretty wooden bridge, separates them from the road. But no walls, no gates, nothing to shut them in from the view of the passer-by. Behind a *façade* of red bricks, enlivened by white wainscotting and large windows spotlessly clean, with their neatly arranged muslin curtains, may be seen large thatch-covered buildings. These are the outbuildings adjoining the dwelling-house, large stables and granaries for housing the corn, and with carts and ploughs, flails and scythes, all ranged in order.

Everywhere the most perfect order and methodical cleanliness; but without any exaggeration I may say the same of the merest trifles one meets with in North Holland. Everywhere, also, evidence of comfort and abundance, and riches seem to spring from the ground, as indeed they do in the shape of verdant pastures and golden harvests. We are, in truth, in the peasants' paradise. They are the kings and masters of the country. The soil does not belong to them; but that troubles them little, as they are sure of its fruits. We are in reality in the region of the *Beklemming*. The *Beklemming* is a peculiar institution, and probably does not exist in any other part of the world. Outside the province of Groningen there is nothing like it in Holland, and probably the Low Countries is the only place in Europe where it is to be found.[1]

The *Beklemming* constitutes, to some extent, a proprietorship over and above the original freehold. It is the right of working the estate, and is a value

---

[1] The Beklemming is not unlike the *Contratto di Livello*, which was practised in days gone by in Lombardy and Tuscany, and the *Aforamento*, which is met with in Portugal. Portuguese and Italian legislation are not, however, suitable to this description of lease, which is sure to disappear before long.

that can be inherited or bought, and in the contract for which, the original proprietor has no right to interfere, and for which he can exact nothing beyond a fixed and unvarying rental, as consideration for the holding of his property under certain conditions.

In order perfectly to understand the working of such an institution, it is necessary to go back to its origin. At that time two men appeared upon the scene, the original proprietor and the cultivator. 'The soil is of no value,' said the latter. 'It brings you in nothing. Give it up to me. By my labour I will fertilise and make it productive; but as it is not just that you alone should profit by my efforts, let us stipulate that all the improvements I effect upon your property shall be for my benefit, and for the payment of a fixed rental, which shall never be increased, I alone shall for ever have the right to work your land. This right, at my death, shall be transmissible to my heirs. During my life I must have the right to dispose of it in any way I may think fit, to sell it, concede it, or give it to whom I please, without you having the power to interfere; and this on the sole condition that my heir or grantee shall undertake to pay you the stipulated rental.'

It will thus be seen that in the first instance the contract was most simple. It was never perfectly equitable. But from the second generation, while still remaining a moral institution, the *Beklemming* lost much of its simplicity. The transmission by inheritance, of this right of working in consideration of a fixed rental, transforms it simply into a capital of a special nature, represented by the accumulation of work expended by the past generation, and the improvements introduced. Like manorial or industrial properties, it might be divided or sold by auction, and in order to arrive at an equal division, the inheritors might have to sell their rights to a stranger, who would benefit by all the advantages of the work previously done.

The complications, which surround a combination so simple in its principle, are numerous, as the right of *Beklemming* is not everywhere observed in the same manner. In certain cantons, together with the '*Regt van beklemming*' is the '*Regt van altijd durende beklemming*,' which constitute two different rights; the one being a lease in perpetuity, the other a long term, the end of which is pre-arranged. In certain other districts, the proprietor of the soil has the right to exact a new rental upon each transmission, whether it is by inheritance, sale, or gift. Therefore, when the French introduced the Civil Code into the Low Countries, with its numerous conditions and clauses, they did not attempt to regulate so complicated a matter. They devoted to the subject but a single Article, verifying and confirming it, and referred to local customs to regulate its effects.[1]

---

[1] The following is the translation of this Article. Art. 1654 (Book III. Chap. 8 of the Civil Code). The right of Beklemming and of perpetual Beklemming, established by contract or other legitimate acts, is regulated by the law and by the stipulated conditions, and where these do not meet the case, by local customs.

Less concise than the Civil Code, the legislators of the country have written a large volume on the subject, but the *Beklemming* is so prolific a source of litigation that it has not by any means been exhausted.[1]

To sum up, the *Beklemming* is, as it were, a dividing of the manorial proprietorship. It divides it into two parts, the one fixed, unchangeable, and bearing always the same rental : that is the soil ; the other is subject to all the vicissitudes of cultivation, and enjoys all the improvements introduced, buildings erected, and material acquired : that is the right of culture. When these two divisions of proprietorship are in the same hands, the estate is in *common right*.

The advantages of such a system are numerous. In the first place it allows the cultivator to enjoy, in return for a small rental, all the advantages of proprietorship without actual purchase. Possessor in perpetuity of the products of the estate, he can improve it and increase its value without fear of its being taken from him. He works it, nevertheless, subject to the supervision of the real proprietor, and he must neither destroy the soil, nor spoil it. On the other hand, the division of the price of the property into two parts enables the original owner of the soil to hold extensive estates. Lowering the price of the

---

[1] The principal jurists who have occupied themselves with the law of Beklemming are Messrs. Van Swinderen, Tresling, Driessen, Nienhuis, Van Houten, &c., &c., and especially Mr. H. O. Teith, whose two works, 'Het Groninger Beklemrigt,' and 'Handboekje over het Beklemrigt,' are authorities.

land prevents its being parcelled out in small lots, which parcelling out is a regular practice in countries under the Civil Code, much to the detriment of agriculture generally. Finally, with regard to the province of which we are speaking, the result of these united advantages is to give to agriculture the greatest prosperity, and to render the country one of the most fertile, rich, and productive in the world. But as to its solving certain social problems, as some writers have pretended, or as to simplifying the relations between labour and capital, the Beklemming has nothing to do with it.

Antagonism, indeed, no longer exists between the proprietor and the peasant, but simply, between the peasant who rents the estate, and his labourers. The *Boer* has become under this system an agricultural contractor, a land worker. The only difference between him and the workman is that the *Boer* lodges and feeds his labourers; but oftener than not the latter hate their master, pretend they are reduced to slavery, and, like working men in general, rave about emancipation. Neither does there exist between the *Boer* and his servants the same relationship that we find in all French farms between the farmer and his men. They neither live nor eat together, and one never sees at mealtimes the long table covered with a coarse cloth, with the master at the head, while the twenty servants are seated round with their soup before them. Here the peasant and the labourer have no relationship, except in work; the *Boer* resides opposite the farm; he has often two or three reception-rooms, as many pianos, a quantity of silver plate and Japanese ware; and all the luxuries for which he has a taste may be found in his rooms. The servants live at the back of the house (*achterhuis*), badly fed they say, and badly housed, and complaining of the hardship of their master, his exorbitant demands and his avarice.

Some of the peasants, it appears, justify these accusations by their parsimony. We were told of some who, for economy's sake, make their servants of both sexes go to bed in the dark, greatly to the detriment of manners and morality. I venture to hope that these rural Harpagons are an exception to the rule, and that the accusations of the '*Knechts*' are often exaggerated. But it is none the less clear that the right of *Beklemming* has not determined the social question.

After an hour's walk, along a road between a double line of well-built farmhouses, we reached the school-house of Nieuw-Beerta. The schoolmaster, M. Bauman, to whom our coming had been announced, received us surrounded by his family. The reception was perfect. He placed himself entirely at our disposal, to show us first his special domain, that is, his school, and afterwards one of the prettiest *boerderijen* of the country.

The school was, for me personally, an object of great astonishment. I expected to find a village-school something like our own, but as the principal of Nieuw-Beerta is quite a gentleman, we might call his establishment an institution. It is divided into four classes, attended by about two hundred and fifty children of both sexes. Each class, if my memory serves me correctly, has some scholars only one or two years old. They attend for eight years, and their education is most comprehensive. It includes reading, writing, grammar, history, geography, and elementary mathematics. There is a room devoted to natural philosophy, and one to drawing, containing plaster models for drawing from the cast. When the scholar leaves he possesses a considerable smattering of useful knowledge. It would be well if French villages were thus happily provided.

The *boerderij*, which we afterwards visited, is like those just described; furnished with rural elegance, and kept with that wonderful neatness which must be numbered among the virtues of the Netherlands.

As we concluded our visit, we were (to use an agricultural term) 'favoured with terrific rain.' We had talked of visiting the outskirts, and pushing on to Nieuwe Schans. The peasant, our host, not wishing us to expose ourselves to the bad weather, harnessed a couple of beautiful black horses to an elegant britzka, and in this light carriage we bowled through the villages of Finsterwolde and Drieborg, and arrived after a couple of hours' ride at Oudezijl, a hamlet adjoining the fortress of Nieuwe Schans.

This hamlet, which is quite modern, possesses no habitations beyond those necessary for the garrison, innkeepers and shopkeepers of all sorts. The foundation-stone of its church was laid in 1751. The fort is a century older; it was constructed in 1665. Seven years after it was besieged by the Bishop of Munster. Delivered by General Rabenhaupt in July 1673, it was occupied by the English in 1794, taken by the Republican troops in 1795, besieged by the Cossacks in 1813, and finally evacuated after a pretence at defence which did not cost the life of a single besieger.

It forms a sort of point which stretches into German territory. In the distance may be seen the clock tower of Bunde, the first Hanoverian town; but these two countries, which join each other, and are only divided by a narrow river, are as widely separated as if they were at different ends of the earth. They have neither the same manners nor the same customs.

'In days gone by,' the obliging M. Bauman informed us, 'the intercourse, without being very active, was somewhat frequent. A few Germans cross the frontier and work among us, but they are not much liked. They have always been found dirty, very careless, and great gluttons. Nevertheless, they speak our language, and that is a good deal. The schools taught Dutch, and it was in Dutch that the pastors addressed the faithful. But since 1866 all that has been changed. The country has been Germanised. Government employés, schoolmasters, pastors, all now come from the interior. All is Prussian. The relationships between the borderers are altogether broken. To-day scarcely a reaper crosses the river to work amongst us, and only the scarcity of labour compels us to receive them civilly.'

'We are a long way out of our calculations,' objected Constant ; 'for we expected to find here numerous German symptoms; we scarcely expected to find a distinction so clearly defined between two neighbouring populations.'

'Ten years ago you would not have found it so,' said the amiable principal. 'On both sides of the frontier they were more Netherlanders than anything else. Language and religion, all were agreed and in unison. But the Prussians came ; and if we have not remained faithful to our ancient traditions, the poor folks have been converted against their will.'

It is a pity, thought I to myself, that M. Kirchhof could not hear this vigorous and sincere language.

At this point we separated, our kind hosts to go back to their pretty village, and we to continue our journey. Nevertheless, we were not permitted to leave them without touching glasses once again, and on the German frontier we drank a last glass of French wine to the prosperity of the Netherlands.

CHAPTER XI.

DRENTHE—THE COUNTRY AND THE PEASANTS—THE '*HUNNEBEDDEN*'—ZUIDLAREN AND TIJNAARLOO—ASSEN AND ITS ETHNOLOGICAL MUSEUM—THE HISTORY OF A CHIGNON.

DO not know any transformation scene more complete than that which takes place in passing from the province of Groningen into the Drenthe. Once the frontier crossed, all is changed. The soil, manners, houses, and inhabitants all differ. The fields have not the same appearance, and the houses are of a different character. The social organisation is altogether different, and agriculture is not carried on in the same manner. The frontier of the two countries is but nominal—no mountain divides them, no stream marks their respective limits, yet an abyss separates them. It is only necessary to cross a road, a ditch, or a field, to find oneself in another world, both physically and morally. In all my life I was never more surprised, nor with better cause.

One of the great landed proprietors of the country, M. Siccama, a near relation to my travelling companion, was desirous that we should acquaint ourselves with this extraordinary metamorphose. He came to meet us at Punt, in the middle of the Groningen country, with one of those good old English chaises, drawings of which may still be seen in the coloured engravings of fifty years ago. Ours dated from the year 1815. We welcomed it with a cry of joy, and declared it a very Phœnix of carriages, for it was at the same time hierarchical and digestive. Hierarchical, inasmuch as the three seats at different elevations permitted the driver to overlook his passengers, and to give the upper seats to those whom he wished to honour. Digestive, by reason of the glorious jolts, which carry us back to our youthful days, to those happy times when the heart beat lustily when we saw the shandry being got ready. It was in this venerable equipage that we made our entry into the territory of the Drenthe; and in visiting the villages of Oosterbroek, Eelde, Peize, and Paterwolde, were able to distinguish the incredible difference between the country of the Drenthe and the two rich provinces by which it is surrounded. The frontier is scarcely crossed before the transformation is complete. There are no longer the rich and heavy meadows, where the cows stand buried to the knee in the grassy and well planted lands, always fertile and producing at will that which is required of them. The soil is poor and sandy, from which nothing is produced without much labour. The domains, cultivated with indefatigable perseverance, stand out in the midst of the moors like oases in the middle of a vast heath. Each year the rink is extended. Trees are planted, a plot of heath cleared away, a canal is cut or a road opened; but each part thus recovered is watered with the sweat of the brow and covered with golden corn. It is necessary to nourish the earth, before she will nourish the inhabitants.

In face of such struggles, it will be understood, that agricultural operations cannot be carried on, on the same principles as in the neighbouring provinces. Here the *Beklemming* would be impossible, for the primitive soil is almost valueless. The agriculturist need no longer be a sort of manufacturer, working one or two branches of agricultural production; he is a country gentleman, living by and upon his estates, and producing that which is necessary for his family and his people.

From this mode of working two things result. First, an excessive variety of cultivation, a parcelling out of the work, which gives the land a peculiar appearance, and also the grouping round the principal house of a number of small farms, which transforms the field labourer into a small agriculturist, and substitutes family life for the grouping together of the servants. Here, each has his work fixed. He is no longer enrolled in a battalion manœuvring under the eye of the master. They work for a master, but leave the field free to his personal initiative, and throw upon him part of the responsibility. To one of these cottagers the master confides the cultivation of the cereals; this one is looked to to furnish corn, &c. Another has charge of the pastures and the raising of cattle; to him they look for butter, milk, cheese, &c. A third looks after the colza, chicory, and general fodder. Another attends to the woods, cuttings, plantations, clearings, and such like. A little turf-pit supplies fuel to everybody. Around each of the farmhouses is a small orchard and a kitchen garden, which, with their fruits, vegetables, and a few flowers, permit these honest workmen to ameliorate and vary their ordinary diet.

These rustic dwellings have an appearance which is peculiar to them. Here they acquire another character than in the north. Here no longer the houses shining with care, which, repainted each year, appear always new, nor the neat farm-yards where not even a straw is out of place. The *boerderijen* of the Drenthe have, on the contrary, somewhat the appearance of those in Normandy. A pleasant sort of negligence prevails: forgotten planks piled up in a corner, creeping plants climbing to the right and left, a broken pail or a half-smashed cart in the angle of the yard. All this is picturesque enough, and has about it just sufficient indifference to suggest an independent existence, where nothing is pre-arranged or supervised.

In the interior, the eye of the master again asserts itself—or rather the eye of the mistress, for this is her real department. Here everything is orderly and well kept, and what Parival said two hundred years ago of the Dutch dames might be said of these rustic housewives: 'They pride themselves upon the neatness of their houses and their furniture, to an extent that one can scarcely imagine.'

The villages present the same appearance as the great houses. They are surrounded by a zone which they call the '*Esch*,'[1] which produces all necessaries for food. It is not, indeed, until after existence has been assured that the little accumulations are sold or exported. Settled in the midst of these immense steppes, in a territory made fertile at the cost of much care and labour, communication with the outer world is difficult. The roads are few, and for the most part bad; the canals are fewer still. The first thought of the inhabitants is therefore for themselves. Hence the occupations and habits are entirely different from those one meets with in Friesland and in the province of Groningen.

Such is the feature of the villages in this isolation. It appears as if, not expecting visitors, they do not care to make their toilette. With the exception of a few elegant houses inhabited by the well-to-do burghers and villagers, all the houses have a perfectly rural appearance. We did not meet everywhere and always the carefully painted woodwork, the polished tiles, the immaculate windows—real public mirrors to which the eye becomes used. Some of the houses are in very bad condition; the great thatched roof descending to the earth, the plaster

---

[1] From the Latin *esca*, nourishment.

walls, the doors of the barns simply barred up, give to these villages of the Drenthe a particularly countrified aspect, which, after all, is not without its charm.

What we have said of the habitations we can equally say about the inhabitants, especially of the women. The costumes are as simple as the houses. It is no longer the everlasting caps braided with gold, the buckles, brooches, and earrings in precious metals. Instead of these expensive ornaments, so generally worn in Friesland on the heads of the kitchen wenches and farm servants, the women of the Drenthe have another ornament, which is not without merit. It is their beautiful fair hair. These luxuriant locks, parted down the centre and bronzed by the air and the sun, are worth all the gold and silver ornaments. The faces of these beautiful country girls would, indeed, ill suit so much jewellery. We are not in the country of the impassive and insensible Madonnas, whose comely proportions are ravishingly enrapt in uniform attire; whose satin complexions, without a wrinkle or a smile, seem to be acquired, according to Propertius, 'by roses steeped in milk.'

Utque rosæ puro lacte natant folia.

The daughters of the Drenthe have another style of beauty. Their olive complexion, brown skin, and great eyes, often brown, but always lively and enquiring, with their lips a bright rose colour and often smiling, contrast greatly with their stouter and more stately neighbours. No more lilies and roses, and certainly no blemishes or suspicious scars. They are, in effect, vigorous and rustic beauties. Their figures are elastic, and the muscles are apparent on their arms, which are always bare, while the little black corsage which covers the bosom indicates a firm and rounded form; their flesh is firm and strong, and their nature is a little wild perhaps, but of the type which always pleases an artist.

The girls of the Drenthe are modestly dressed, without ornament or laces or jewels; but they are always neat, and their costume is, on the whole, very picturesque. It generally consists of a dark blue dress with short sleeves, a small corsage underneath, either black or brown, without sleeves and simply covering the breast; this, with a striped black and white petticoat, completes their toilette, which, though very simple, is gracefully worn, and is not without character.

It must not be concluded that the poverty of the country is the cause of this simplicity. The peasant of Drenthe is generally in comfortable circumstances; but, like French countrymen, he hides his money and makes no display of his wealth. He is industrious and economical, stubborn and hard to a degree. 'The Drenthers are very difficult to manage,' as an old chronicler has said, 'being a far-seeing people.' Their circumstances differ from those of the peasants of Friesland and Groningen; the latter not being able to extend their operations, while the former are surrounded by arid and uncultivated plains, which they can cultivate or not as they choose. In this they embark most of their capital, and not in golden kickshaws, like their neighbours of the North.

All these good people are not, however, as simple as one might suppose. At Punt, where we passed the night at a rustic inn kept by an honest peasant, I had in my room a pretty marqueterie cabinet, filled with china ware, Delft pottery, and curiosities. By its side the beds were disposed, after the fashion of Schiermonnikoog, that is, enclosed in a wainscot, and composed of half down and half straw. Five or six mice endeavoured all night to run over me.

The next day at dawn we continued our journey. We followed the course of a small river called the Aa, a name borne by most of the rivers in the country, and took the road to Midlaren, where we expected to find some of the earliest Celtic monuments. On the way we met some wandering bees. They were in a cart, enclosed in their hives, and continued during the journey to make that sweet honey which, in the graceful language of Montaigne, ' is no longer thyme or marjoram.' Twice a year they journey in this way, from the north to the south and from the south to the north, keeping near the flowering colza fields, where they 'suck' without hindrance.

After having traversed many kilomètres of moors, intersected here and there by a spare field of buckwheat, we reached those primitive monuments, enormous piles of granite rocks, which in the country are called *Hunnebedden*, 'the beds of the Huns.'[1] Beds a little hard indeed, and somewhat primitive! What is their origin and signification? They are to be met with all over the world. In France we count them by hundreds; Wormius has described the Danish ones, Rudbek those in Sweden; Spartmann has seen them among the Caffres, Jefferson in Virginia, Barrow among the Hottentots. Everywhere their presence is attempted to be accounted for by the most improbable stories. I have had the curiosity to read what ancient authors have written respecting the *Hunnebedden* of the Drenthe, and their contradictory ideas do but little to clear up the mystery which hovers about the gigantic ruins.

Originally it was said they were the work of evil spirits. That is the religious explanation. For it must not be forgotten that long after the establishment of Christianity, these stones, regarded as idols, were worshipped in secret. The Council of Arles in 452, and that of Tours in 587, exercised all their authority to suppress this idolatry, and in order to stop it, attributed an infernal origin to the monuments. Schœvonius, on the other hand, believes them to be the remains of the columns of Hercules.

J. A. Mellen inclines to the idea that they are

---

[1] According to another version, first admitted by Nicholas Westerdorp, the word *Hun* means *death*, and thence *Hunnebed* would appear to be *bed of the dead*, or *tomb*, an explanation now generally accepted.

altars or sacrificial stones erected by the Cimbri, while Dr. Jean Picardt, pastor at Koevorden, took them to be the work of giants who inhabited the country in days gone by, and has even described these giants and their manners and costumes. He has gone even further, and has given us the portraits of some of these gigantic phantoms as conjured up in his mind.[1]

Others, again, more sensible or less fantastic, see in these primitive monuments tombs erected by the Celts, to their venerated chiefs; sepulchres grand but nameless, which have existed for ages, outlasting the strength of those who erected them, but leaving us in ignorance of the names of those whose memories they are intended to consecrate.

In this last opinion the *savants* of our day agree, and that which justifies this view is the excavations that have been made during many years past in digging round about them, and which have led to the discovery, under a large number of these monuments, of urns of baked clay containing human ashes. Unfortunately, from the commencement of this century, a large number of these *Hunnebedden* have already been rummaged by careless hands, who, believing

---

[1] See his 'Korte Beschrijving' &c. (Amsterdam, 1660). This belief in giants was very general in the Low Countries. Guicciardini refers to it several times. In his 'Grande Chronique,' M. Jean le Petit grows very indignant against those who doubt their existence: 'Car de nyer généralement qu'il n'y auroit eu nuls géants, ce seroit trop ridicule! Voir desmentir les sainctes Ecritures qui en font assés mention,' he exclaims in anger.

they should find other treasures there, have neglected to preserve the result of their researches.[1]

Although a large number of these monuments has been destroyed, there are still fifty-one in the Drenthe, to which may be added a number of *tumuli*, and of those mortuary chambers which, in the language of the country, are called *grafkelders*, but of which, up to the present time, but little notice has been taken.

The *Hunnebedden* of the Drenthe are scattered about somewhat unequally, but on the map their position seems to be almost regular. The localities in which they occur most frequently are Borger, which contains eleven, and Emmen nine. Odoorn has eight, and in and about Anloo are seven.

Of these fifty-one *Hunnebedden*, twenty-nine have been acquired by the Government by means of the Credits opened from 1869 to 1872. Twenty belong to the province, and two are private property. The monuments of Zuidlaren and Middlaren are the property of the Government.[2]

I will not here describe these burying-places. He who has seen one has seen all. Their principal architectural feature is a vast slab resting on two

---

[1] Most of these early researches were made at the commencement of this century, notably in 1809. At Loor the results of the first search have been found, the *débris* discovered having been buried in the neighbourhood. Unfortunately the pottery had been broken, and the shattered urns rested amidst the ashes they should have enclosed.

[2] See the pamphlet published by M. R. W. Kymmel, entitled, 'De Hunnebedden in Drenthe.'

THE HUNNEBEDDEN OF TIJSAARLOO.

other stones, which form its supports. By the repetition of this principle the constructors built a sort of gallery, closed at both ends by two other blocks. The number of tables, and the dimensions of the numerous slabs of which they are composed, constitute the only difference existing between all these monuments. Beyond this, there is not a sign of human industry. The blocks are in their natural state—unshaped, and bearing neither inscription nor sculpture.

Under the influence of time and by the incredible force of vegetation, some of these *Hunnebedden* have been overturned. A sapling, in forcing its way between the gigantic stones, has disunited them, and caused the edifice to collapse. This has been the case with the monuments of Middlaren, the blocks of which are now piled up without order, and are imposing only through their massiveness. Those of Tijnaarloo, which ought to be seen the same day, are, on the contrary, entirely complete and beautifully preserved. They alone, in the midst of an immense country, attest the presence of man and bear witness of his power.

Before arriving at Tijnaarloo, we passed through the pretty village of Zuidlaren, where we made an excellent breakfast at the Maison de Ville—not an official repast, but a friendly one, for according to the custom of the country, the Town Hall is installed in a large inn.

Throughout the whole of the Drenthe, every

municipality is similarly circumstanced. Each principal inn contains a large and beautiful hall, decorated in the old style. There the Council assembles, meetings are held, and there the host receives travellers of distinction. The hall of Zuidlaren, with its pictures and its grand chimney-piece, appeared to us all the more worthy of note as we were there served with a delicious repast. In these modest villages of Drenthe the French traveller finds two valuable resources: the ham, justly praised throughout the whole of the Netherlands, and excellent rye bread, such as is not to be met with in any of the other eleven provinces.

The good cheer, however, did not prevent our visiting the village, which is most picturesque, with its sandy lanes and large open greens, surrounded by thatched cottages and grand trees. The church, though largely restored, still wears a venerable aspect. The interior is cold and bare, the only woodwork being the pew of the Counts of Heiden Reinestein, which illustrious family hold a magnificent château close by the church. This château is called Laarwoud. It is one of the oldest estates in the province. The buildings are relatively modern, having been reconstructed in the middle of the last century by Count Alexander Charles, who was then 'drossaard'[1] of Koevorden. It is a real castle, of lordly appearance, with two large projecting wings.

---

[1] The post of 'drost' or 'drossaard' is equivalent to that of seneschal, or rather bailiff.

In front of the *façade* is a magnificent flower-garden, enclosed by an iron railing. In the rear of the buildings extends a magnificent park. Nothing is wanting about this noble dwelling, which leaves the miniature castles of Groningen far behind, in point of beauty and grandeur.

The park is, above all, admirably laid out and kept up in princely style, with its majestic avenues ending in lovely perspectives, and its grand old trees interlacing their branches overhead, and forming an immense cradle, about the summit of which innumerable herons are continually fluttering.

If the stories we were told are to be believed, the lords of Heiden owe to a singular custom the splendid condition of these beautiful plantations. In the good old times they enjoyed a curious privilege. Each newly married peasant who became a father before the regular time—that is to say, whose wife increased the population in less than nine months after the nuptial benediction—had to work for the counts of Heiden, for as long a time as they were in advance of the prescribed period. As these things, it appears, happened pretty frequently, the lords of Laarwoud had always a numerous company at work on their estates.

It was certainly very hard upon the poor husbands thus to render them responsible for the caprices of nature. Perhaps it is owing to the sense of this heavy responsibility that the origin of another custom, equally strange, may be found. Every man, on the morning of his wedding-day, purchased his coffin, a purchase at least peculiar. This curious custom is still in existence.

Zuidlaren visited, we resumed our route through the desolate moors. Nothing could be more melancholy than the slow and painful journey across this immense heath. The carriages were buried to the axle in the sand; everywhere around, silence and solitude; on the horizon a line of hillocks entirely destitute of vegetation; not a human form in the vast solitude, and the only living beings to be perceived, the birds, appear like unquiet spirits wandering at hazard in the midst of this desert.

Thus we followed Tijnaarloo, Taarloo, and Loon. In the evening we arrived at Assen, the modern capital of this dreary country.

Certainly, no one having seen Assen would doubt the *rôle* that contemporary politics had assigned to it. It has the appearance of a splendid village, not at all that of a town, much less a capital. It is so nevertheless, and the grand edifices, occupied by the Government of the province and the administration of the young city, clash almost with its low houses, its unpretentious streets, its old trees, and the vast meadows stretching out on every side.

Assen is altogether a modern town. You would search there in vain for the closely packed houses, the sinuous and tortuous streets and gloomy lanes, the inevitable traces of the narrow and cramped existence which was the ordinary life in the cities of the middle ages. Throughout you have light and verdure—absolute necessaries in these days. And this is not surprising, for Assen dates but from yesterday. A century ago it was a hamlet of five hundred souls; to-day it has six thousand inhabitants.

When the National Government organised the provinces under the Batavian Republic, it sought to fix upon a capital for the Drenthe; Koevorden, which held that position in the middle ages, was not sufficiently central. It became necessary to establish a principal town. Assen was chosen on account of its position, and was constituted the capital. Later on, King Louis came to see it. He felt, as it were, a secret affinity between this desert and desolate country and the state of his mind. A sweet sympathy drew him to this official village, which he treated like a beloved child, endowing it with wealth. He even entertained the idea of building himself a shooting-box, a sort of quiet retreat, where he might come for calm and repose. He was, however, prevented from carrying out his designs, by events which are known to all, and which hastened his retreat.

Among the properties given by King Louis to the town of Assen is a magnificent wood, which is to this day one of the two attractions of the place. Young couples love to wander beneath the beech trees and to picnic in their green shades. It is at once a paradise for the poet and the lover.

The other attraction is more interesting to geologists and archæologists. It is a museum of prehistoric antiquities, justly held in great repute in the surrounding provinces. Some years ago there were collected and brought together, in a large room of the provincial palace, all the antique *débris* that could be found in the country. For, independently of the scientific researches carried on round the *Hunnebedden* and in the *grafkelders*, the Drenthe possesses two almost inexhaustible mines of antiquities of all sorts, its peat beds and its sand.

It is in the latter that the most ancient vestiges of the presence of man in these countries are met with. Flint-dressed and polished knives, arrows, hatchets, and hammers of prehistoric times abound in the glass cases of the museum of Assen. The peat beds furnish evidence of the age of bronze only. This age is represented in the museum by bracelets, but, above all, by a magnificent sacrificial knife, the geometrical ornamentation of which, together with its elegant shape, give ample evidence of a highly developed æsthetic idea. Of more modern times, however, these beds have yielded articles of all kinds. Amongst them are found specimens of almost everything—clothes, purses, jewels, rings of fine gold, cameos, and rich and precious relics of the period of the Roman occupation. There have also been found complete the wheels of an ancient Roman chariot, entire bridges, well-preserved human remains, caps and hats—what more shall I say? The sand has also furnished some bronze statuettes and a fragment in alabaster of the abduction of Proserpine. Then come the stone tombs, like those of *Schierstins*, with their collection of swords, rings, bracelets, and daggers. All these ethnographical treasures have been preserved with great care by the erudite M. R. W. Kijmmel, who has devoted a large portion of his time to them, and who is constantly augmenting the collection, by fresh discoveries. Amongst them is a singular object, which I cannot pass in silence. The ladies certainly would not wish me to do so. It is— a chignon, and is sufficiently peculiar to merit description. It is composed of a card head-piece, of an almost oval shape. The bottom is embellished with plaited fair hair; the top, that part which is technically called the turban, is covered with seven rows of small plaits. Some silver-threaded plaited ribands seem to hold the structure together. The shade of the hair is very well preserved. The ribands are more damaged, having almost lost their colour.

This chignon was found in 1814 in an ancient sepulchre. It surmounted a skull white and polished like ivory. It was all that remained intact. The adornment had outlived the head that wore it, and it was through her vanity alone that the souvenir of this fair person is handed down to our time.

CHAPTER XII.

STEENWIJK—A HEROIC SIEGE—MEPPEL.—THE PENITENTIARY COLONY OF VEENHUIZEN.

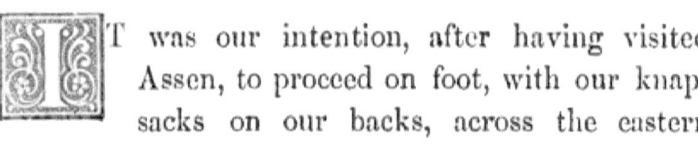T was our intention, after having visited Assen, to proceed on foot, with our knapsacks on our backs, across the eastern portion of the province of Drenthe. We wished to leave by Rolde, reach Eext and Gieten, and descend by Gasselte, Borger, Exlo, Odoorn, and all those charming villages so justly renowned, follow the road parallel with the German frontier, and in this way reach the little town of Koevorden, that celebrated fortress, placed like an advanced sentinel at the extreme limit of Netherland territory.

But, before putting our project into execution, and starting across the arid steppes and endless moors, we resolved to visit two little towns, Steenwijk and Meppel, situated between the capital of the Drenthe and the Zuyder Zee, and also to see in detail a penitentiary establishment of a special nature, lying to the north-west of Assen, and known as the colony of Veenhuizen. It was by Steenwijk that we commenced this series of excursions.

'Steenwijk is an old town, situated on a small river called the Aa. It is small, and measures but sixteen hundred yards along the river, in the form of a bow.'

In these terms the author of the 'Grande Chronique de Hollande et Zeeland' describes the little city at the close of the sixteenth century, at a period when, by reason of the sieges she had sustained, all eyes were turned towards her. As he saw her then, so she appears to us to-day, holding always the same place, surrounded with grass fortifications which have been altered into boulevards, neither greater nor more extended than they have been for three hundred years, and always retaining the same style.

Steenwijk is not, however, as old as Jean le Petit would have us suppose. It was not until the year 1232 that she appeared in the history of the Low Countries, where, indeed, she never played but a secondary part. She was counted among the eight close towns of the Overyssel; but she figured at the bottom of the list among the unimportant ones, and belonged ecclesiastically to the Chapter of Deventer. Her principal church is nevertheless one of the great religious monuments of the country. It was built in the twelfth century, and in 1205 raised to the dignity of a parish church. Almost entirely rebuilt in the fourteenth century, it presents to-day a high central nave covered in wood, and two low vaulted sides in brick, the whole overtopped by an enormous tower of three storys, each pierced by a dozen diamond-shaped windows. This tower has been lowered, or remains unfinished; and in order to improve its incomplete appearance, a wretched, painful wooden balustrade, and a small clock tower have lately been added. Its interior is vast and bare, whitewashed according to the custom of the country. As to works of art, it contains nothing beyond a few beautiful tombstones, now unfortunately much worn by the footsteps of the faithful.

This grand church, in days gone by dedicated to St. Clement, is not the only religious monument in Steenwijk. There is another church, dedicated to Our Lady, which is a handsome specimen of the architecture of the fifteenth century. According to an inscription on the *façade*, it was almost entirely rebuilt in 1477. It has been restored in our time, with great care and much taste.

These two monuments are the more interesting, as very old houses are extremely rare in Steenwijk. This is easily explained: the town was nearly razed to the ground in 1592. In order to reduce it, Prince Maurice was obliged to mine the ramparts and bombard the town. When it was carried by assault, ' les maysons et les églises estoyent presque toutes abbatues et les autres percées de part en part, de sorte qu'il falloit que le peuple se tint ès caves.' Let us add that this memorable siege, of which Blaeu has preserved the plan of operations in one of his beautiful tracings, was neither the first nor the last that the valiant little town had to endure. In the year

1552 it was besieged by Count de Meurs, but without success. The following year, however, it was less fortunate; it was then occupied by the troops of Charles the Fifth, and its castle razed to the ground by order of the Emperor. But all the vicissitudes of these different attacks are unimportant compared with the memorable siege of 1580.

On this occasion resistance was carried to the utmost extremity, and rendered for ever famous the name of the little city. On the 18th October Count de Renneberg invested the town. He led against it six thousand infantry and twelve companies of cavalry. Steenwijk possessed but six hundred soldiers and three hundred townsmen, of whom not more than a fiftieth were free from suspicion of disloyalty. As to cavalry and artillery, the besieged were absolutely without them.

It was in this deplorable condition, badly supported by the populace and badly provided with provisions and ammunition, that the two brave captains, Cornput and Olthof, undertook the heroic defence, of which Frison Remigo Fresinga has preserved minute details.[1] I should like to trace, here on the spot, all the episodes, too little known, of this siege. It is among those which read like legends. One would imagine oneself suddenly transported back to the time of the Paladins. Though it is not practicable to recount them all here, the following two or three will enable the reader to judge of the valour

---

[1] Published in 1584, at Deventer, by Fridsert of Campen.

of the besieged and of the spirit which animated them.

On the 25th October the soldiers of Renneberg, after several fruitless attempts, managed to fasten a cask filled with tar and sulphur to one of the gates of the town. In the evening they set fire to it, and the flames, which began to lick the framework of the gate, caused great uneasiness to the people of Steenwijk. It was impossible to extinguish the fire without opening the gate, and thus delivering the place to the enemy. The consternation was great, and the people commenced to barricade their houses, when there suddenly appeared on the top of the ramparts a tall black figure. It was one of Cornput's soldiers, brandishing an enormous cutlass. 'Wretched thieves,' cried he, 'I am Arent of Groningen, son of a brewer, and I am going to extinguish your fire.' This said, and without hesitation, the tall phantom glided down the embankment and into the water, struck out, and amidst a shower of projectiles cut the cords that held the cask and pushed it into the middle of the moat, where he in turn disappeared. A profound darkness succeeded the blaze of the fire, while a deathlike silence followed the crash of the fusilade. People held their breath in anxiety, and all eyes turned enquiringly towards the dark and stagnant waters. The uncertainty did not last long. The black form reappeared upon the top of the rampart, and in the silence of the night cried aloud, 'Wretched thieves, I am Arent of Groningen, son of a brewer, and your fire is extinguished.'

1552 it was besieged by Count de Meurs, but without success. The following year, however, it was less fortunate; it was then occupied by the troops of Charles the Fifth, and its castle razed to the ground by order of the Emperor. But all the vicissitudes of these different attacks are unimportant compared with the memorable siege of 1580.

On this occasion resistance was carried to the utmost extremity, and rendered for ever famous the name of the little city. On the 18th October Count de Renneberg invested the town. He led against it six thousand infantry and twelve companies of cavalry. Steenwijk possessed but six hundred soldiers and three hundred townsmen, of whom not more than a fiftieth were free from suspicion of disloyalty. As to cavalry and artillery, the besieged were absolutely without them.

It was in this deplorable condition, badly supported by the populace and badly provided with provisions and ammunition, that the two brave captains, Cornput and Olthof, undertook the heroic defence, of which Frison Remigo Fresinga has preserved minute details.[1] I should like to trace, here on the spot, all the episodes, too little known, of this siege. It is among those which read like legends. One would imagine oneself suddenly transported back to the time of the Paladins. Though it is not practicable to recount them all here, the following two or three will enable the reader to judge of the valour

[1] Published in 1584, at Deventer, by Fridsert of Campen.

of the besieged and of the spirit which animated them.

On the 25th October the soldiers of Renneberg, after several fruitless attempts, managed to fasten a cask filled with tar and sulphur to one of the gates of the town. In the evening they set fire to it, and the flames, which began to lick the framework of the gate, caused great uneasiness to the people of Steenwijk. It was impossible to extinguish the fire without opening the gate, and thus delivering the place to the enemy. The consternation was great, and the people commenced to barricade their houses, when there suddenly appeared on the top of the ramparts a tall black figure. It was one of Cornput's soldiers, brandishing an enormous cutlass. 'Wretched thieves,' cried he, 'I am Arent of Groningen, son of a brewer, and I am going to extinguish your fire.' This said, and without hesitation, the tall phantom glided down the embankment and into the water, struck out, and amidst a shower of projectiles cut the cords that held the cask and pushed it into the middle of the moat, where he in turn disappeared. A profound darkness succeeded the blaze of the fire, while a deathlike silence followed the crash of the fusilade. People held their breath in anxiety, and all eyes turned enquiringly towards the dark and stagnant waters. The uncertainty did not last long. The black form reappeared upon the top of the rampart, and in the silence of the night cried aloud, 'Wretched thieves, I am Arent of Groningen, son of a brewer, and your fire is extinguished.'

On the 15th January—for the siege lasted no less than four months—the spectacle was of a different nature. Pretending that they were bored, the officers of Renneberg sent a challenge to those of Cornput, who accepted, and the Captains William and Thomas, after exchanging cards in the usual manner, fought on the ramparts before the two armies.

But the most curious of all these episodes is without doubt the scene that passed on the 4th February in Steenwijk itself. By this time the provisions had failed, and as it appeared impossible longer to sustain the siege, the townsmen assembled in the middle of that large and beautiful square which is to be seen to-day, murmuring loudly against the governor, when, to the surprise of everybody, three partridges fell in the midst of a group of the most turbulent.

Cornput having been informed of this extraordinary event, rushed hurriedly to the place, and then, taking from those around him the three little birds, cried in a tone of inspiration, 'Courage, my children, this is the hand of God. Behold in this the dove of promise. In three weeks we shall be delivered.' The most curious thing was that the prophecy of the plucky Huguenot was exactly realised. Colonel Norrits soon appeared with the States army. On the 21st February he managed to send into Steenwijk one hundred and fifty cheeses, three hundred and fifty loaves, and some powder. On the 23rd February

Renneberg retired, abandoned his camp and all his war material, and the town was saved.[1]

So much heroism was, however, but badly rewarded. It was with great difficulty that the troops, who comported themselves so bravely, could recover their pay from the State. As to the citizens, ruined by the siege, they were afterwards decimated by the plague. So when, in the following year, the town was again besieged by the Spaniards and the Malcontents, the inhabitants were unable to offer any resistance, and on the 15th November, Verdugo appearing suddenly before the town, forded the moat with his troops, and scaled the ramparts without opposition.

Some days before, the Spanish general had reconnoitred the environs of the place, and the means he adopted so as not to excite suspicion are too original to be passed in silence. A very pretty girl went to walk along the edge of the moat. All of a sudden her hat, caught by the wind no doubt, fell into the water. The efforts she made to recover it only increased its distance from the bank. She then called some boys to her assistance, who, by throwing stones round the hat, guided it to that part of the moat where the water was shallowest. Here they waded in, thus discovering the weak side of the place.

Steenwijk had remained ten years subject to Spain,

---

[1] An old and very rare book, the 'Polemographia Avraico Belgica,' contains a very curious engraving representing this siege of 1580-81, and gives a perspective view of the town, which is most interesting.

when Maurice came in person to retake it. We have seen to what state the town was reduced as the result of these six weeks' siege.[1] Since then it has been visited by the troops of the Bishop of Munster, who occupied it in 1672, and abandoned it the following year, after obtaining ransom. Riots in 1749 and the inundation in 1825 were afterwards the only two sorrowful pages that darkened her history.

To-day Steenwijk is a nice little town, with its irregular streets overlooking the surrounding country, the source of its riches; for she 'is situated in a territory fertile in corn, in which she does a large trade.' Her grain and butter markets are renowned, and sometimes a thousand head of cattle may be seen on the boulevards and on the *grande place*, where three hundred years ago the Puritan Cornput took the partridges and gave out his oracles. Close by, in a little street, is to be found the 'Weighhouse,' a pretty construction, ornamented with two bas-reliefs, and bearing date 1642. From the 'Weighhouse' to the place, and from the place to the 'Weigh-house,' there is on market-days a perpetual coming and going; and if on these days one takes refuge on the boulevards, there may be seen in the distance long processions of peasants and carts coming

---

[1] It is a curious fact, that the heroes of the first siege took part in the second, but this time in the ranks of the besiegers and not of the defenders. The brave Captain Osthof, who commanded one of Maurice's regiments, was killed by a projectile shot from the place, and the States army served the engines of war invented by the old governor Cornput.

to the town or returning joyously to their peaceful villages.

Steenwijk was already an old town before Meppel came into existence. At the commencement of the seventeenth century it was counted in the province of Overyssel among the 'very respectable places which enjoy great privileges, and are boroughs of importance.'[1] In 1580 it was surrounded by a moat and a wall, on account of the wars which desolated the country. But it was nothing redoubtable, for on the 11th September, 1587, a dozen of the States cavaliers sufficed to take possession of it. They presented themselves on foot at the gates, requesting permission to enter to make some purchases. As they displayed their gold they were allowed, but they had scarcely cleared the gate when they knocked down the sentinel, and called their captain, who was hidden close by. Thus the town was occupied. The moat still exists, but the walls have been demolished. Meppel is built lengthwise, forming a large and beautiful street, into which run numerous smaller ones. This principal street is divided by two canals into three nearly equal parts, which open up pleasant views on either side. Of ancient monuments there are none, but there are some old houses of a cheerful and pleasant appearance. These specimens of ancient architecture are more particularly to be met with in the centre of the town and at one of its extremities, the *Kruisstraat*. The Hôtel de Ville dates from the

[1] Guicciardini, 'Description of the Low Countries.'

last century. If it were not for the coat of arms over the door, one would readily take it for the house of a respectable citizen.

Nevertheless it has a simple and unostentatious appearance, which is not without a certain odour of municipality. With its quiet but important appearance, it looks like a burgomaster's residence of days gone by.

Meppel has two churches: one, quite modern, built at the entrance to the town, in that transition style so much affected by our own architects; the other dates from 1498, but was so extensively restored during the last century, that it affords very little of interest. It is easily overlooked in the midst of this handsome and cheerful yet unpretentious little city, which has altogether the air of a small provincial town.

Our third excursion to the west of Assen, it will be remembered, was to the penitentiary establishment of Veenhuizen. It is an agricultural colony, where poor people convicted of mendicancy are detained, and is situated in the midst of a veritable desert. It is reached by a two hours' journey across barren moors. 'Not a tree, not a shrub is to be seen on these immense plains, which would be condemned to eternal sterility if man's industry had not effected one of the most admirable transformations it is possible to imagine.'[1] Nothing can convey an idea of

---

[1] Ramon de la Sagra, 'Voyage en Hollande et Belgique.' The history of this journey, undertaken in order to study the Penitentiary system of the Low Countries, contains a quantity of technical details respecting these establishments, of the highest interest.

the charm one experiences when, after having crossed these barren wastes, one suddenly finds oneself in the midst of a golden harvest, fields of colza and clumps of oaks.

The colony of Veenhuizen possesses about 300,000 acres of land. Of this quantity, about 100,000 acres are in full cultivation. The working is divided into three departments: the first is reserved for the women, the second for the men, and the third is occupied by men and orphans. In the centre are the manager's offices and three churches, one for the Protestants, one for the Catholics, and the third for the Jews. Separated in their churches, the different sects are also separated in their domiciles; and the Catholics and the Jews have each a special quarter.

At the time of our visit there were nearly 1,800 people in Veenhuizen, of whom 400 were women, and only 60 children. The whole establishment is employed in the fields during the summer time, and in the winter at different trades that can be followed indoors, such as weaving and matmaking.

The honours of the colony were supported with the most perfect courtesy by Capt. Neetesen, the director. We visited in turn the three establishments, each of which is built after the same plan, that is, round a large courtyard planted with trees, bordered on each side by a long row of low houses, each of the same height. These houses form a suite of large chambers, which serve at the same time as sitting-rooms, eating-rooms, and dormitories for the inhabitants of the colony. They sleep in hammocks, which they roll up in the daytime to make more room. They are fully as comfortable as the beds of most field labourers. Their food is also much the same as that of ordinary farm servants. Two, three, and even four times a week they have meat or bacon, and every day a certain quantity of vegetables, and they are also entitled to a ration of bread and coffee.[1]

The bread is black, but it could, with a slight addition, be made whiter, and thus improve their daily fare. They are not entirely deprived of resources. They receive a portion of the money they earn, and their labour is paid for according to a detailed tariff.

A man with a little industry will thus make for himself a florin a day; there are, indeed, some who have made as much as eight florins in the six days comprising the week's work. Upon the product of their labour they are allowed fifteen per cent., of which ten per cent. is paid to them immediately, and the remaining five per cent. is capitalised, to be

---

[1] The colonists are divided for work into three classes: the first comprises men and women over sixteen years of age; the second, boys and girls from eight to sixteen years of age; the third, children of less than eight years of age. As to the little ones of two years and under, they remain with their mothers. The food is divided by quantity into three classes also: Children under thirteen receive three-fifths of a portion; those of thirteen to seventeen four-fifths of a portion; and those above the latter age an entire portion. For further details, a notice, published in 1872, by M. A. F. Eilerts de Haan, and entitled 'De Noordnederlandsche Landbouwkolonien,' may be consulted.

handed over to them upon their leaving the place. With what they receive on the spot they are able to procure for themselves some little delicacies; and the proof that the régime thus mitigated is not unwholesome is to be found in the good health they nearly all enjoy. We visited the infirmary attached to the establishment of No. 2: it contained but twenty-eight patients. Out of six hundred prisoners, this number is but small, especially if the fact is borne in mind that a large number of these poor people have been forced into mendicity through physical weakness, sickness, or the consequent infirmities.

The régime is not unwholesome, nor is the discipline too harsh, for numbers of these unfortunates, after having passed some time in the colony, conceive a liking for it, and leave it only to return.

We were shown the book in which were entered the names of some who had been sent back for the eleventh or twelfth time. The maximum period for each condemnation is two years; and as those who return always get the maximum, they will thus have passed there twenty years of their existence.

On the other hand, some make their escape, but these are quickly brought back and put in the prison. They also lock up the insubordinate, and those who refuse to work. But the prison of Veenhuizen has not a very terrible appearance. It is a neat little house divided into cells, guarded by a sleepy veteran who is anything but fierce.

The insubordinate are not very numerous; the

lazy are more so. The ranks of the prisoners are recruited from among the aged, the invalided, or those cowardly vagabonds altogether indisposed to exchange, for a laborious existence, their habits of idleness and licence. The women above all, it appears, are difficult to manage. Quarrelsome and spiteful, lazier than the men, they require the most constant watching; and although they are never lost sight of, more than one leaves the establishment in a situation that would be more interesting if it were more legitimate.

In establishing this colony it had been hoped to form, without any great expense, an agricultural population capable of rendering real services. This idea, however, was soon abandoned. They calculated that each prisoner would easily earn his own living. But the number of incapables and invalids was much too great, and the *Société Neerlandaise de Bienfaisance* which took the initiative in these Penitentiary colonies, have found it necessary to transfer them to the Government, who annually disburse a considerable sum for their support.[1]

Veenhuizen and Ommerschans were founded in 1818. The years 1816 and 1817 were very disastrous. The dearth had become a famine. The small cultivators and the workpeople were reduced to begging for their bread, and mendicancy assumed

[1] The two colonies of Veenhuizen and Ommerschaus cost the Netherlands Government nearly 350,000 florins. Ommerschaus, which is established on the same footing as Veenhuizen, contains from eight to nine hundred prisoners.

such proportions that it became a public danger. Some feeling men then hit upon the idea of utilising these inactive forces, with a view to giving bread to those who needed it.

Such was the beginning of this institution, which has been variously judged. Certain philanthropists have sadly asked if the solution of this terrible problem of misery is to treat as malefactors those who, urged by hunger, have held out their hands for public charity. Others again, by the light of a reasoning more economical than sentimental, argue that a work must be judged by its results; and that charity, public or private, when it offers a certainty of assistance, does more to increase improvidence than to assist the unfortunate.

Such was the opinion expressed by Mr. Batbie, when commencing, at the School of Law, on the 10th April, 1866, his course of lectures on Political Economy; this opinion was also expressed in the same year by Pierluigi Bembo, a magistrate of Venice, to his colleagues of the Lagune; also, six years previously, in one of his works,[1] by M. E. Duceptiaux, a Belgian economist.

[1] The Association, in its dealings with the bettering of the condition of the working classes.

CHAPTER XIII.

THE VILLAGES OF DRENTHE, ROLDE, EEXT, GIETEN, BORGER, AND EXLO— A RURAL PRINTING-OFFICE—LOST!—THE PASTOR OF ZWEELO— KOEVORDEN.

UR excursions in the west terminated, we forwarded our luggage to Zweelo, and with our knapsacks on our backs started for the eastern villages. Our intention, as I have already said, was to reach Eext by passing through Rolde, then on to Koevorden by the road that runs parallel with the German frontier.

I know few pleasanter roads in Europe than the one from Assen to Rolde. Like those in Friesland, it makes many turnings and windings; but no one would think of complaining, so many beautiful and attractive views succeed each other. The grand trees, the rustic houses, and the hedges bordering on the road, are most charmingly grouped. Every ten steps reveal a perfect picture, admirably composed, which would delight the eye of a landscape painter. Sometimes the hedges and trees open suddenly and then a long stretch of country is to be seen, with vast fields of golden grain beautified with corn flowers and red poppies, or beautiful sketches of green pasturage, with black and white cows browsing on the short but nourishing grass.

Sometimes, also, there may be seen in the distance a barren and uncultivated country, the dark outline of which stands out in bold relief against the clear sky; or, again, a series of small hillocks placed in regular order, which carries us back to prehistoric times, and denotes the presence of one of those mysterious burying-places, of the inhabitants of which but very little is known in these days.

Thus everything combines to interest the mind and charm the eye. But we soon came in sight of Rolde, where the beauty of the scenery is even greater; for with Rolde commences that series of villages of the Drenthe so much admired by artists, and which indeed justifies their admiration, for it is impossible to see anything more picturesque.

These cheerful hamlets are hidden amidst the grand trees, and in their nest of foliage one catches a glimpse on each side of charming rustic cottages, with their roofs reaching to the ground, and of ancient walls, with their warm-coloured bricks peeping through the white plaster.

In the centre of this lovely picture stands a church, with its tapering spire, and its little churchyard filled with flowers. In one corner is a smithy with the usual farrier's shop, and the smith in knee-breeches and leather apron. On the ground axle-trees and wheels, and secured to the wall large black long-tailed horses prancing while waiting their turn. There are no streets or squares, and the houses appear as if thrown about promiscuously, and forming one of the most charming medleys of grey roofs, white or red walls, and grand old trees that one could well imagine.

Such is Rolde ; such also are Eext, Gieten, Gasselte, and Borger. You know them—these charming villages of the Drenthe—it is they who have inspired the first landscape painters of the Dutch school.

The farrier's shop, to which allusion has just been made, has been painted ten times by Wouverman, who enlivened the picture with his brilliant cavaliers, his weather-beaten old soldiers, and his smiling serving-women. It is from the entrance to one of these pretty villages that Waterloo has taken his 'Voyageurs au Repos,' and his ' Mère aux Trois Enfants.' Old Wynants came here for inspiration, and Jacob van Ruysdaël, a lover of solitude and an admirer of wild scenery, would also come here before proceeding on his wanderings among the Norwegian gorges. Here he painted his 'Champ de Blé.' But no one has depicted these charming little nooks with such admirable truth and loving tenderness as Minderhout Hobbema, thus justifying the local tradition that his birthplace was, not Antwerp, as Pilkington pretends ; not Haarlem, as Smith affirms ; not even Guelderland, as Van Eynde and Van der Willigen suppose ; nor Friesland, as MM. Henri Herris and Charles Blanc believe ; but Koevorden, on the frontiers of Guelderland and the Drenthe, on the confines of the two provinces, from which he borrowed all his ideas and most of his subjects.

From Rolde to Borger all the pretty villages along the route have quite a homely appearance, but nevertheless each is distinguished from the other by some interesting peculiarity. Beyond that, the *Hunnebedden* and the ancient burying-places to be met with in the neighbourhood, which suffice to reconcile them to the esteem of archæologists, and the appearance of the surrounding country, remove anything approaching to monotony. The sites on which these monuments are erected are infinitely varied.

Everything about Rolde indicates abundance. Its two beautiful dolmen are placed in the centre of the *Esch*, and are consequently surrounded by the golden harvest. A thick tree has demolished the most important of the two; this patriarch of the plain almost entirely envelopes in the folds of its trunk one of the enormous blocks of which the monument is composed. A hundred steps from there the church stands, a beautiful construction of the fifteenth century, of which the graceful outlines and the strong buttresses tower above the surrounding fields.

Eext and Gieten are totally different. They are both situated in the midst of a veritable desert. No fertile fields, no refreshing shades; but everywhere dusky moors, and on the horizon a few clumps of trees; not a soul is on the road; not a cry, not a sound is heard but the buzzing of insects and the cadence of our own footfall. It is in the midst of this desolate solitude and impressive silence, that the Celtic monuments of Eext and Gieten are to be found; and the two villages which are five hundred mètres from there, seem to hide themselves behind a rampart of verdure that they may have no part in the pitiless desolation.

Once within this verdant boundary, all is changed: again the smiling, picturesque, and charming aspect of these favoured hamlets, gay without bustle and pretty without ornament, with their old houses, their new church, and in one corner of the road a neat and unpretentious inn, recognised by the sign swinging above the door, and by the half-filled trough awaiting the tired horse.

At Gasselte and at Borger the country changes again. It is half moor and half fields, and the grand trees to be seen in the distance indicate the vicinity of a forest. The road is winding and the undulations of the heath form the little hills which diversify the horizon. There is nothing monotonous to be seen in this country of wild aspect and ungrateful soil, where man carries on a constant struggle for existence, always to finish triumphantly.

Add to this a thousand joyous things, the hearty welcome at the inns, the salutations on the road, and the lively joke, all which tend to banish monotony.

In the inn at Gieten we fell upon two wretched

lithographs, hanging in the full light among the polished and shining cupboards. They were the 'Pont d'Arcole' and 'Napoléon blessé devant Ratisbonne.'

At Gasselte the scene changes again. It is now a poor country tavern, patronised by rustic customers and kept by a young female peasant. In a corner the baby is sleeping, and the young mother, in order that she may attend to the cradle and the business at the same time, carries with her, as she passes backwards and forwards, a piece of twine which is fastened to the cradle, and by means of which she keeps it gently rocking.

At Borger we experienced another instance of maternal solicitude. An unfortunate woman had lost her son, a child of two years of age, who, the people said, was lost on the heath. All the gossips of the hamlet, spreading themselves out like sharpshooters, beat the plain, calling the lost little one. In the midst of them was the mother, crying and tearing her hair. Her despair is explained by the fact that these barren wastes swarm with black-headed vipers. Each year they find many victims. This gave rise to the fears of these good people and to the battue-like form of their movements. The child was found. While it was being sought for on the moors it was in the house of a neighbour, quietly occupied in playing with a large cat.

Notwithstanding the sociability of the inhabitants of Borger, we were obliged to leave and to direct our course to Exlo. But this day's journey, which was the most painful of all our excursions, deserves to be narrated by itself.

We were called at four o'clock, and started at five. Two gamekeepers accompanied us to show us the road. Calculating that we should arrive at Odoorn by eleven o'clock, and that we should be able to breakfast there, we took only a cup of black coffee, but had nothing to eat. We struck at once on to the moor, in order to get a closer view of the superb *Hunnebedden* of Borger; then afterwards, by a road ankle deep in sand, we arrived at Exlo. To this point the road had been almost agreeable. The morning was fresh, and the vestiges of departed people were sufficiently numerous on this desolate plain to occupy both the mind and the eye. Not only do *tumuli* and stone monuments abound, but there are to be met with immense circular excavations in the form of an enormous funnel, perfectly regular, and comprising a radius of from fifty to sixty mètres. What could have been the origin of these strange excavations? Legend attributes them to witches escaped from the infernal regions. The lugubrious aspect of this dismal country would almost justify this fantastic explanation; but archæologists, who are less poetical, pretend they have found a more plausible one. According to some they are ancient Celtic camps, dug by the primitive population to guard them against their enemies, and to shelter them from the icy winds, from which there is nothing in this desert to break the force; according to others, they are immense rain-water cisterns— the only water obtainable in these parched solitudes. It is, however, impossible in these days to confirm the correctness of these opinions; they must be taken for what they are worth, that is, simple suppositions.

At Exlo we made but a short stay. It is a charming hamlet. An old chronicler, Picardt, affirms that it dates from the early years of the ninth century; and the existence of a large Celtic burying place, that must be crossed before the village is reached, would appear to assign to it an origin even more remote. It was not, however, either the picturesque cottages or the prehistoric sepulchres that attracted us. We came to Exlo almost exclusively to see a *confrère*.

This hamlet of a hundred hearths, lost in the midst of the moors, hardly connected with the outer world, and numbering at most but three hundred inhabitants, possesses a printer and a printing-office, a newspaper and a journalist. The 'Drentsche Courant' is a nice little journal, well got up, on good paper and with pretty type. Its columns abound in weighty articles and local news, while its fourth page is devoted to advertisements, &c. It is often quoted by the great papers of Amsterdam, and I imagine they have but little idea of the place from whence this publication is issued.

It is in a small, well-lighted room that all is done;

—the editing, the setting-up, and the printing. It joins a dining-room at one end and a stable at the other.

While listening to M. de Ros, the proprietor of this rural printing establishment, we could not help admiring the primitive but ingenious arrangements; and my mind, making a bound through space, went back to one of our principal Parisian artists, one of our master printers, my old comrade, Jouaust. How many times in our friendly chats have I not heard him wish for a similar retreat, where he could, far from noise and bustle, produce irreproachable works of art. Here would have been the realisation of his dream!

Notwithstanding the charm with which we contemplated this village 'office,' the sun reminded us that it was time to continue our journey. Ten o'clock chimed. We began to feel the heat, and we must reach Odoorn for breakfast. It being but little more than an hour's walk from Exlo we took leave of our kind cicerone and gaily continued our road. At Odoorn our first disappointment awaited us. Not an inn! Not a cottage where we could find anything to eat! Most of the inhabitants were in the fields, and the others said it was too late or too early for eating, for the country people here do not possess the culinary talents of our French villagers, who know how to prepare a tasty repast quickly. We tried to console ourselves in our enforced fast by visiting an old church, which is partly built of blocks of granite taken from the neighbouring *Hunnebedden*; and but slightly comforted by our archæological repast, we continued our route, deciding to push on to Zweelo, where we were expected.

It would take, as we have said, about a couple of hours' walking; but in the Drenthe, as in Friesland, hours are somewhat elastic. Half an hour after leaving Odoorn our guides left us, and, following their instructions, we took a road across the moors.

For the first hour all went well. The road was so sandy we sank at every step to the ankle, and could follow its dusty windings into the far distance. We thought it would take us to Zweelo, and our impression was confirmed by the Ordnance map, upon which the road is marked, besides which the governor of the province had declared, during my sojourn at Assen, that the roads of Drenthe were in tolerable condition.

Unfortunately we were deceived. As soon as we had cleared the *Oranje Kanaal*, the road became simply a track, traversed by country carts, and furrowing in painful zig-zags the uneven surface of the moor, which was full of bogs. Very soon, indeed, all trace of the road disappeared, and we searched for it in vain for it was covered by sand. Nevertheless we persevered, and soon the heath appeared again, with its tough shrubs and the rushing of the adders as they started away at our approach. Thus another hour passed, we advancing all the time, but without a trace of a road or a path before us. We walked straight on, not knowing whither this weary road would lead us, with overhead the burning sun, under foot the black heath, overpowered by the heat, crushed by the weight of our luggage, fasting since the night before, and buried at each step in the moving sand; while around us not a habitation, nor a human form was visible. We were lost. At last, towards half-past one o'clock, we perceived a church spire, which seemed to spring from a clump of foliage. Constant, who had never ceased sweeping the horizon with his glass, was the first to discover it. 'Is it Zweelo?' he asked. 'I don't know the place,' I replied. 'Let us go on at any rate, we will enquire later on.'

It was Zweelo! An hour later we reached the limit of the *Esch*. We had still to pass through the cultivated portion of the place, and it was not until three o'clock that we entered the village.

Our principal attraction at Zweelo was to visit a learned man, the pastor of Lesturgeon. But, knocked up by our ten hours' tramp through the moor, overpowered by the heat, and exhausted with fatigue, our first thought was to obtain some refreshment and attend to our disordered attire. We enquired for the inn. We thought we should there, at least, find the necessary accommodation. Alas! we had reckoned without our host, or rather, our hostess, a regular shrew, who refused to receive us. 'What do you want?' cried she, 'a room? There isn't one here for you; there's the door; be off!' We protested strongly against such treatment, but we had to go; so we went without any further hesitation to the house of the venerable pastor, and sought from him the hospitality which the innkeeper had refused us for our money. This time the reception was totally different, as one would suppose. Though I had never seen M. Lesturgeon, I had known him for a long time. I knew him to be a very deeply read man. I had corresponded with him, and I had been able to judge of the kindness of his heart and of the shrewdness of his mind. Surrounded by his family, he inhabited a charming villa, situated in the midst of a beautiful garden filled with flowers, and shaded by grand trees. He threw open to us his house, his wine cellar, and his kitchen. All the worse for him, for we played havoc everywhere. The wine cellar, in particular, was subject to rude assaults. When we told him of the fashion in which we had been received by the innkeeper, he said, ' I am the more indignant as these Mensingh are well off, and are looked upon as among the wealthy people of the neighbourhood, and the brother of this woman, who received you so badly, is one of our magistrates.'

The worthy pastor, when he had seen us refreshed and restored, offered to do the honours of his church, a modest structure of Roman architecture, surrounded by a small churchyard. We rested awhile in this peaceful asylum of the dead; and in the midst of these modest tombs, some of which had only just been closed, we passed the remainder of the day, meditating meekly, and forgetting in our friendly chat that we then saw each other for the first time and perhaps for the last.

In the evening we returned to the house, where the family awaited us. Mdlle. Lesturgeon, a charming and amiable girl, asked me many questions about Paris. Paris! that magical place which she had read of in books, and which she had imagined a species of paradise. 'Your houses must be beautiful,' said she, 'and what pretty gardens you must have!' I had to undeceive her, and to tell her of the niggardly life led there, of the houses divided into flats, of the dark and narrow courts, and to depict the gloomy and cheerless streets. She opened her eyes in astonishment. I had evidently dispelled an illusion. Later on she recompensed me for my frankness: 'If you have no garden,' said she, with a charming smile, 'you must be all the more fond of flowers; permit me to offer you these,' and she presented me with a superb bouquet which she had just gathered.

Just then her brother arrived with a carriage and a capital horse. As we could not sleep at Zweelo, he was anxious that we should reach Koevorden without fatigue. The hour of our departure had arrived, and we were obliged to quit, not without regret, this amiable family. As our carriage moved away, M. Lesturgeon gave us a last shake of the hand. 'Do not altogether forget,' cried he, 'the little village of Zweelo and its modest pastor.' We readily promised him not to do so, and the promise has been religiously kept.

It was nearly one o'clock in the morning when we arrived at Koevorden. We had trouble enough to secure a room. Everyone at the inn and in the town was fast asleep, and as soon as possible we followed this excellent example—and our rest was well earned.

The next day we were awakened by a malicious dwarf, who bawled with all his might a fantastic rendering of the *Fille de Madame Angot.* I profited by the morning sunshine to thoroughly examine my little room. What was my surprise to perceive, hanging on the wall, a first-class old painting! It was the portrait of the family. The father, palette in hand, is represented playing with a pretty little girl, whose mother held her on her knee. The costumes were curiously drawn, and the faces were remarkably interesting, for it was the portrait of that Rotius whose genealogy had puzzled me so much two years before.[1] It was impossible to be mistaken about it, besides the inscription removed all doubt. Put in good humour by this discovery, we wandered about the town in the hope of meeting a few precious monuments. But we were disappointed. Apart from a pretty house, the graceful *façade* of which was constructed after the fashion of those of Groningen, and bearing date 1641, there was nothing worth speaking of.

The Town Hall is a heavy, modern, plastered building; and the church, built in 1641, is devoid of

---

[1] See 'Dead Cities of the Zuyder Zee,' p. 58, 2nd edition.

THE CHURCH OF KOEVORDEN.

interest or character. The streets are large, irregular, and badly paved. The whole beauty of the town is confined to the superb bastions surrounding it, and to the fine avenues of trees which shade it with their rich foliage. One would imagine that Koevorden desired no other ornament than that of its ramparts, which, after all, is easily understood, for the town is essentially a military town. From its earliest date it has always been more a citadel than a town; and according to its old historians it owes its very foundation to a Roman camp. Bizot confirms this in his description of an ancient medal referring to this town, bearing the inscription, 'Covordia capta Drenthe a Romanis constructa Anno Domini X......' Picardt thinks that it is the *Villa Cruporicis* referred to by Tacitus. However, one fact is certain, and that is, that in 1024 the place became the residence of the Counts of Drenthe, and that the sovereignty of its territory was conceded to the Bishops of Utrecht by the Emperor Henry II.

The first act of these new sovereigns was to endow Koevorden with a castle, and thus make sure of a position which, at that time, was of no little importance, considering it was situated between two undrained marshes, was a military point, and the key, so to speak, to the whole country. This precaution, however, was eventually turned against those who had taken it. Profiting by the continual wars and vexations which occupied their episcopal sovereigns for nearly three centuries, the lords of Drenthe deprived their lawful rulers of their power, and for two hundred years played the part of sovereigns themselves. This usurpation of their rights was not submitted to by the bishops without a show of violent objection. In the winter of 1288 the 'episcopal troops took advantage of a hard frost, which enabled them to cross the marshes on horseback,' to besiege the rebellious town; but 'their design was frustrated by the advent of a strong southern wind and heavy rain,' which obliged them to beat a hasty retreat.

It was not till a century later that the town returned to its original state of obedience, under the following circumstances:

One day Frederic of Blankenheim, who was a man given to studying the laws and rights concerning his own property, and fond of increasing his domains where he could, while rummaging over some papers and records, discovered certain old letters of value. These letters, sealed and authenticated, mentioned that the country of Drenthe, with the town and castle of Cœvorden, was the property of the bishopric, and that the predecessors of those who now possessed it had only held it for a certain sum, to be redeemed whenever it pleased the bishopric to reimburse it. This sum Bishop Frederic of Blanckenheim now demanded, and on the owner of the castle refusing, the town was besieged and the castle invested, and, after a siege of six weeks' duration, the rebel vassal was forced to open his gates and to return to obedience to his lawful sovereign.

Until 1552, the town and castle remained in the power of the bishops of Utrecht, and then both were occupied by the troops of Charles V. Koevorden had no ramparts at that time, and remained without fortifications of any sort till the War of Independence was at an end, although it had been occupied alternately by Holenlo, Cornput, and Ranneberg.

Its last Spanish governor, Éverard Ens, repaired the oversight of his predecessors by fortifying the town with a redoubt of earth and adding ramparts to the castle, which enabled him to hold out, in 1592, for six weeks against Prince Maurice, the State troops, and a formidable artillery. Koevorden was taken nevertheless, and the news was received with such joy by the States that a medal was struck to commemorate the happy event. Maurice did not remain idle after his victory, but ordered able engineers to surround the town with the fine solid bulwarks which, thirty-six years later, formed the base of those marvellous defences by which Coehoorn protected it.

From that time forward (1592) the town was regarded as impregnable. Still it was not so; for, in 1672, being besieged by the Bishop of Munster, 'and cowardly defended by Colonel Burum, and betrayed by Colonel Broersma,' it capitulated, although the warrior bishop had only 18,000 indifferent troops under his command.

This triumph, however, was not of long duration. In December of the same year, Rabenhaupt, who was operating in the neighbourhood with an army of the States, learned that the garrison, confident of their position, were somewhat careless of their guard. He therefore resolved to take advantage of the severity of the season to surprise the town. Profiting by indications offered him by a man called Van Thienen, who had formerly been a churchwarden of Koevorden Church, but was now an engineer, he made his troops advance slowly as far as the frozen marshes, and then, by a forced march, cross the marshes and surround the rampart of the town, where they arrived about three o'clock in the morning. The attack, under Colonel Eybergen, was so unexpected that the Dutch army carried the place the same day, and the garrison, reduced to 300 men, after fighting as bravely as was in their power, were taken prisoners and sent to Groningen.

This victory produced great excitement and delight in the country. Vondel made himself the mouthpiece of the general joy by composing a stanza full of puns, as was the fashion in those days, which remained a popular ditty for a century afterwards:—

> De Raven roepen : Kras, kras !
> Maer Ravenshooft roept : huiden !
> Men laet' de klokken luiden
> Daer helpt noch sterkte, noch macras.[1]

---

[1] The ravens cry, 'To-morrow, to-morrow ! But the head of the raven says, "To-day !" The bells may ring. Neither fortifications nor marshes can avail.' Vondel puns on the word *kras* (*cras*), the cry of the raven, and signifying in Latin *to-morrow*, as also on the name of Rabenhaupt, which means *raven's head*.

Since then, Koevorden has only had one other siege to support. In 1813 it was invested by the allies while occupied by the French; but the garrison, though few in number, held out for some time, and did not capitulate till May 3, 1814, and then only by order of Louis XVIII., thirty-four days after the taking of Paris, and twenty-two after the abdication at Fontainebleau.

Koevorden is no longer a stronghold. Its gates have been demolished and its ramparts destroyed; for, under a new system of defence recently adopted by the Low Countries, it was placed in the list of useless frontier fortresses.

Wandering along the earthwork which surrounds the town with its formidable bastions, one cannot help regretting that such fine works should have been destroyed. They were grand works of art, and for that reason alone ought to have been preserved, even if patriotic reminiscences could not save them from their sad fate.

CHAPTER XIV.

THE OLD SALIAN COUNTRY—DEVENTER—ITS MILITARY HISTORY—EDWARD STANLEY AND COLONEL TAXIS—ST. LIEVIN AND THE BERGKERK—A PAINTING BY TERBURG—THE '*DONAT*' OF THE ATHENÆUM AND THE '*REYNARDUS VULPES*'—'*KIJKINDEPOT.*'

N quitting Koevorden, we passed through Dalen, which has the reputation of being the first village of the Drenthe. Its pretty houses and grand avenues of trees, bordering the streets, have given it the name of *Drentsche Haag*, in allusion to the royal residence in the Low Countries, which for a long time was reported by travellers to be the handsomest and largest village in the world.

On leaving Dalen, we left the bogs of Noord and Zuid Borge on the east, and the village of Emmen on the north, in order to pursue our road to the west by the *Drentsch Kanaal* and reach Hoogwan and the railroad.

We did not pass by Emmen and the bogs, because they are not worth a visit; on the contrary, Emmen is a very pretty village abounding in old Celtic remains. Its *Hunnebedden* are the largest if not the most interesting in the Province, and several wooden bridges which are attributed to Roman construction, and no doubt are the *Pontes Longi* referred to by Tacitus, are well worthy of special attention. On the other hand Nieuw-Amsterdam ought to interest, on account of its being a fair example of what man's activity and labour can accomplish, in a country of bogs and peat. Not twenty years ago this part of the Province was one vast piece of marshy ground, pestilential in summer, and useless in winter, besides being a constant source of danger to the neighbouring land.

Two intelligent men soon changed the aspect of this desolate ground. Holthe tot Echten and H. F. Gorselaar, the former a landed proprietor at Assen, the latter a native of Emmen, worked together to accomplish this purpose. The bed of a canal was dug, the ground was drained, and certain parts were rendered habitable, and then the enterprise of clearing the bog itself began. Very soon several of the owners of land in Amsterdam joined the undertaking, and imitated the good example set them by these intrepid men, and after a while 2,500 acres were cleared, and a village founded, which although it has only been twenty years in existence, possesses already about three thousand inhabitants, one church, and two schools.

In every direction around the purified soil produces potatoes, buck wheat, barley, beans and vegetables, and as the work of clearing the bogs goes on in proportion to the demands of the village, a certain amount of material is excavated from the bogs, under the direction of M. Corver, an engineer of the country, which by a certain process is converted into a very good substitute for pit coal. All these things were great inducements for us to linger about the spot, but we were anxious to push on to Zwolle, besides travelling is a very difficult matter in this Drenthe country, and each place is so difficult to reach that this, in itself, was a sufficient reason for deferring the pleasure at that time.

We had no intention of staying long at Zwolle. We intended indeed remaining but a few hours at the capital of Overyssel, as I had already visited the town, and had described it elsewhere.[1] We thought of merely staying sufficient time to pay our respects to the governor of the Province, and to obtain from him letters of introduction to the burgomaster of the principal towns of the old Salian country. But we counted without our host, or the excessive kindness and courtesy of the high functionary, to whom we appealed to grant our request. Baron Nahuys would not hear of our leaving his pretty capital so soon. In spite of our wish to hasten onwards, and our pre-arranged determination not to be persuaded into staying, we found ourselves accepting a gracious invitation to meet at the Governor's table the most distinguished men of the Province.

We were not in the least surprised at the hospitable kindness of the Baron, for both he and his wife are known throughout the Netherlands for their courtesy and hospitality. The king made a happy

---

[1] 'The Dead Cities of the Zuyder Zee.'

choice when he placed this gentleman at the head of Overyssel, for the Province prides itself on its hospitality and kindness, and naturally looks to its governor to carry out the traditions of the country.

The borders of the Yssel (*Issala* in Latin) are regarded by all old authors as the original country of the Salian Franks. Oldenzaal (*Salia vetus*) must have been their capital. The Seigneurie of Salland (country of the Salians) and the village of Salicum, would justify this pretension which was gathered by Hadrianus Junius, accepted by Revius, and confirmed by Guicciardini.

'L'isle de Crète, glorieuse pour le berceau de Iupeter, et la ville de Thèves, superbe par le naissance de Hercules, doibvent à bon droit donner place à toi, ô Over-Issel. Car ... en toy sont trouvez les sources at les parents de la très puissante et célèbre nation des Francs.'

The time we did stay at Zwolle was devoted to pleasure, and to the enjoyment of the society of our hospitable entertainers, for no one could have been received more cordially than we were; and then we started on our journey to Deventer.

The route we chose to reach the episcopal city, which played such an important part in the history of Guelderland, was by the Yssel.

The Yssel is a fine broad river, bordered on either side by rich country, fertile meadows, and powerful villages. Every moment we caught sight of pointed steeples, surrounded by bright-looking houses, farms, and cottages. First came Hattum with its strange look of antiquity, then Wijhe, Veessen, and Olst, were reflected in the river, after which came the groves around Diepenveen, Nijbroek, and Terwolde, skirting the sides of the river like long avenues. At last the steeples of Deventer appeared on the horizon, grand and firm in their position like lords governing their domains, or mitred bishops keeping watch over their diocese.

These steeples can be seen from a long distance, and their imposing appearance gives one a favourable impression of the valiant city, which is not diminished as we draw nearer the town. Indeed the approach to Deventer has the effect of a magnificent panorama. The quay, still bordered by its old walls, shaded here and there, and commanded by a mass of pointed gabled roofs, high towers and numerous steeples and belfries, forms on the whole the most attractive entrance to a town one could wish to see. On the other side superb plantations, and grand trees with enormous out-spreading branches, and heads so tall they seem to vie in height with the opposite steeples, greet the eye the instant one turns one's head from looking at the town. The banks of the river are joined by a bridge of boats, the simplicity of which seems slightly out of place in connection with the noble appearance of its surroundings. Formerly there existed here a very handsome wooden bridge, the erection of which had cost no less than 16,000 florins of gold (*Rijnsche goudgulden*), but it was destroyed by fire in 1521 and 1578, carried away by ice in 1570, and finally cut down in 1592, in which year it was replaced by the bridge of boats, which still exists, although in constant need of repair and restoration.

At the head of this bridge there are still to be seen the ruins of the old walls, the glorious remains of the first fortifications of Deventer. It was the same enormous brick wall which resisted the assault of the Burgundians, in 1457. The town had refused to acknowledge for its legitimate sovereign, David of Burgundy, Bishop of Utrecht, Philip the Good's bastard; and the old duke, furious at this insult to his son, swore he would bring the town to reason. Happily the Duke of Guelders interfered in time, and the rebellious city was spared from devastation. The grand old walls protected the inhabitants for a period of many years, and even in 1578 resisted the troops of the States General for a space of three months.

The gallant and populous city was not on very good terms with Spain. It was Dutch and Huguenot to the core, and very proud of its independence. Hence, when taken, it refused to receive the garrison, and the citizens organised a militia and declared they would guard the town and its ramparts themselves. But in 1586 when the Spanish threatened the borders of the Yssel anew, the Earl of Leicester forced Deventer to receive certain troops, whereupon 1,200 entered the place. According to Leclerc's 'Histoire des Pays Bas,' these troops were 'Irish Savages,' coarse, rough, half-naked men, headed by an extraordinary man whose history demands a few words from us.

Edward Stanley, the Englishman in command of this cohort, was a knight of adventure. He distinguished himself at the taking of Zutphen, by a brilliant action. Just as he was scaling the ramparts a pike was advanced by one of the enemy with the intention of running him through; but he seized hold of it so firmly that he was dragged by the soldier who held the other end into the fort, where he laid about him so lustily with his sword, that he vanquished all those who attacked him. This heroic action attracted the attention of Leicester, who forthwith dubbed him knight and pensioned him. Later on Stanley managed to slip into the circle around the earl, became a great favourite, and thus obtained in a sort of way the command of Deventer. It was worse than imprudent to place such a man at the head of so important a place. The States soon found this out to their cost. The moment Stanley found himself master of the town, he sought an opportunity to sell the place to the Spaniards. In league with Colonel Taxis and the Duke of Palma, he proceeded very early on the morning of the 29th January, 1587, to the Burgomaster's house, and demanded that the gates of the town should be opened in order to effect a sortie and to surprise the enemy who were approaching the town. His demand was complied with, and he rode out after announcing that he would be back in an hour, and begging that the gates might be opened again the moment he was seen approaching. He returned at the appointed hour, but with Colonel Taxis, and six companies of Spaniards, who penetrated the town, marched straight to the market-place, put themselves in battle order, and took possession of all the posts. All this was done so quickly and with so little noise, that no one in the town knew or noticed what was going on. When the citizens awoke their surprise was immense. A few of the Protestants were so frightened that they endeavoured to escape by throwing themselves over the ramparts. But Colonel Taxis reassured the inhabitants, who very soon perceived that the Spanish soldiers were far preferable to the Irish savages belonging to Leicester.

Stanley's treachery did not bring him any reward. He had delivered the town for a certain sum of money and the promise of advancement, both of which were very scantily paid to him—and being suspected by both parties, he took refuge in Spain, where he died in the greatest misery and obscurity.

Count Herman de Berghen succeeded Colonel de Taxis as governor of Deventer. It was from him that Prince Maurice retook the town in 1591. On the day of Pentecost, June 9th, 1591, the prince surrounded and attacked the town with twenty-eight double pounders, and called upon it to capitulate. Count de Berghen replied, 'that he wished happiness to his cousin, but that he would keep the town for the king, his master, while he had breath in his body.'

Before the end of the day Deventer had received four thousand shots, and Count de Berghen, wounded himself in his face, ordered the white flag to be hoisted. 'Thus the town was taken in so short a time,' says De Meteren, an historian of the time, 'that one heard of the attack and surrender at the same time.'

No sooner were the States in possession of Deventer, than they proposed enlarging its fortifications, and charged an engineer called Adriaan Metius to render it impregnable. But in spite of all his science, Metius did not succeed, which however can hardly be imputed to him as a crime. He did not count on the treachery of Governor Steeke, who, terrified by the cannon of the Bishop of Munster, surrendered the place in 1672, without firing a shot. Happily for its military honour, the last siege Deventer underwent was of a singularly glorious type. It had been prepared beforehand, and when it was invested by the allies early in November, 1813, everything was ready to receive them. The captain increased his defences, and the garrison, few in number as they were, were nevertheless determined to do as well as they could. The place was still intact, when on the 15th April, 1814, the French troops received an order to evacuate it. As this order was signed by King Louis XVIII., the commander demanded that it should be confirmed hierarchically, hence it was not before the 26th April, after the return of the officers sent to the French staff, that the troops commenced their retreat, leaving the town with arms and baggage, and military honours.

It would not have been astonishing if Deventer had been partially destroyed through so many military agitations. But happily it was not, and it is still, as it was in the days of Guicciardini, 'a large spacious town full of fine edifices both public and private.' The few injuries inflicted by the besiegers' cannon have been tolerably well hidden, and war has not had much more effect on the town than the lapse of time.

Deventer is certainly one of the oldest cities in the country. J. Revius, who wrote its history in the seventeenth century, assigns a certain man called Davon as its founder. He was powerful, respected, very pious and learned, and a friend of the St. Lievin who died at Deventer in 770. Others assert that the town is still more ancient, and pretend that it was founded in the year 130, by the Catti, a Germanic tribe, who took refuge in Spain, when they were turned out by the Salians, and became the origin of the people of Catalonia. If this is the case, the name of Deventer must be derived, not from the castle built by Davon (Dava's Slot); but from the noun *aventurium*, which means in the Catti language 'fortune,' from which we might have derived the word 'adventure,' if the Romans had not transmitted for our benefit the noun *eventum* and the verb *advenire*. However, whether it was founded in the second or eighth century, it was not till the eleventh that it began to take any important position in the world.

Deventer is indebted to Bernulphe, Bishop of Utrecht, for its Cathedral. It was after having obtained from the Emperor Henry III. a spiritual and temporal power over the town and its environs, that this prelate organised a council of canons, invited twenty prebendaries from the church of St. Saviour, of Utrecht, to the town, and then had the first church dedicated to St. Lievin, constructed in 1046. However this building did not last long. In 1235 it was rebuilt, and again in 1334 it was found necessary to reconstruct it, in consequence of a fire which took place that year.

It is this church, erected in 1334, that we visited, and which remains in existence to this day—which in spite of the alterations and enlargements it has undergone at various periods, is still one of the finest churches in the Low Countries. The centre nave and the crypt immediately under the high altar, are the only parts left of the original building. Two naves of similar height were added in the fifteenth century, and at the same time five brick vaults were built over all three naves, which considerably enhanced the grace of the outline, and completed the noble appearance of the structure.

The south *façade*, constructed in freestone and ivory elaborately ornamented, dates from this same period. There is a tower also at the head of this *façade*, but in an unfinished state. In 1613 a belfry was added which has not a bad effect, although it has a more modern appearance. It is of octagon shape, with several attics and pilasters, on four sides of which are four mottoes, worth meditating on: FIDE-DEO —CONSVLE—VIGILA—FORTIS AGE: precepts which are valuable in themselves, even when written high in the air.

Evidently this handsome tower was not intended to remain alone, the intention being to erect a similar one on the north side—but the project was abandoned early, and replaced by a large chapel. The western door is a half-circle, standing between the unfinished tower and the one in project. It is an architectural curiosity, being, besides the doors of St. Pancras, of Leyden, and the windows of the Abbey of Middelburg, the only known specimen of half-circle construction, at a time when ogive architectural was at its height. Formerly the interior was covered with paintings on the walls. But at the epoch of the Reformation these beautiful decorations were destroyed by the whitewashing of the iconoclastic. Here and there a fragment of these paintings escaped destruction; and just at the time when we visited the town, a rather large portion of one of them, representing a kind of last judgment, in which devils are torturing penal sinners, was discovered. But unfortunately, although the plaster is only half-an-inch thick, it cannot be removed without destroying the painting it covers; hence it is impossible to find a single one of these old specimens of art intact.

Two or three of the minor bas-reliefs have happily escaped much damage, and are in such a state of preservation as to give us a very good idea of the beautiful sculpture formerly ornamenting the church. One indicates the place where a certain *Johan van Leyden* reposes, and is very curiously executed. One must not confound this *Johan van Leyden* with the well-known John of Leyden. He was a simple citizen and respectable burgomaster, who died in 1435, and had nothing in common with the famous prophet of Munster. By his side lies his wife, Dame Mitchell.

This large Church of St. Lievin is not the only one of the same name in Deventer. There is a Catholic St. Lievin, as well as this Protestant St. Lievin, although its construction is of a much more simple style. It has only two naves, terminating in three sides of an octagon; hence I believe it is in an unfinished state. However, in spite of the simplicity of its design, and built as it is, entirely of brick, it has a very presentable appearance in the interior. Its coloured windows, carved and gilded altars, and wall paintings, although modern, nevertheless give it an imposing appearance, which as a rule is wanting in temples of the Reformed religion. It was not till 1803 that this church was made use of for the Catholic form of worship. Since 1579 it had been occupied by Calvinists, and before that period— for it dates from 1338—it had formed part of a monastery, perhaps that of the Frères de la Vie Commune, or most probably that of the Récollets, founded in 1335 by Eleanor of England. These dates coincide too distinctly to admit of any other hypothesis. This church is described in old parchments as *Broerkirk* (Church of the Brothers). When it was restored to the Catholics they remembered that St. Lievin had been the patron saint of this little city ; that he had, in fact, established the first chapel in 760, and that it was owing to his protection the pretty little town had not been destroyed in 882 by the Normans, and in 1178 by the Duke of Guelderland ; and, remembering all these good offices, they consecrated their only church to him, indifferent to the fact of the name being already possessed by the large church.

If there is any doubt about the exact religious order to which the Catholic Church of Deventer once belonged, there is no such doubt about St. Nicholas, also called the *Bergkirk* (Church of the Mountain). The Prémonté monks were in possession of the parish. Their convent was the most ancient in the town, having been founded in 1123; and their prior, as pastor of St. Nicholas, was generally called *pastoor op den Berg* (pastor up the mountain). Yet to visit St. Nicholas it is not necessary to climb steep places, nor to round sharp corners. Here the slightest undulation appears like a mountain—even a hill or a small eminence—for one could hide a hundred such mountains as Deventer in the rise of Montmartre.

The position of the *Bergkirk* is tolerably picturesque, if one takes into consideration that in this flat country the slightest approach to a rise assumes the appearance of a hill. The building stands out boldly from the surrounding landscape. It was erected in 1198 by Thierry van der Arc, Bishop of Utrecht; but the only portions in existence of that date are the *façade* and the towers, with their tiled roofs, though in the arches of the choir there is still a trace left of the half-circle period. The columns without capitals, and with ornamented round bases, the arches of the nave, and the brick vault above, date very probably from 1463, the epoch when the side aisles and the circumference, with its seven sides, were built. The interior is bare and desolate. It is said that it contains the tomb of Eleanor of England, who died at Deventer in 1356. But we could not find it. No doubt it has been destroyed. In fact, it is of no use to expect paintings or statues in the *Bergkirk*. The building was scratched, pumice-stoned, plastered, white-washed, and done up afresh about three years ago; and the only fault its *koster* finds with it now, is, that it is not lit with gas.

This destruction of churches in Deventer is all the more to be regretted, because formerly they were very richly decorated. From the earliest times they were provided with prebends and canons of considerable importance, and they must have had gifts in their possession of immense value, when they were governed by a bishop. The archives of the town prove this, and refer to a number of tithes, belonging to the chief churches of Deventer, of great value. The bishopric of Deventer did not exist for a very long period. It was first established by Paul V. to combat the progress of Protestantism, and counted in all only three possessors: Jean Mathiew, whose bad health obliged him to retire from his see, and who, living among the Récollets of Oudenarde, was cruelly tortured by the Huguenots; Egidius de Monte, called also Gilles van den Berg, or Gilles Dumont; and Gilbert Cœverinx, dean of the chapter of Bois-le-Duc, who was instituted in 1589, but was not able to take possession of the episcopal see owing to the disordered state of the Provinces, and the decline of spiritual before civil authority.

The Town Hall is built on the site where the cemetery was formerly, close to the large church. The place is still called the *Kerkhof*. The building dates from 1693. To mention its date is to mention its style, though the Dutch architects rarely succeeded in their Greek or Latin reminiscences. The large vestibule is decorated in the best style of the Louis XIV. period. The simple white walls bring out in strong relief the grand carved frame-work of the doors, and form a sharp contrast to the bright vivid tints of the armorial shields of the old guilds. Amongst these emblems of industry and peace a dozen swords hanging over our heads reminded us that the *Magistrat* of Deventer formerly possessed the right of high and low justice on all the city and its dependencies.

Twelve magistrates and four counsellors formed the body invested with these rights. Each year, on the 23rd February, they were elected by an assembly of citizens. These citizen-electors were forty-eight in number, and swore they would only choose such magistrates as were honest, and had the good of the State at heart. Each quarter furnished six, the town being divided into eight quarters. The privileges of these men were various. Amongst others they might assemble four times a year for the purpose of deliberating on the affairs of the Province, comprising peace and war, which, according to a writer of the time, gave them considerable authority over their fellow-townsmen. The hall where the Council of Magistrates was held and where also the Municipal Council held their meetings, is still in existence. A magnificent picture, dated 1667, which still hangs in the Council Chamber, gives one a very good idea of what those Assemblies of Justice were like a couple of centuries ago. It is the portrait of the sixteen magistrates and four secretaries holding office at that time. Each one is sitting in his place. The two men, who were elected every quarter, occupy the President's desk, and the four secretaries the small table in front. Each figure is robed in black, as becomes the office of judge. Each face is expressive of strong character, and a conscientious honesty. The picture is by Terburg, and it certainly is a marvellous display of the exactness and power of observation generally attributed to that gifted being. The colouring and style are very charming. Terburg was born at Zwolle, in

1608 ; but it was not till he was about sixty years of age that he established himself among his relations in Deventer, where he married one of his cousins, and died thirteen years later, without leaving behind him any children. No doubt while he was painting this marvellous *chef-d'œuvre* he himself sat under the swords and administered justice in his turn. He deserved honouring by a town which he honoured so much by his talents and his just character. It would be a good thing if M. Ch. Blanc could see this noble picture. He would not again say of Terburg that he was a 'painter without any depth.'

It is with very great regret that we turn from this grand picture to a Biblical painting by Hardenberg, and four others of the four Evangelists, by Henry ter Brugghen. This latter artist was born at Deventer, but, unlike Terburg, he quitted the pretty town to go and live at Utrecht. He was born in 1588, and died in his adopted town in 1629. His son, at the age of ninety-nine, restored these paintings to his father's native town.

Before leaving the Town Hall we paid a visit to the Burgomaster's chamber, and the library of the Athenæum, which has gained a well-merited reputation. The Municipal Cabinet contains three interesting pictures of views of Deventer, and a very handsome chimney-piece. There are more than 6,000 volumes in the library, many of which are rare and valuable. There is a goodly collection of

Oriental works and manuscripts,[1] 130 volumes of incunabula containing about 500 different works, among which are two of very great value, two bibliographical treasures—a xylographic *Donat*, and the only known copy of a certain *Reynardus Vulpes*. The *Donat* has had the honour of a *fac-simile* reproduction. In his *Monuments Typographiques*, M. Holtrop has compared it with an identical copy in the Royal Library at the Hague. The special value of the Deventer *Donat* consists not in its being unknown, but that it is the only complete copy extant. The *Reynardus Vulpes* dates from the thirteenth century. The library is well taken care of. M. Van Eyck, the real librarian, to whom we are indebted for the catalogue, is not only a careful keeper of manuscripts, but a scholar. He has devoted a great deal of time and attention to the origin of printing in his native town, and his researches have been crowned with success. To him we are indebted for the knowledge that between 1470 and 1475 this marvellous discovery was brought to Deventer by one Rykert, or Richard Paffroed, who established himself in the neighbourhood, and worked at his printing till 1486. In this year he seems to have handed over his block and plant to a man called Jacques de Breda. However, he returned to his art about the year 1488 with a new set of implements, and from that time the town of Deventer possessed two printers.

---

[1] M. de Goeje has drawn up a catalogue of these works. It can be found in his *Codius orientalis*.

Although this early establishment of the art of printing proves that the inhabitants of Deventer were cultivated people, it does not account for the extreme richness of the Athenæum library. The treasures it contains were obtained from the library of Hardewijk when the Academy, which was the principal ornament of that little town, was suppressed.

The books comprising this academical library were divided, by command of the king, into two parts. The one, consisting of the larger number of ordinary books, went to Arnhem; while Deventer became the happy possessor of the second part, consisting of rare and precious treasures. Not very far from the library are to be found the archives, classed in order, docketed and described with the greatest care. It is a pleasure to look at archives in this condition; all the more so because Deventer having been the capital of the Province, and an episcopal town, its archives, of necessity, are very valuable. The catalogue refers to 1,600 principal documents, several of which are a kind of combination of others. We had no time to stop and look over these interesting papers, much as we should have enjoyed studying their contents.

Close to the Town Hall, and built on the same site of the old *Kerkhof*, is a handsome edifice used as a police-office. The *façade* is of brick and stone. It has five storeys, the two highest of which, including the gable, have no openings, and are surmounted by a figure of a warrior, carrying on his shield the arms of the town, said to be the statue of Charles V. This handsome *façade* is in very good taste and style. The doors of the ground-floor, especially the centre one, are veritable triumphal arches of most elegant form and style.

This building is not the only one in Deventer either of this period or of this style. One could point out half-a-dozen others—one especially, built near to the *Brink*—and the Palace of Justice, standing in a corner, and shaded by grand trees; but the Police Office is perhaps the finest and the one most beautifully ornamented.

There are fewer traces of the fifteenth and sixteenth centuries to be found in this town. However, the pretty little city need not complain of this, as the Weigh-house, and a house near the *Kerkhof*, will prove. This house has a pointed gable, two jutting storeys, and eight consoles supporting curious figures—not only very rare, but full of interest when one takes into consideration that all the wooden houses of the fifteenth century were carefully destroyed for fear of fire.

The Weigh-house dates from 1528, although it has triangular windows, towers, and turrets; in fact, all the attractions of the Gothic style. It was erected close to the shady place called the *Brink*, and is altogether a very charming building. It has been several times restored—in 1620, 1755, and 1873—but never disfigured. It was completed in

1643, by the addition of a staircase with double balustrades and an elegant flight of steps in front. In olden times it was the rendezvous of the business men of Deventer, the place where most of the commercial transactions took place. The importance of these transactions was much greater at that epoch than might generally be imagined, for Deventer was a rich, industrial town, with large revenues. Besides the yearly income accruing from its 'free Weighhouse,' which was a gift from Count Florent V., the town received special privileges from the Emperor Henry V., who loaded it with gifts in order to attach it firmly to himself. His example was followed by Count Otho I., next by Renaud of Guelderland, and later on by the Bishops of Utrecht, each with the same object in view—only his own benefit. Then the importance of the town was considerably increased by its joining the Hanseatic League, and by signing treaties with the King of Denmark, and the sovereigns of England. No wonder, then, that the 'Weigh-house' reflected the importance and prosperity of the town which had made it the centre of its industrial and agricultural commerce.

Even now, Deventer is a town of no mean importance. Besides its markets, which still continue very important, it carries on an active manufacture of cotton, wool, and silk, and especially a certain kind of carpet which is celebrated throughout Europe.

While we are on the subject of industry, we may

as well mention the manufacture of gingerbread (*Deventerkoek*) and of wine. For Deventer does manufacture its own wine, and is very proud of it too. The hotel-keepers announce it on their cards, and make a great distinction between the native wine (*onversneden*) and that which is not.

The 'Weigh-house' has two or three sculptured pieces about it which must not be passed over in silence. First we have the sun, moon, and stars, as a magic lantern; and then a couple of curious figures in high relief on either side of the building, one representing a very ugly fellow looking into a pot, called *kijkindepot* (glancing in the pot); the other, the same fellow looking away from the pot while cooking something in it, called *kijkuitdepot* (glancing out of the pot). We wished to know a little more concerning the subject treated in this double way, but we could find out nothing of any importance. We were told that an immense cauldron, hanging close by, and pierced by several balls, had once served as a means for boiling a coiner of false money. The execution took place on the *Brink*. It was the punishment in those days for the crime of forging coin.[1]

This was not the only execution which took place on the *Brink*, in front of the Weigh-house. A certain number of heretics were burned there. In

---

[1] There is a drawing of this mode of death on the margin of one of the archives of Lille, close to the sentence passed the 12th July, 1560, condemning a coiner of gold to be boiled in a cauldron.

1544 Marie van Beekum and her sister met their deaths on this identical spot, and in 1571 a dozen other unfortunate victims shared the same fate. I mention these specially because Jan Luiken has preserved a record of their memory.

Looking at the *Brink* now, one finds it difficult to believe it has such a sinister history. It is the most charming little place in the world, and is surrounded with handsome houses, one or two of which are so ancient and attractive that I must describe them. The first is a genuine specimen of the Renaissance period. It is a small building, only one storey high, surmounted by an immense roof. The mullioned windows are placed between two friezes ornamented with scrolls. The entrance to the building is composed of a grand portico, with an enormous arched door, above which are two storeys decorated with windows, niches, and statues. The *façade* terminates in a pinnacle, with an enormous grotesque head at the top. The niches are crowned with attics or with arches, and arabesque designs of graceful form and outline connect them with a series of scrolls bearing inscriptions. It is scarcely necessary to add that the statues represent a remarkable collection of rare virtues—Courage, Prudence, Faith, &c. The other house is situated a little farther away, but also on the *Brink*. It only dates from 1739, hence is not very old. It is occupied now by a silk merchant.

In spite of its bastard style, which might be called the Louis XIV. of the Low Countries; in spite of the heavy entablature surmounting it; in spite of its flower-pots and such things, it has such a grand, noble appearance, with its two fine statues towering above, that it forms an exception to its age, and proves the fact that a good architect can always master every style. It is certainly not paying an empty compliment to Deventer to tell the world that such grand edifices are to be found within its walls. These houses are in themselves proof positive of the intelligence and artistic tastes of the population. It is one of the brightest and prettiest towns possible, and pleasant and instructive to visit. A town also that one would like to see more than once, and where one would not be sorry to settle down for a time.

CHAPTER XV.

APELDOORN—THE LOO—AN ABDICATION—ZUTPHEN—PILLAGE—HOL-
LANDSCHE TUIN—A LETTER FROM LOUVOIS—ARCHIVES—THE
MUSEUM—ST. WALBURGUS AND NOTRE DAME.

THE environs of Deventer are as charming and coquettish as the town is full of artistic houses, and rich in reminiscences. The silver Yssel winds in and out, green meadows, groves and shady walks abound along its banks; and, turn in whichever direction one will from the town, a pleasant promenade is sure to invite, and then claim, our attention. The country is superb all around, but the road to Apeldoorn is specially interesting from a variety of causes. Apeldoorn is certainly one of the finest villages, not only in the provinces, but in the whole of the Low Countries; and it is there that the favourite residence of the King of Holland is situated. The castle is called Loo.

The distance between Deventer and Apeldoorn is about eight or nine miles. We started early in the morning, and walked this distance with the greatest ease, for the route was shady, and the cottages we passed, ornamented with flower-gardens and large verandahs, beguiled the monotony of the way.

No such village as Apeldoorn is to be found in France. Imagine several majestic avenues of elm-trees a century old, with elegant houses emerging from beneath their shade, surrounded by beautiful flower-gardens. Each house leaves its hall-door open, and chairs are placed outside. They are divided from the road by no wall or barrier of any kind, and the owners of these charming habitations appear to live altogether in the greatest harmony and peace, like one immense family party.

Apeldoorn is by no means a village of to-day. Otho III. and Lothair III. refer to it in their letters. In 1629 it was considered sufficiently rich and prosperous for a band of Spaniards, commanded by Count Salazar, to pay it a visit. Burned and pillaged as it was, it sprung up again after a time, and in 1770 the widow of William V., Princess Frederica Sophia, endowed it with the church still in existence. This church is not very handsome, being heavy and massive; but its austere appearance enhances, by pleasant contrast, the beauty of the elegant and flower-covered cottages around.

The Castle of Loo is reached through these magnificent elm-avenues. It is an imposing-looking building, with an immense white frontage broken by a number of windows with outside shutters of a very dark colour. A large court of honour is in front, with a peristyle, leading to a magnificent vestibule, by a staircase ornamented from top to bottom with trophies and scutcheons. Armour, banners, and flags, and a few Indian pictures, painted by Radhen Salé, a painter of Batavia, complete the decoration of the vestibule.

The private reception-rooms are on the first floor; two or three of which are still ornamented in the magisterial style of the eighteenth century. The others have been arranged according to the good taste of the royal owner, and are profusely ornamented with works of art, and furnished in a very costly manner. These rooms have a pleasant and charming appearance, and give one the impression that they have been furnished and adorned by one who had an affection for the place.

The dining-room is on the ground-floor, furnished in a rich style, and decorated here and there with precious mementoes of bygone heroes. Side by side with silver pyx and silver-gilt jugs, one notices the knife which belonged to the great William the Taciturn, and a glass which William V. drank from. The original decorations of the room are preserved as they were.

Next to this apartment is the library; and then come the rooms set apart for Prince Frederic, the King's uncle.

Through a series of passages one arrives at the theatre. It was just receiving its finishing touches when we visited it, and it certainly is one of the most charming places of the kind I ever saw.

It is impossible to imagine anything more grandly beautiful than the park and garden belonging to this castle. Lawns, rich beds of exquisite-coloured flowers, gigantic black birch-trees, chestnut-trees in groups and apart, meet the eye at every turn, forming the most perfect landscape and charming scenery. Each step brings one to a fresh surprise in the form of a lovely nook or exquisite grove, and whichever way one walks one appears to be in a fairy land of beauty.

At the end of the magnificent alleys is the ancient castle called now, the little Loo, the residence of the young Prince of Orange. It is an old feudal building with machicoulis and turrets half covered with creeping-plants, ivy, and honeysuckle. This simple edifice, destitute of any official pretension, was erected about the beginning of the sixteenth century by the Seigneur Johan Bentink.

First of all it was a sort of hunting castle (Jachtslot); then later on it became a lordly habitation, and the owner, knowing the advantage of having a powerful protector, paid homage to Duke Charles in 1537. The result of this was that it became a transmissible fief, subject to the singular annual rent of a hunting-horn and two white greyhounds.[1] Johan Bentink's sons dying without issue, Loo passed into the hands of Zeger van Arnhem, his son-in-law. From him it went to the Van Voorst family;

---

[1] Van der Aa says, 'two white hinds;' more difficult still to be obtained.

from them it was inherited by Van Isendoorn; then later on by Van Stepracht; till finally it fell to the possession of Van Dornick, who yielded it to the Stadholder William III. This prince conceived a great affection for the place, and had the ground laid out in the marvellously beautiful manner so much admired in the present day; commanded the erection of the new castle, the great Loo, and, in order to ornament and decorate it in the best style, he employed the highest talent of the age to carry out his wishes. In the meantime the little Loo was turned into a menagerie.

In 1795, when the Republican troops invaded the country, this property was considered as no longer belonging to the Princes of Orange, so the castle was confiscated and converted into barracks, and the furniture and menagerie sold. Two elephants, deemed worthy of a place in the Jardin des Plantes, were reserved by the victors, shut up in enormous wooden cages, and sent to Paris. These animals were called Hans and Parkie, and the account of their journey to the French capital is to be found in a book called 'Les Animaux célébres et intelligents.' Elephants at that time were very rarely seen in Europe; hence these two afforded ample amusement to the public for a long time, till finally one day they took cold and died of inflammation of the lungs.

During his short reign King Louis made great efforts to have the castle restored to its original splendour; but time failed him, and his intentions were very imperfectly carried out.

On their return to the country, the Princes of Orange naturally regained possession of their magnificent domain. William I. was very fond of the place; he lived there constantly, and it was in the great hall of this castle that he abdicated on the 17th October, 1840. In the presence of his son and grandson, the ministers and members of the Council of State, the old King passed his crown to the Prince of Orange. The President of the Council read the form of abdication; it was signed by all present, and then the ceremony was over.

Was it the remembrance of this ceremony, or some other cause, which kept William II. from enjoying the shades of this peaceful retreat? He rarely, if ever, set foot in the place. Fortunately his successor, William III., was particularly attached to the old castle, and not only lived there continually, but had the domain restored to its original grandeur, and the park and gardens improved, as we have already remarked.

An enormous forest, stretching to the north as far as Elspeet and to the west as far as the heaths of Milligen, joins the park and gardens of this princely residence. The desolate heaths of Milligen are admirably adapted, by their great extent, for military evolutions, and it is there that the grand manœuvres of the army take place in summer and autumn.

ZUTPHEN (BANKS OF THE BERKEL).

A beautiful wide road connects Loo with Milligen, leading on to Apeldoorn, and from thence to Zutphen. To reach this last-named town requires three good hours' walking; the moment the border of the Yssel is reached, fatigue is forgotten in admiration of the charming and picturesque appearance of this city. In the distance it looks like a great lake of red roofs instead of shimmering waves; but on approaching nearer one can perceive the little river Berkel dividing the town into two parts, washing its old ramparts, and opening to view such delicious bits of colour and form that a painter might go mad with joy at sight of them.

The old moat and the wall, which formerly enclosed the *enceinte* of the town, form a very attractive picture, though the latter is party hidden by houses which have been built out of it by some of the inhabitants of Zutphen. An opening here and there, and a bit of roof, and behold the house was considered fit for habitation! Here and there a wall had been whitewashed, or a little plaster stuck on, and the windows ornamented with shutters or blinds; but as a rule these places have been left in their original state, and the impression of the old machicoulis is still to be seen under the shadow of their roofs.

Add to all this a mass of plants and flowers, white inclining barriers, and black, worm-eaten staircases, red roofs and grey walls, surrounded by tiny gardens gay with colours, and with the branches of their trees drooping in the bright water beneath.

Then, by way of contrast, we see on the opposite side of the moat clean, well-kept houses, painted pale yellow or grey, their outlines all perfect, their angles sharp, and the mouldings above the windows as fresh and new as if only just finished by the hand of the workman. They are the backs of the houses of *Ijsselkade*, facing the large river.

These houses are the pride of the town, but I am inclined to find them too stiff and slightly pretentious; so we will leave them behind, and follow the course of the river, which will interest us a great deal more, and show us at every dozen yards something worth seeing. First, we have a row of shaky houses with their walls full of cracks; then comes the fish-market, situated close to the water's edge, but deceitful in appearance, for the eels and plaice are brought there in carts, and carried away in baskets on the arms of the buyers. Fish is sold by auction. At first a high price is called out; then, in a monotonous tone, the price is gradually lowered till it is in accordance with the pocket of the purchaser, who cries out 'Ja,' and the lot is knocked down to him, unless, of course, two persons happen to pronounce the fatal 'Ja' at the same moment, in which case a great deal of joking and discussing goes on, ending sometimes in blows.

Beyond the markets we have the mills—genuine mills—with enormous wheels, half rotten by constant immersion in the water, continually in need of repair. They are picturesque marks of olden time, and were given to the town,[1] in 1312, by Count Reinoldt—a gift that was truly appreciated by the grateful inhabitants.

Following the mills are the bridges, with their arched vaults overtopping the street below. On either side of the river, which has no quay, there are curious groups of tumble-down roofs, laticed balconies, boarded terraces, leaden spouts, worm-eaten steps, and decayed walls covered with verdure and moss. All this, in bright warm tints, is to be seen along the road, till a grand and majestic ruin intercepts the view and draws one's attention to itself. This ruin was formerly the gate to the town—one of those called *Waterpoort*. Standing on two enormous piles, it stretches across the water like a bridge, thus commanding and defending the access to the river. Above the arches, open during the day for boats to pass under, is a long gallery, with windows and loopholes, formerly crowned with battlements. Two small towers, completing the warlike appearance of the old ruin, have fallen a prey to the ravages of time, and form support for the creeping ivy and iris.

Beyond this old gate is the new rampart, with its large bastions and grand trees, commanding the surrounding country, which, although flat and marshy, is very fertile. This new rampart encircles the city, here and there following the ancient walls, for the *Waterpoort* is not the only vestige of the old defences still remaining. Portions of the wall are still visible

---

[1] The letter bestowing the gift is among the archives of the town.

in various places, and in the distance can be seen the double platform of the *Drogenapstoren*.

In spite of time and ill-treatment at the hands of men, the old tower holds its machicolated battlements high in the air, frowns down on the picturesque assemblage of gabled-roof, belfries, and old trees around it, and reflects its haughty head in the stagnating waters at its base.

On the opposite side of the ramparts the eye catches sight of a little island, full of wooden houses, inns, and dockyards, and hemmed in by *Tjalks*, with red-coloured sails and masts gay with flags, which seems to be at once the naval quarter, and gate of the town.

It is pleasant to contemplate this mass of lines and colour, to listen to the subdued hum from the busy streets, and then to glance one's eye over the golden fields beyond, glistening in the warm noonday sun.

The richness of the soil of this country has long been proverbial. 'It is a special favourite of Heaven,' cries Bleau, the geographer, in a sort of ecstasy. 'The atmosphere around it and the air it breathes are salubrious and strengthening. The fields and meadows are fertile and productive, as fattening for beasts as abundant in harvest.' However, unfortunately, this much-boasted salubrity of climate has not prevented Zutphen from being visited at various epochs by terrible epidemics. From 1458 to 1617 it was ravaged no less than ten times by the plague, and each time the inhabitants were frightfully thinned in numbers.

The plague was not the worst disaster which happened to this charming city in those sinister times. Sieges, assaults, massacres, and devastation of every kind periodically assailed it.

It was almost depopulated by the Spaniards in 1572.

In spite of the inhabitants making no difficulty or resistance to receiving the Duke of Alva's troops, the soldiers had no sooner entered the town than 'they began murdering, hanging, strangling, drowning, and cruelly ill-treating the women and children.'

The author of the *Polemographia* has given us a touching account of these horrors, in a print entitled 'Horrenda ab Hispanis commissa latrocinia.' 'They were hung up by their feet,' he says, 'officers and soldiers alike; several of the inhabitants were tied together and flung naked into the river, while others were deprived of their clothing and driven out of the town, where they perished with cold and hunger.'

It was next besieged by the States' troops. In 1586 Leicester attacked it, but in vain, for the Duke of Palma prevented his entering the town by giving him battle outside, in which 'the English were rudely repulsed.' Revictualled and refurnished, Zutphen held out till 1591, when Maurice himself invested it. This time it was carried by a genuine stratagem. On the 22nd May a dozen soldiers belonging to the garrison of Doesborg arrived early in the morning, and posted themselves at the door of the large fort the Spaniards had established on the left bank of the Yssel. They were disguised as simple country fellows, carrying for sale butter, eggs, milk, and cheese. The moment the gates were open they entered the guard-room under pretence of selling their wares, and while the unarmed soldiers were making their purchases they threw themselves upon them, killed a portion of the guard, made prisoners of the others, and were soon joined by the rest of their accomplices hanging about the neighbourhood.

As soon as Prince Maurice heard of the success of this stratagem, he hastened with all speed to invest the town, and call upon it to surrender. For want of ammunition and salt the garrison capitulated, not daring to hazard an assault, or to attempt to prolong the siege. The Spaniards marched out of the town with sword and dagger, and with as much of their personal property as they could carry round their necks; and I think there is no manner of doubt that they took advantage of this permission to pillage the town to perfection.

However, in spite of epidemics, wars, assaults of arms, and pillage, Zutphen continued in a rich and flourishing state. Her wealth even became proverbial, passing into a ballad, and sung about the streets of Guelderland.

Nymegen de oudste,	Nymegen the oldest,
Roermond de grootste,	Roermond the largest,
Arnhem de lugtigste,	Arnhem the gayest,
Zutphen de rykste.	Zutphen the richest.

Even at the present time Zutphen is a very wealthy place, with considerable agricultural and commercial importance. If we are inclined to believe the statistics, which tell us of seven hundred boats moored each year along the quay, of ten thousand horned cattle in the markets, five thousand sheep bleating in the streets, and eight thousand pigs grunting behind doors, surely the town merits its reputation. Besides its traditional wealth, it has other points worthy of attention. Although not as old as 'Nymegen the oldest,' Zutphen is, nevertheless, an ancient city and noble to boot, for it was the capital of a province bearing its name.

The history of this province is neither very important nor very clear in its origin. According to Pontanus, who has written a history of the country, the first titular lord was a certain Count Reimer, who lived about the year 833. Berchemius says that in 810 a certain Wichard, or Wichman, belonging to the House of Saxony, bore the title of Count of Zutphen. Be this as it may, it was certainly not before 914 that any serious mention is made of the country, and then it was in reference to the marriage of Adelaide, 'Countess of Zutphen,' with Robert de Heusden. Later on, by the marriage of Sophia, daughter of Wichman, with Otho of Nassau, Count of Guelderland, Zutphen and its territory were united to the neighbouring province. When the latter was raised to the dignity of a Duchy, Zutphen was definitely absorbed in the more powerful province. Hence the reason for the province of Zutphen figuring among the titles and dependencies of the Emperor Charles V.

But to return to the town itself. In its aristocratic quarters Zutphen is decidedly elegant and well built; the streets are large and cleanly, and have the winding appearance of an old city. Plenty of life is always stirring in this gay old town. The principal hotel bears a name that is very suggestive and agreeable to the ear.

It is called *Hollandsche Tuin* (the Dutch Garden). Certainly it is a very curious, even peculiar garden, for it has neither flowers, nor plants, nor a blade of grass. Its only grove is a straight sombre-looking courtyard full of niches, which by no means carries out the promise suggested by the signboard. It is true that the absence of flowers is, to a certain extent, compensated for by a number of talking, laughing girls hurrying to and fro the passages, and that the sweet song of the nightingale is substituted by a peal of bells constantly ringing close by.

That this peal of bells is still in existence is not due to the present inhabitants of Zutphen, or to those of bygone days either—but rather to Louvois, the austere minister of Louis XIV. Allow me to explain.

When, on the 26th June, 1672, after five days of trenches, the Duke of Orleans carried Zutphen by assault and took the garrison prisoners, the French artillery officers, in accordance with their right, laid an *embargo* on all bells and belfries, and every description of copperwork to be found in the town. Then the authorities of the town were invited, according to the custom of the time, to redeem these articles, by a sum of money, fixed by the officers at ten thousand crowns.

Taking advantage of this to rid the town of its numerous peals of bells, church bells, and bell towers, the authorities turned a deaf ear to the proposition, and offered instead to pay half the sum, and to write to that effect to M. de Louvois.

Now to address M. de Louvois in writing was looked upon as a very audacious proceeding, and the Duke of Orleans, who knew the terrible man, tried to dissuade the authorities from any such hazardous undertaking. 'It will be quite useless, and you will lose your bells into the bargain,' he said. But the brave men persisted, and their letter was written and despatched.

To their great astonishment they received the following reply from the haughty minister:—

Messieurs,—

J'ay receu la lettre que vous m'avez escrite, par laquelle vous me faites connoistre l'jmpuissance dans laquelle vous estes de payer dix mil escus, pour les droitz que les officiers d'artillerie ont sur vous cloches. J'en ay rendu compte au Roy, et Sa Ma^e a bien voulu modérer cette somme à la moitié. Mais après cela, il faut que vous sortiez promptement de cette affaire. Je suis, Messieurs,

Votre affectionné serviteur,

DE LOUVOIS.

Saint Germain, ce X's Aoust 1672.

Les Bourguemestres de Zutphen *

---

* Gentlemen,—

I have received the letter that you have written, in which you inform me of your inability to pay the ten thousand crowns, the indemnity

This interesting letter from Louvois is preserved in the archives of Zutphen.

Hence it is certainly de Louvois' fault that the peal of bells, which awakens the inhabitants of Zutphen night after night, is still in existence.

The pedestal supporting this belfry of Zutphen is the tower of the 'Weigh-house,' which stands in the centre of the town, at the cross-road of the long street where the market is held. This 'Weigh-house,' composed of a kind of fore-building of very solid architecture of the year 1618, soars high above a grand display of market stalls, butchers' shops, and *spekslagers*, and a noisy talking crowd of buyers and sellers. The fore-building is divided into two storeys, surmounted by a long roof and high tower, in the same style as the *Westerkirk* of Amsterdam. The first storey of this tower, on a height with that of the main building, forms a sort of balcony, to which is attached a double flight of steep steps, adding greatly to the picturesque appearance of the *façade*. This balcony with its flight of steps is the place from whence in olden times proclamations, edicts, and condemnations were read, or, more literally speaking, were 'cried on the steps.'

In 1660 this building was called the *Wynhus* (wine-

---

claimed by the officers of artillery on your bells. I have submitted the matter to the King, and his Majesty is willing to reduce the sum by one-half. But after that, the sooner you settle this affair the better.

I am, gentlemen, your affectionate servant,

DE LOUVOIS.

house), owing to the duties levied there on wines, since which time, however, the *prestige* of the name has gone for ever, and a police-office, superintending fresh laws, has been established on the ground-floor to the terror of drunkards.

The first floor of the *Wynhus* contains many artistic relics of the town, comprising the beginning of a local museum, an interesting collection of archives, and the foundation of a tolerable library. We will not say a single word of the library, for we found nothing new or attractive in it; but the collection of archives is really good. These documents number about a thousand, and have been arranged in order by M. Van de Velde, a scholar and man of taste. The most ancient of these charters go back as far as the close of the tenth century, but are all of mere local interest. Some few among them are excessively curious, on account of the strange way they are illustrated. There is one, a *Remonstrance* of Count de Meurs to the Count of Guelderland, dated the 20th November, 1493, covered with very amusing scenes and little figures curiously drawn. Among the illustrated autographs are many of illustrious persons : as, for example, the permission given by Maximilian and the Archduke Philip to the inhabitants of Zutphen to erect a bridge over the Yssel ; a letter of Charles of Guelderland, rewarding a valiant soldier for brave actions by the office of executioner ; also 'the Letter of Pardon,' sent by Philip II., in 1585 (after the pillage), to his 'good people of Zutphen,' with a black seal as sinister as its master; also letters from Charles V., Maximilian of Egmont, Gilles de Barlaymont, Margaret of Parma, the Prince of Orange, and a hundred others.

In the museum there are also a few manuscripts remarkably illustrated. This museum contains also a fair collection of arms, amongst which are several superb halberds, ancient seals of state, sceptres of burgomasters, and specimens of wrought gold of the sixteenth century; besides sundry pieces of sandstone of mere local value, and a few glass cups engraved with the arms of the town. Two of the latter have a special interest for the Zutpheners. They are enormous goblets, the feet of which are blown, and veined inside with white in imitation of the productions of Marano. They were manufactured at Zutphen in 1668, by a man called Simon, a native of Tournay, who had established in the town a large glass manufactory—a trade which has long since disappeared there.

Notwithstanding these various collections, the 'Weigh-house' is neither the most interesting nor the most remarkable monument possessed by Zutphen. The Town Hall is a modern edifice without any special character, so we will say nothing about it, but pass on to describe minutely the three churches, one of which, St. Walburgus, decidedly merits its architectural fame.

It is situated near the ramparts, on an uneven but

pleasant spot. It was built in 1105, but in 1406 a fire broke out in the tower, which in falling crushed the church and partly destroyed it. It was rebuilt in the ogive style with side aisles, but in 1466 the interior walls were pulled down and new ones raised to the height of the nave, so as to form three naves of equal height. Thus transformed, St. Walburgus presented grand, noble proportions, harmonising well with the crowd who formerly worshipped on its flagstones. For in the fifteenth and sixteenth centuries this large church had a widespread reputation in consequence of its possessing the relics of St. Justus, a young neophyte who died a martyr's death in the neighbourhood of Beauvais, during the reign of Diocletian. These relics were supposed to have miraculous power, and pilgrimages were undertaken to worship at the shrine wherein they were kept.

But if we are to believe an old song inserted by Aubertus Miræus in his *Annals of Belgium*, there is no reason to doubt that Treves really possessed the best portion of the body of this young martyr, and that the head presented for the veneration of visitors was genuine.

> Ejus caput nunc habetur,
> Magna Treviris reverentia;
> Sed corpus obtinetur
> Diligenter in Zutphania.
> Laudetur hinc Dei clementia!

Hence the grand church at Zutphen could only possess a part, and not the whole of the sacred body.

However, be that as it may, it is undoubtedly

owing to the presence of these holy relics that the town still possesses two beautiful specimens of wrought and cast iron work. The first is one of those chandeliers known as 'coronas,' and was presented to the Church by Count Otho II.; hence it must have been made during the latter half of the thirteenth century. It is made of a fine piece of forged iron in the form of a tiara, very elegant, but rather too slight. The other is an enormous bronze baptismal font in the form of a cup, with a pedestal supported by crouching lions, and ornamented with the figures of the Four Evangelists. The lid is a kind of double structure of figures and small pinnacles, surmounted at the top by a pelican. This superb metal monument is about sixteen feet high, and the basin about four in diameter.

St. Walburgus possesses still another curiosity, which, in its way, is unique. It is a library—not such a one as is usually to be seen everywhere nowadays containing common rows of books, and presses and tables—but exactly in the same state as libraries used to be three hundred years ago. This library is a low, narrow, badly-lighted room, with a vaulted ceiling, supported by four old pillars ornamented with curious capitals and animals in basrelief. Twenty double desks extend perpendicularly along the wall, covered with enormous folios, with a chain attached to keep them in their places. There are only about three hundred volumes, none of them very varied in their contents, as Blaeu[1] remarks, for the celebrity of this resort does not date from yesterday. But the three hundred folios are genuine treasures. The greater number of them came from Venice and Cologne, works of the Bapistas Tortis, of the Andreas Thoresanus, Johannes Alemanus, and twenty others, among which we find the celebrated name of Petrus Schoiffer's famous Bible, dated 1469. Of more recent works there are several very precious ones—the *Homer*, printed at Basle for Jean Froben, the friend of Erasmus; Aristotle's *Logic*, and the *Prodigiorum ac Ostentorum Chronicon*, with its twenty strange vignettes and peculiar plates, which seem oddly out of place amongst such a religious and learned collection.

Unfortunately, the riches enshrined in this ancient crypt are under the care of a sacristan who scarcely appreciates the importance of his charge. Fresh air is rarely allowed to enter the room, and damp is slowly doing its silent work; and from time to time the precious books are soiled and torn by those who turn them over out of curiosity, but with careless and indifferent hands. We did our best to inspire the good *koster* with affection and solicitude for the treasures he has to guard, but our words had no effect. The good man's dinner was on the fire, and all his thoughts were concentrated on that, and

---

[1] 'Ad partem templi orientalem bibliotheca est publica varietate librorum, mediocriter instructa.'—*Blaeu.*

that alone. He paid no heed to our wise and earnest exhortations.

We quitted this scientific resort somewhat downhearted, for we felt bitterly the danger of destruction these typographical treasures incur in such hands, added to which we knew that the churchwardens of St. Walburgus have never been noted for the careful preservation of treasures. Indeed, no less than ten acts of Vandalism have been brought home to them at various times. Formerly the church was decorated by magnificent painted windows. Guicciardini confirms this with a sigh of regret, for, with his Italian taste, he found the edifice too obscure, but he excuses it by remembering that 'it was the opinion of saintly persons at that time, and also of our wise fathers and ancestors, that sacred places of worship ought, on first entering, to have the appearance of a great devotion and contrition for sins, and not distract our thoughts from prayer by dazzling our eyes with too much light.' And yet in that very century these beautiful windows were destroyed! One day a carpenter conceived the insane idea of replacing these grand windows by common glass ones; his idea was approved of and acted on. But the sacrilege did not end there. We were shown, in the museum, a couple of beautiful panels, exquisitely decorated with charming figures, and dating from at latest the fifteenth century. These panels bear the marks of nails and planing. Just imagine—they had been employed as an inside lining to a press! After that, can any one wonder that we were downhearted on leaving these library treasures in such hands?

It appears, also, that formerly it was a real pleasure to the magistrates of Zutphen to associate their names with works of destruction. Now, St. Walburgus is surmounted by an enormous tower five storeys high, very massive, and almost devoid of openings. Twice, at different epochs, in 1406 and 1600, this tower fell a prey to flames. Each time it was struck by lightning, and naturally those in office had nothing to do with it. But each time this misfortune happened, the magistrates in office at the moment had their names inscribed on a plate with the date, and the plate fastened to the wall of the unhappy tower. Truly, such a love for fame is a little too much!

Besides St. Walburgus, there are two other churches worth mentioning in Zutphen—the Dominican Church, standing in the centre of the town; and another occupied by the Catholics, which, if I remember rightly, is called Notre Dame, but designated, I do not know why, in old maps under the name of Nieuwstadskerk (church of the new town).

The most remarkable thing about the Dominican Church is the way it is entered on ordinary days. One has to traverse a suite of small, deserted, queer-looking courts, enclosed in old walls, ornamented and variegated with honeysuckle and petunia, all of which, richly coloured, represent the ancient dependencies of the cloister. The main building has been transformed into barracks for the infantry, and is reached through one of those passages called by the Venetians *sotto portico*.

The interior of the Dominican Church has not much to boast of. It is of brick, consequently very simple, and whitewashed throughout. Like the majority of convent churches, the choir terminates in three sides of an octagon. It has no aisles, and the ten round, short, and thick columns supporting the vault, by no means enhance the elegance of the building.

The exterior is just as bad. There is no steeple, but in its stead the edifice is surmounted by a bell-tower, which looks as if it had been taken off a Savoy cake; and to embellish its general appearance, a lateral entrance of columns and attics has been added, which is simply atrocious.

The church of *Nieuwstad* is better off than that of the Dominicans, inasmuch as it possesses an elevated steeple, a sort of immense tower in the style of that of St. Walburgus, with small arched openings, partly hidden by brickwork and surmounted by a high tapering roof twice its height.

The interior, however, does not correspond with the proportions of the immense steeple. It is heavy, with three low naves, supported by enormous octagonal pillars, and lighted by ten windows, the panes of which are so happily decorated that they hide the bareness of the interior. According to Jacob Clinge this church dates from 1361, but according to other authorities from 1272. The altars, pulpit, and ornaments, which are all new, are in Gothic style, and would be in good taste were it not that they are too much gilded, and the colours too bright for the severe and austere aspect of the building.

The church of *Nieuwstad* is near the ramparts, and close to one of the gates of the town, surrounded by barracks. Beyond the gates is a charming promenade, bordered by water and clumps of verdure, which leads on one side to the Yssel, on the other to a grand highway shaded by superb trees. This road turns in the opposite direction from the river, traversing a rich country bordering upon the pretty little town, and leads to the agricultural colony which bears the name of *Mettray hollandais*.

CHAPTER XVI.

NEDERLANDSCH METTRAY — HENGELO — EUSCHEDE — CONFLAGRATION — ALMELO — OLDENZAAL — ST. PLECHELME — THE HUNNEBED OF OLDENZAAL.

THE *Nederlandsch Mettray* is an hour's walk from Zutphen. It is not necessary to describe it minutely or at length, for it is a miniature but faithful copy of the other colony on the borders of the Loire, a few miles from Tours, and near the village from which it takes its name of Mettray. Every one is acquainted with this model establishment, which is well deserving of a visit.

Nothing is more touching and instructive than a walk through these pretty cottages in the midst of their gardens and lawns, or than an excursion on the land cultivated by the colony. In a few hours one discerns the narrow limit which separates good from evil better than by reading a host of books. For here the possibility of transmuting wasted powers which might otherwise have been dangerous, into useful forces, is demonstrated. The principles of action and their application are identical. The former Mettray had been in full action for ten years, and had vindicated the excellence of the institution, when a brave-hearted man, M. Suringar, generously thought of introducing into his own country an establishment which produced such good fruits. He knew M. Demetry, the founder of Mettray. He was also aware of the devotion and goodness on which his doctrine was based. He had felt the persuasion and power of his captivating eloquence, and became in turn an apostle. He pleaded the cause of poor children, innocent by law, yet imprisoned as if guilty. He tapped the inexhaustible spring of Dutch charity; and on the 21st June, 1851, he laid the first stone of the establishment we are about to visit.

Ties of family and affection, broken only by death, had long attached me to the founder of our Mettray, so that it was not without emotion that I visited upon Dutch soil the faithful reproduction of the noble work to which his life was devoted. The same principles were applied in the same manner, a similar division in the small houses, and each taking the name of a family, which extend their simple and elegant *façades* along a green lawn. At the base of the parallelogram were the workshops and offices; at its summit the church, all on a reduced scale, for the *Dutch Mettray* has only ten cottages, containing 120 children —scarcely a fourth of the number contained in the original institution.

Each of these pretty cottages bears on its front the name of the donor, each being a special donation and pious foundation. The King contributed three, to which he gave the names of Anna Paulowna, William II., and Prince Mauritz. The late Queen-mother gave one called after her grandson, Alexander. The others were given by Prince Frederick, by the towns of the Hague and Rotterdam, and by the three private families of Valkart, Boelens, and Dubois.

Each of these houses is inhabited by a number of children who live together as one family, and form a home of itself, whose softening influence has produced the very best results on these poor little outcasts. As a rule they look very well in their working clothes; and their happy faces, straight figures, and respectful manner, bear witness to their return to better ways.

As in France, farming is the chief part of the work done here. The grand principle which guided M. Demetry is applied 'to improve the earth by man, and man by means of the earth.' Although the ground at the disposal of this colony is not very extensive, nevertheless it keeps the young colonists hard at work together with their horticultural labours, the keeping of the stables clean, and the care of the animals.[1]

Several boys are put to trades which have more or less to do with farming or the wants of the colony, such as wheelwrights, blacksmiths, tailors,

---

[1] The colony possesses fifteen cows, two bulls, one ox, six heifers, and eight calves; most of these animals are of French race. They have also three horses, a colt, and a donkey, to go to and fro to market.

shoemakers, &c., &c. There are even two or three future artists among the boys, for we saw several drawings hanging on the walls of the large reception-room, which were not badly executed and are in themselves decided proofs that the arts are not forgotten in the general education received by the inmates of the little colony.

If the principles upon which the Dutch Mettray is worked are borrowed from the French institution, the recruiting of the establishment, as also its means of support, are not obtained in the same way. In France, the institution was built from the proceeds of public charity, and is maintained chiefly from the same source, aided by the Government, which pays a certain sum for the support of each child. This is quite right, for Mettray only receives such boys as are bound by Article 66 of the Penal Code to be kept in houses of correction at the expense of the State, for having committed offences for which they are not responsible, owing to their tender age. Hence it is natural that the State should pay the sum to Mettray that it would have to spend on the lad, if kept in a house of correction.

On the other hand, the Dutch Mettray is absolutely and entirely supported by private charity. The Government has nothing to do with it from a financial point of view. All it does is to give up the children to be educated there. Not a farthing of money is paid for the support of the children. The expenses of the establishment are paid by subscribers. Thirty-four towns and villages contribute to this work; and if among the large towns we read the names of Amsterdam, Lieuwarden, the Hague, Rotterdam, and Utrecht, we must not forget that small villages, and even tiny hamlets like Zeist, Apeldoorn, and Velp do their best to help on such a good work. Each of these subscribers has either a direct or indirect share in the administration of the establishment. He can place a child there, and yet keep him to a certain extent under his own surveillance. All the boys have not entered under Article 66. There are many orphans, and a few viciously inclined. In the French Mettray the latter are kept apart in more severe discipline in a house called the *Father's House*, and the former are not admitted.

The result of this difference of management and means of support is, that authority is not so severe in the Dutch Mettray as in its French model. Discipline is more lax, and rules are less strict; and, unhappily, it requires a very firm hand to make good men out of these poor outcasts from society.

The director of the institute deplores this want of discipline very much, and has already somewhat raised the tone of the establishment on this point. Still, he cannot assert what the celebrated founder of the French Mettray proclaimed a few years ago before the *Congrès de l'Alliance Universelle*: 'Thirty-three years our Mettray has existed, and we have not once had to inform the Minister of the Interior of a deserter.'

Desertion is a very frequent occurrence in the

Dutch Mettray, though certainly it has not taken place quite so often lately. 'I had more bacon put in their soup,' said the director to me, with a smile; 'so the bad boys were more willing to stay with me.' Not being able to touch them by kindness, he appealed to them through their stomachs, a practical way of acting—but will he succeed always?

With all its faults, the Dutch Mettray is an excellent institution, and very well cared for. It cannot fail to have good results, and Holland ought to be eternally grateful to the memory of M. Suringar, its generous and honourable founder. The good man sleeps his last sleep in the little cemetery of Mettray, under the modest-looking tombstone raised to his memory.

There is another name I looked for in vain in the colony, that of M. Demetry. If it is well to honour the one who accomplished the good work, surely it is well also to honour the man who first conceived the idea; and I confess I should have liked to see a portrait or an inscription in memory of the generous-hearted man who first started this noble work, of which Lord Brougham said before Parliament, 'Mettray is a work which will suffice for the glory of a nation, for a whole century.'

In order to visit the various towns on the frontier of the country—Almelo, Enschedé, and Oldenzaal—and carefully to study their characteristics and appearance, on quitting Mettray we took up our quarters at Hengelo, a village about half-way to the above towns, and a centre-point from whence we could direct our movements whichever way we chose.

Hengelo is a sort of outlying hamlet, partly rural and partly industrial, not very ancient, and with no special history. It was in existence about two centuries and a half ago, and possessed a church at that time, for in 1608, on the 3rd July, the *Drossaard* of Twenthe complained of mass being performed in his territory.[1] Fifty years later, in 1650, a horse and cattle fair was held there, which afterwards became an annual affair, held on the eve of St. Michael.[2]

Situated in the centre of a rich country, some of the houses in the principal street of Hengelo are newly erected, elegant in appearance, and in the style of those built at Arnhem and Zutphen of late years along the *Ysselkade*. A dozen smaller streets branch off from the principal one, all of which have a rural aspect, with their one-storeyed picturesque houses of brick, surmounted by enormous wooden lofts. There are two churches, one built in 1750, in the pretentious antique style, so much admired about that time, and which the inhabitants were so proud of, that they sent a sketch of it to the Governor of the Province. The sketch is preserved in the archives of Arnhem. The sister church belongs to the Catholics, and is as tasteless as possible. It is built in that irregular

---

[1] This complaint exists among the archives of Deventer.

[2] I have found out since, among the *Kronijk van Arnhem*, that the place is supposed to be more ancient. There is mention made of a certain grant of land to the Abbey of St. Sauvour, dated 1405, held by a certain Gérard de Hengelo.

style in vogue at the beginning of the present century, called in derision 'Troubadour style;' but it is not even a good specimen of that period: on the contrary, it is simply a detestable monument, and the sooner the inhabitants of Hengelo repair this mistake of the past, the better.

From Hengelo we went on to Enschedé. Although it does not seem so, this small town is much more ancient than Hengelo. In the thirteenth century its name appears in history, for in 1288 it was burned to the ground by Otho II., thirty-fourth Bishop of Utrecht. It lost no time in rising from its ashes, for it was rebuilt within a century; and its sovereigns, the bishops, as a kind of reparation for their predecessor's cruelty, endowed it with a number of privileges. It gradually increased in wealth till the sixteenth century, when Guicciardini speaks of it as an 'important hamlet.' In 1597 Maurice occupied it, but did not fortify it; and from that time it has never had any ramparts.

However, that did not much affect the industrious little town, for its inclinations were not warlike; on the contrary, it loved peaceful occupations, and preferred the arts of pleasing to those of intimidating. Unfortunately, its old houses and neat little cottages were all destroyed by fire in May, 1862. In a few hours the flames had taken possession of two-thirds of the town, and completely destroyed it. The Town Hall did not escape the conflagration. Even the Church, an old basilica of freestone, and the legitimate pride of the town, fell a victim to the flames. The inhabitants, hoping the sacred edifice might escape the general destruction, placed all their treasures within its stone walls; but, alas! their hopes were doomed to disappointment, and the poor houseless creatures saw their effects and household treasures consumed by the remorseless flames before their eyes. The only part remaining of this ancient church is the steeple.

From our position in the tower of the Town Hall we could note the course of this terrible conflagration by the red roofs and new fronts to the houses.

The only ancient monument left in this town is the steeple already mentioned, which would have a very handsome appearance were it not for the octagonal bell-tower—*pseudo*-Gothic, and in very bad taste—which tops it.

The other Church, belonging to the Catholics, is of modern architecture, and of elegant and graceful appearance. The same cannot be said of the Town Hall, which is also modern, and was reconstructed in 1863, in a vulgar, irregular style, and surmounted by a belfry, from whence can be obtained a most magnificent view of the surrounding country.

Rich and fertile as the country is, it is not from this source entirely that Enschedé obtains her large revenues. The town is essentially industrial, and the manufactures of its cotton materials realise large sums yearly.

Perhaps the secret of its having doubled, during the past twenty years, its industrial resources, is that the manufacturers do not look upon their workmen as mere human machines, but rather as useful fellow-labourers. Hence the masters do all in their power to improve the condition and provide for the future peace and repose of their men. To this end a society has been formed, with funds of about 16,000 florins, to aid the sick and wounded. There is also a school for the children of the workmen, bearing the significant name of *Jabriekschoof*.[1]

Then, as rest and repose are as good for the workman after his day's toil, as play is for boys out of school, a large public garden has been laid out just beyond the gates of the town, called the *Volkspark* (people's park). It is a fine promenade, with ornamental water, beds of flowers, and large restaurant. When the trees are grown it will be quite a beautiful park; in the meantime the heat is rather trying there in summer, which perhaps accounts for the enormous quantity of drink sold there during a few short months. No less than 30,000 pints of beer, 300 bottles of Sitzer water, 300 pounds of coffee, and 500 pounds of sugar, were sold in the space of eight months. The two latter, of course, were sold in the form of cups of coffee, so I leave the number of cups to be imagined.

I have already observed that everything is new

---

[1] Five hundred and seventy-two children attended this school in 1872 and in 1873 the numbers were increased to 631.

about Enschedé, both houses and streets. The same may be said of Almelo. Its houses are clean and neat, its streets wide and quiet, and appear to be about fifty years old. The only proof that the place has been inhabited for several centuries exists in a portion of an old church, which has not been destroyed by fire. However, appearances are deceitful as regards this little town, for Africus, the historian of Saint Ludger, refers to 'Almaloh.' Hence it must have existed in the ninth century. It was also referred to during the thirteenth and fourteenth centuries, for in the archives of Deventer there are several documents relating to the Heekeren, the lords of Richteren and Almelo and their castle, and even to the town itself. In 1318 the said lords paid homage for their fief to Renaud the Fair, Duke of Guelderland. In 1393, the 'Sunday before Easter;' in 1394, and in 1405, agreements were signed with the Bishops of Utrecht. In 1421 Egbert, Seigneur of Almelo, accorded to the town the right of choosing magistrates; and from that time forward the city became almost independent of its lords, who lived in their castle, and spent their time at the chase and in the management of their immense estates. In 1664 the castle was pulled down, and reconstructed in a modern style, with two large wings, pilasters, and attics, as it remains to this day. The present legitimate owner, Count Adolf, is a direct descendant of the old Richterens, and one of the most kindhearted men in Holland.

Better still, the old family not only retains the castle in its possession, but almost the whole of the ancient domain. The *Ambt Almelo,* as it is called, comprises the town of Almelo and its territory, in the same manner as the department Seine-et-Oise comprises that of the Seine. The town, too closely confined within the narrow limits, which it cannot extend without changing its jurisdiction, is constantly in danger of encroaching on the domain surrounding it. The dead have already stepped over the fatal barrier which confines the living. After passing their lives under the sceptre of the burgomaster, they take their last sleep in the ground of their rival; a privilege which has not been obtained without numberless contests, as those will understand who know anything of the municipal spirit of such small countries.

As we expressed a great desire to visit the *Ambt Almelo,* Count Adolf offered to accompany us and show us over it. Mounted on a high dog-cart, drawn by a couple of thorough-breds, we drove over his property for about two hours, looking at his majestic woods, rich golden harvests, green pasturage, and the *polders.*[1] We also visited his farms and dairies, and were greatly interested in a new kind of agricultural enterprise which our host was carrying out extensively.

In the evening, when we returned to Almelo, the town had assumed quite a different aspect. The

[1] Drained marshes.

factories had turned out their hands from their day's labour, and the streets were full. Of its 4,000 inhabitants 2,000 are artisans employed in textile trades, and in the branches affecting those trades, such as dyeing and bleaching. This industrial population is Dutch in origin, and especially so in habit and feeling. Manners, customs, language, and character are all essentially Dutch; and as to their patriotic sentiments, the following will prove their genuineness.

A few years since the manufacturers of Almelo contracted the habit of paying their workmen in German coin, on account of the depreciation their money is subject to in the bordering countries. This went on for some time under difficulties. But one day the workmen declared that 'they were Dutch, and had a right to be paid in the money of their own country.' Plausible as this reason was, the masters refused, and a strike ensued. The troops were had out, but intimidation was of no use. At last, after a great deal of misery, matters were arranged, but the brave workmen preferred loss and the payment of exchange rather than continue to receive German thalers. Their patriotism was stronger than their personal interests, and they proved it. How many industrial populations would do the same?

From Almelo we went on to Oldenzaal, an old town, with a picturesque appearance. It does not give one the impression now of having once been a capital. Still it has had a glorious history.

Founded about 700 years before Christ, it was at first inhabited by the **Teutons**, who erected a temple consecrated to their god Tanfana, close to the town. This temple existed in the time of Germanicus. In due time the Teutons were replaced by the Franks, who enlarged Oldenzaal, and chose it as their capital. Then later on, when the Germanic populations were moving towards the west, the Franks were replaced by the **Huns**, who, according to Marcellinus, gave way in their turn to the Saxons.

It was these **Saxons** whom St. Plechelm endeavoured to convert by mildness, but whom Charlemagne converted by stronger means. Oldenzaal fell under the hands of the Carlovingians, and was comprised by Louis the **Debonnaire** in the county of Twenthe, the investiture of which he gave to Bandouin of Cleves. At that time it was known as the *Salia Vetus* (the old Salian town).

Fifty years later (970) Count Balderic, its noble possessor, having been nominated Bishop of Utrecht, added this family fief to his new dignity, from which day Oldenzaal was incorporated in the bishopric.

It had no need to complain, for Balderic endowed it with a church, to which he attached rich prebendaries. In 1049 the Emperor Henry III. conceded to it important privileges, from which time the town has ever been devotedly attached to the bishops and the Catholic religion, an attachment which exists to this day.

At the time of the Reformation Oldenzaal was

a rich, strong, and very important place. An old chronicler, Francois le Petit, describes it as 'large and well-peopled, surrounded by three double walls, and as many moats;' and the formal, exact Meterin speaks of it as 'a tolerably reasonable town, having no river, but several good high walls, and many antique towers.' The States regarded it as a military point worth possessing, and they did their best to obtain it, but in vain. On two occasions their generals seized it—Hohenlo in 1580, and Prince Maurice in 1597—but each time the inhabitants, 'leaning towards the Spaniards,' escaped from their power. It remained one of the last bulwarks of Catholicism; and it was not till 1626 that the Prince of Orange subdued it.

That year, on the 25th July, the town was suddenly invested by seventeen troops of cavalry. The following day Count Ernest Casimir of Nassau arrived with the infantry, and attacked it at once. A breach was made on the 2nd August, and the commander of the garrison, Baron de Moncle, was summoned to surrender. While the parleying went on, some slight misunderstanding brought about a panic. A few shots were fired, and treason was cried on both sides; an assault took place, the town was invested, and battle raged in the streets. Both parties were determined not to give way, so the day was a terribly bloody one. Partly overcome by the besiegers, the Spaniards retreated to the church, where they sustained a fresh siege, and it was two days before they could be dislodged from their place of refuge. As an example and punishment, Oldenzaal was dismantled, and its fortifications razed to the ground, since which time it has been an unprotected town.

The church still bears traces of the terrible combats which then took place. Part of the southern wall is covered with holes, and one ball is incrusted in the *façade*. We looked at those marks of past glory with a great amount of respect, while the venerable old dean, who was with us, retraced their history with spirited ardour.

Suddenly pointing to his church, he cried out enthusiastically, ' That belongs to us, and no one can take it from us during our life-time ! '

' But no one thinks of doing so,' remarked Constant. ' The Catholics in Holland are as free as elsewhere, and as much masters of their own property.'

' The danger is not from that quarter,' replied the dean. ' It is there ! ' and he pointed in the direction of Germany.

' Yes, indeed,' I thought to myself ; ' at Almelo it was the workmen, here it is the clergy ! What a pity M. Kirchhoff is not here ! '

Dropping the subject, we entered the church, an interesting specimen of the Roman style, erected about the middle of the eleventh century, under the auspices of St. Bernulph, in place of the oratory of stone constructed a century earlier by Bishop Balderic, and dedicated to St. Sylvester.

It is built in the style of the basilicæ on the borders of the Rhine. The choir originally terminated in a hemicycle, with a niche to correspond at each end of the transept. The interior is of great interest architecturally, for it distinctly marks the effect certain materials employed may have on architecture. In reality St. Plechelm differs considerably from all other basilicæ of that period, that I could find in the diocese of Utrecht. The majority of these churches, constructed in pumice-stone, the relative weight of which is not heavy, have their walls supported by light columns or very thin pillars; whereas the stone this church is built of is a yellow sandstone, obtained from the quarries of Gilhuis, two or three leagues off; and the architecture being heavy the pillars are very thick, and the walls very massive.

Partly destroyed by the fire which ravaged the town in 1492, St. Plechelm was restored and enlarged towards the end of the fifteeth century. The south aisle was done away with, and the original construction, still in existence, was put in its place; a sacristy was also added and the tower finished. In 1809, the church being occupied by the Catholics, it underwent restoration again. An altar, chairs, and 'prie-Dieu' were added; but its ancient ornaments could not be restored, and the only vestiges left of its primitive contents are the chandeliers. Fortunately the clergy were able to retain and preserve such precious relics as the head of St. Plechelm and the shrine in which it was enclosed. Although the making of this shrine is imputed to St. Balderic's time, it cannot be older than the fourteenth century.

It has the form of the saint's head crosiered and mitred, and belongs, by its style and its severity, to the Gothic period. It is in silver, with the cap and mitre gilded and covered with enamel work. The crosier especially is an exquisite piece of work. Raised on a pedestal at the entrance to the choir, this austere-looking visage seems to exhort and reprimand at the same time, and produces an impression on the crowd of peasants the more profound because they know that the precious shrine contains the head of the venerable saint. This treasure is taken great care of. It is allowed to be seen only once a year, and by a fortunate coincidence our visit took place on the very day appointed for this annual exhibition. Thus we saw, not only the shrine, but the crowd of worshippers dressed in their best,[1] and kneeling with solemn earnestness repeating their prayers.

St. Plechelm is not the only church in Oldenzaal. The Reformers, though few in number, possess a little temple of rather singular appearance in which to worship. It was built in 1809, when the old church was handed over to the Catholics. Is it necessary to describe it? The little sanctuary has an antique aspect with its pilasters, arches, and attics, with its garlands and its miniature dome. On the whole it is a very neat specimen of the architecture of this special

---

[1] R. P. Pitra endorses this opinion (see the 'Hollande Catholique.')

style. It is surrounded by a garden, carefully laid out, with shady paths and walks, and enclosed by a wall with two large pedestals bearing simple vases; a gate to enter by is also there. This little place has such a genuine antique air that we seem to expect to see a girl in ancient dress issuing from its portals with bare arms and short waist, accompanied by a sweetheart with costume to match.

There is another religious monument in the neighbourhood of St. Plechelm, but it belonged to a sect long since passed away, and is a vestige of the first inhabitants of this fertile soil. It is a *hunnebed*, anterior no doubt to the presence even of the Teutons. It stands about a dozen steps off the church to the north, in a deliciously picturesque corner. The outline of the church, half Byzantine, half Gothic, the houses near, and the huge trees surrounding an immense arch, and shading the colossal table of this *hunnebed*, the most ancient human monument in the country, form a most refreshing picture, full of calm and poetic tranquillity, which impresses itself on the mind as a scene not likely to be forgotten.

CHAPTER XVII.

DOESBURG — DŒTINCHEM — THE *KRUISBERG* — THE **KOLONIAAL MILITAIR INVALIDENHUIS** — DUTCH SWITZERLAND — ROSENDAAL — ZONSBEEK AND BILJOEN.

N quitting Oldenzaal we were anxious to go straight to Arnhem, but there were two towns—Doesburg and Dœtinchem—on the road, far too attractive to us to be passed without paying them a visit ; besides, the latter contains a penitentiary which we wished to compare with Mettray. We determined, therefore, to push on to Dieren, and from there to visit the above-named places, and while examining the neighbourhood to put up, for the time being, at the *Kruisberg.*

Doesburg is a stronghold on the borders of the water, one of the line of defences on the Yssel; to reach it we were obliged to cross the river, on a very singular bridge, partly wooden and partly made of boats. The town is said to be very ancient, dating from the time of Claudius Drusus, the adopted son of Augustus, who founded it, and after the celebrated canal was cut, to which he gave his name, he colonised the country and built several castles. *Drusi-*

S

bergum, the burg or Castle of Drusus, is the etymology of the name Doesburg. It is certainly one of the oldest towns in the country, for in 884 it was pillaged by the Normans, and in 1230 raised to the dignity of a town endowed with privileges[1] by Otho the Limper, Count of Guelderland and Zutphen.

Several old houses are still standing with their trebled arcades in front and crossed gables, presenting a strange contrast to the modern buildings close by, with large bedizened shops, the fronts of which, being of glass, show off the brilliantly-coloured contents within.

In the centre of the well-formed, clean-looking little streets is the Church, a handsome building, erected in 1340, on the site of the one formerly destroyed by the overflow of the Yssel. The magistrate who ordered this church to be erected named it St. Martin. But ill-luck seemed to pursue the unfortunate place of worship, for in 1483, and later on (1548) it was partly destroyed by fire, and on the 1st September, 1717, the very day of the *Kermesse*, a fire again broke out in the steeple. The Reformation destroyed in the interior what the flames had spared. Coloured windows, statues, and paintings have all disappeared, to be replaced by plain glass windows, oak benches, and the inevitable white-washing; hence there is nothing interesting to be seen there.

For some distance beyond the gates of the town

---

[1] An edict of Count Otho dated 1230 accords to the town the right of having a weekly market and an annual fair. This and several other edicts are preserved in the archives of Doesburg.

redoubts and advance-works extend along the road, bordered farther on by pleasant shady walks, which are as fresh and green, as it is dry and bare at the gates of Doesburg. The Castle of Keppel midway between Doesburg and Dœtinchem, and surrounded by clumps of trees, is close to the borders of the old Yssel. It has an impressive and bright appearance. Its gabled advance-building, with its layers of brick and stone, and bulging bell-towers give it the air of an old warrior who has given up fighting, in order to pass his last days in rural felicity. A couple of leagues farther on, one catches sight of Dœtinchem, a pretty little town, less ancient and of fewer inhabitants than its neighbour Doesburg. Mention was first made of *Villa Dutthinge* on the day of the consecration of its church, 23rd March, 838, by Bishop Balderic. That building was replaced in the thirteenth century by another which was burned in 1527; nothing of which remains but the walls. It was reconstructed almost immediately, but in spite of having been repaired at several epochs it is still in a very dilapidated state.

In 1100 mention is again made of the little town, this time in reference to the construction of a wall to enclose it, some portion or fragments of which are still to be seen on the side towards the river. In the fourteenth century it became rich and prosperous, and generous to boot, for Pontanus boasts of its gifts to the Abbey of Bethlehem.[1]

---

[1] See Pontanus, *Historia Gelrica*. This Abbey of Bethlehem was founded by Count Henry of Guelderland in the neighbourhood of Dœtinchem.

The Town Hall (the only monument it possesses) was destroyed by the fire of 1527, which also destroyed the Church; but reconstructed that same year, it was again destroyed, this time by the terrible tempest of 1724. It is to this double disaster that we must attribute its poverty in the way of archives.

Dœtinchem never played any important part in the annals of the country. For three hundred years it enjoyed peace and quiet, and peace and quiet it enjoys to this day. It is proud of having given birth to the diplomatist Christian Verhuell—who took a leading part in the famous deputation charged to offer to Louis Bonaparte the crown of Holland—and his brother, Admiral Charles Verhuell, whom Queen Hortense in her sorrowful days called her 'beau ténébreux.'

In the neighbourhood of Dœtinchem is the *Kruisberg*. Its name signifying 'Mountain of the Cross' proves pretty plainly that the word *berg* (mountain) has not always in Holland a very exact meaning. This 'colony' is built at the foot of a gentle rise planted with trees, where the air is fresh and the situation agreeable, giving to the building more the appearance of a castle or country house than that of a prison. In fact it was once an old fortress, and has only changed its destination during the last few years.[1] Its old lugubrious aspect has been done away

---

[1] Since 1866. In an almanack published that year by the Maatschappij van Weldadigheid, called *Erica*, there is an article on the colony of Kruisberg, by M. A. F. Eilerts de Haan, containing a mass of information of great interest.

with by strengthening the walls and constructing new buildings. There are no longer any battlements, or iron gates, or garrison, or grim warders. Large windows, open doors, and plenty of space, with here and there a keeper to preserve order and immediately to repress insubordination, in case of need. Such is the place now, where the young lads pass the time of their detention.

The inmates have not much to recommend them, nor can one have much confidence in their future. They are not young lads who have committed faults, of the gravity of which they were scarcely able to judge, but the majority of them are criminals of deep dye. Thieves, incendiaries, and, in some few instances, murderers. Notwithstanding, they are allowed to come and go about the place freely, even to take long walks outside, under the eye of their keepers. On our way to the *Kruisberg* we met several small parties resting on the roadside; some keep the roads in order, others are told off to pull up vegetables, and while some are occupied in haymaking, others are employed in the kitchen garden.

The *Kruisberg*, however, cannot, like Mettray, be called an agricultural establishment, for it only farms about forty acres, which is very little in proportion to the number of the establishment. To extend their labours farther would be to deprive the inmates of surveillance, as even now evasions take place from time to time, with all their care and watching; the numbers would considerably decrease if no precautions could be taken. The director kindly guided our steps over the establishment, taking us first to the workshops of the younger inmates. The rooms are well lighted and well ventilated, and each boy is taught a trade which will enable him to gain an honest livelihood on leaving prison.

Many even are able to gain money **for themselves, long** before their **term of** detention is expired, **as each** one has a right to a certain sum for work done beyond the appointed task, which money is saved **up and** forms a resource in hand, when they depart. The director pointed out to our notice the chapel, which, he informed us with no little pride, had been built and furnished entirely by the convicts.

We may as **well** add here, that such trades as slaters, tilers, and **masons** are very little exercised in **the colony,** for the very good reason that such work is **rarely required;** besides, the majority of the inmates **would not** physically be strong enough for such employments. At the time we were there, the **place** contained one hundred and fifty-nine inmates, of whom thirty-eight were under thirteen years of age!

The trades more especially taught are tailoring, shoemaking, carpentering, and tinning. The diet is similar to that in the large **prisons,** coarse and unsavoury, and at night the boys retire to similar small **iron** cells resembling cages.

Kruisberg is, without doubt, a wonderful improvement on establishments of the kind formerly in Holland, **as** also on those of other countries at the present time. Its system is somewhat similar to that carried on at *Mettray*, but more extensive, and applicable to great criminals, as well as to those who have committed minor crimes.

Instead of being shut up in an unhealthy place, which they quit corrupted in mind and body, the boys brought up at *Kruisberg* have a healthy tone given to them, both physically and morally, which, unless they are irretrievably bad, corrects their inclinations and lessens their faults. They enter life with the consciousness of having committed a fault, it is true, but also with the certainty that, by hard work and honest dealing, they may redeem their past, and reconquer the respect of their companions and fellow-citizens.

A couple of days later, we were enabled to extol, by a strange coincidence, the excellence of this open-air system on children and old men.

On quitting *Kruisberg* we passed on to Arnhem, where we arrived the following Saturday evening; and as we had promised General Smits, Governor of the *Koloniaal militair invalidenhuis* (establishment for the disabled soldiers of the Indian army), that we would visit Bronbeck immediately on our arrival at Arnhem, we took advantage of the next day, being Sunday, to spend a few hours with him. The *Koloniaal militair invalidenhuis* is about an hour's walk from Arnhem, in that part of Guelderland called 'Dutch Switzerland.' The road to it is certainly lovely—shaded by grand trees, bordered by limpid streams, and interspersed by handsome houses, the gardens of which extend as far as the footpath, without any barrier or enclosure of any kind to hide their bright-coloured flower-beds from view. Most of these villas are inhabited by enormously rich men, who, having gained their wealth in the Dutch Indies, have returned home to enjoy it; which accounts for the luxury prevailing in these charming habitations.

The building occupied by the disabled soldiers stands in the midst of a magnificent lawn, enclosed by large trees, with an artificial river meandering through the grounds around. An elegant little pavilion, ornamented with a large verandah, fronts the main building. It is now the residence of the Governor, but formerly it was inhabited by the Count de Chambord. On the threshold of this pavilion stood General Smits, with a smile of welcome on his kind face as he greeted us; and I remarked, with a warm glow at my heart, that he had hoisted the French flag above his house, in honour of our arrival. He proposed showing us over his establishment himself; a pleasure we were glad to accept.

The number of soldiers amounts to 210, including 40 non-commissioned officers. The house they inhabit is an enormous, but handsome brick and iron edifice, plastered in grey, and not having the appearance of either a barracks or a hospital. It is divided into two storeys, and is very lofty and well ventilated. The ground-floor is employed for general use. It contains the dining-halls, coffee and billiard rooms, and conversation-rooms, besides two others we shall speak about presently—the chapel and library. Above are the private rooms of the old soldiers.

On both floors the rooms are divided by long corridors, the walls of which are ornamented with arms and the colours captured from the enemy. Some few of these trophies are of rich workmanship, mounted in gold, enriched with diamonds, and covered with marvellous engravings. Several very remarkable cannon are on the ground-floor. These long corridors, or rather galleries, serve for the soldiers to take exercise in, when the weather is too inclement for them to take a turn in the park, or go on without-door occupations.

The extent of this park is about a dozen acres. The river, winding through it, is ornamented here and there with graceful cascades, while white swans and brilliantly-coloured ducks flap their wings on its banks or swim along its surface. The old soldiers are very proud of their river, besides having a great affection for it, which is not to be wondered at considering the fine trout and carp to be found in it, and that both fish are great favourites with the soldiers. Besides this river, the inmates of the hospital have a cowhouse, containing a dozen animals for the supply of milk and butter; a pigsty, with fifty grunters, each of which in turn supplies bacon, ham, and sausages; and a well-kept kitchen garden and a fowl-yard.

Each and all of these stables and outhouses are kept in a perfect state of cleanliness and order, as indeed is the case with the kitchen, and the establishment generally. Care and due attention to the slightest detail is observable everywhere, both in the persons of the old soldiers and in the house and grounds belonging to them, which, added to a happy, contented expression on every face, rather surprised us. As most of the inmates are old men, we asked for an explanation of this phenomenon.

'We have very stern discipline here,' replied our amiable *cicerone*. 'The old fellows belong to every nation—Spanish, Belgian, German, Prussian, and French—and not one of them is allowed to infringe the rules; consequently we have adopted a principle from which we never swerve—work and amusement. Each man owes it to his neighbour, to do as much work as his strength permits. Besides our agricultural labour, we have various trades carried on—carpenters, tailors, bootmakers, wheelwrights, blacksmiths, joiners, even bookbinders; so that, while we increase the comfort of the house, we lessen expenses, and the money thus saved is spent in giving the old fellows as much amusement as possible, both in winter and summer.

'We will not say anything about the thirty or forty days a year on which they play at dominoes, or skittles, or billiards, and enjoy a promenade to music, for that is their right; but we have besides concerts, discussions, theatricals, and evenings spent in the enjoyment of literature and other improving subjects. The moment we hear of the arrival of a conjuror or a musician, he is sent for to perform here; and when we can get no foreign artist of distinction, the singing-hall in the neighbourhood supplies us regularly with the best singers to be had.'

'It seems to me, my dear General,' I could not help remarking, 'that all you want, to complete your list of amusements, is to give a ball.'

'Ah! you think so? But to do that we should have to admit women, and that is strictly forbidden——,'

'What! you think it might be dangerous for the old fellows——?'

'There is no knowing; they might fall in love, you know,' added the General, smiling.

This existence, passed in work and amusement, is very pleasant for the old soldiers accustomed to discipline, and certainly very conducive to health, for they live to a good old age at Bronbeck, and very rarely think of taking their last voyage till a very advanced period of life. Before they can be admitted to this retreat they must have seen forty years' service, and, considering that service in India is continual expeditions full of fatigue, and that the climate is bad, the peaceful pleasures and life they enjoy after entering the hospital, are somewhat dearly earned.

Each soldier is entitled to 1s. 3d. per week, the non-commissioned officers receiving double. This does not sound very much, but being well housed, well nourished, clothed, and amused, it is sufficient in plenty to supply them with gin and tobacco, the only **two** things not furnished by the administration. In Holland both gin and tobacco are very cheap, and a great deal of both can be obtained for very little money. Besides, the very best guarantee we have, that existence in this place **is pleasant** and complete **is, that** many who need not enter **at all,** do so from choice. Lately an old man died at Bronbeck who was found on his death to be in possession of **two** hundred thousand **francs,** besides five hundred **francs** in gold. He was **a** subaltern adjutant, and no one had any idea he possessed such a fortune.

Born in Switzerland, at first he served in the Helvetian army, and retired from that as an ensign. He next entered the Papal army, from which he voluntarily retired with the rank of second lieutenant. A few years later he enlisted in the army in India, as a **common** soldier, where he gained **promotion; after** which, **wounded in** an engagement, he had **himself** admitted to **the** *Kolonaal militair invalidenhuis,* at Bronbeck. Certainly such a singular life as his had a halo of mystery about it; but, whatever secret **he** had, he guarded it carefully, **and** carried it **with** him to **the tomb.**

The two rooms we **said we** should refer to again are the **library and** the chapel. The former contains **about a dozen** or thirteen hundred volumes, for the **use of the inmates;** a privilege they take good care to **avail** themselves of largely. A librarian has charge **of** the room, and keeps a record of the books lent to and returned by each man, for the last one must be brought back before a fresh one is allowed out.

The chapel is a very simple building, and is used alike for the Catholic and Protestant service. The pulpit faces the altar, both of which are furnished with large green curtains. When the Catholic priest officiates, the pulpit of the *predikant* is hidden by the curtain; and when the *predikant* mounts the pulpit to expound the word of God, the altar is veiled from sight by its curtain. I was particularly touched with this simplicity of treatment.

We have already remarked that Bronbeck is situated in that part of Guelderland called 'Dutch Switzerland.' This term may appear somewhat pretentious, but it is nevertheless perfectly justifiable. The country stretching to the north of Arnhem is covered with extensive woods, and very hilly. Of course, there are no steep mountains or eternal snows; but the scenery has a wild beauty of its own which is very attractive, with its hills and springs and leaping cascades in the midst of wide-spreading heaths, forming a contrast it would be difficult to find elsewhere, and which is very charming to behold.

It is not much to be wondered at, I think, that the nobility of Guelderland made choice of this pretty corner of the province in which to build their country seats. Later on their good example was followed by the patricians of the neighbouring province, who liked to pass a few days under the shade of its grand old trees; hence the origin of the Beckhuizen, Rosendaal, and Duinoog *Chalets*, or inns, analogous to those in Oberland. Then after a while this inn accommodation was found to be insufficient, for those who came to stay a few days wished to live there altogether; so country-houses were built in every direction, and handsome villas and pretty cottages sprang up as by enchantment; but, elegant and showy as these latter are, one cannot prefer them to the lordly residences which were first built there.

Rosendaal is incontestably the handsomest and most illustrious of these residences, both as regards position and appearance. Situated at the mouth of the gorge, surrounded by wooded heights, shaded by gigantic beech-trees, with its park and glistening lakes and limpid streams and marble statues, no wonder it was compared more than once to the Valley of Tempe:—

Roosendaalsche Tempé, o pronkcieraad der Hoven![1]

The magnificence of this castle is, to a certain extent, accounted for by its having remained in the same family for several centuries; and, the family bearing the same name as their residence, they have done all in their power to keep up its reputation, and add to the charm and beauty of their place. It is inhabited at present by the last descendant of the old name.

---

[1] 'Tempe of Rosendaal, queen of residences!' Such is the beginning of some pompous verses in praise of Rosendaal, written last century by J. d'Outrien.

Formerly Rosendaal[1] was a regular old manor, with machicolated battlements. An old tower still standing, reflecting its magnificent top in the moat at its feet, bears ample proof of the strength of the walls and the assaults they could have sustained. When artillery came to be employed, these walls were no longer of any use; and from that time the castle was turned into a country-house, the park improved, the bridges, grottoes, cascades, and fountains renovated and embellished, and old tritons in marble holding their traditional urns to the limpid streams, and figures of nymphs half hidden in the shade of the trees, were added in every direction. It was well to render this dignified retreat worthy of the august visitors likely to become its guests. William III. sojourned there at different times; for, as King of England, he did not forget the early companions of the Prince of Orange, nor the friends devoted to him when he was Stadholder of Holland. He loved to find himself among those friends who had aided him to mount one of the finest thrones in the world; and there is still at Rosendaal a reminiscence of his last stay there, or rather of that of Queen Mary. It is a screen, embroidered entirely by hand, which was presented to the mistress of the castle by the ladies of honour of the Queen of England.[2]

[1] Rosendaal signifies valley of roses.
[2] This royal visit inspired the poetical talents of John d'Outrien, *predikant* of Dort. He published, in 1699, in Amsterdam, a long poem called *Wegwyzer door de Hurligkheid Roozendaal*, in which he celebrated, in pompous verse, the beauties of this superb domain. The book must

William **III.** was not the first great personage to visit the old castle. Long before his time, Renaud III., **Duke of** Guelderland, was brought there in **1361 by** his unnatural brother, who kept **him ' confined in** a close prison**' during a period of ten long years.** The dungeon where this **unhappy man was incarcerated is still in existence. It is a kind of** recess formed in the thickness **of the wall, lighted by** an imperceptible grated window. **A man of ordinary size could scarcely move in it. It was approached by a dozen steps and through two barred iron doors, which made any attempt at escape impossible.** **It makes one shudder to think that a human** being was once incarcerated in **such** a hole for so long a space of time. When the poor fellow was at last set free, he had lost the use of his limbs, and his **forced immobility had produced** an *embonpoint* that **prevented his being able to pass through the doors, which had to be broken apart before he could be dragged out of his dungeon.**[1]

Another fine **place in** this Dutch Switzerland, also possessing **a** good position and a good name, **is** Zonsbeek. It belongs to Baron de Heeckeren, a rich landowner, of Holland. The park contains fine timber, streams, **ponds, cascades, and a** small belvi-

---

have been a success, for **in 1718 a third edition** was brought out, enriched by a great many very interesting plates, showing the different views of the castle at that time.

[1] In 1808 M. G. Van Hasselt published an **account of all the documents he could find,** referring to Rosendaal, from **the earliest, dating** 1304, to 1793. His **work** is entitled *Rosendaal als de prachtizste Arzitting van de geldersche graven en hertogen*.

dere tower, from whence a grand panorama can be seen, stretching as far as Cleves. Its situation, however, is not so picturesque as that of Rosendaal, and the castle is entirely devoid of character.

The same cannot be said of Biljoen, its appearance being most warlike, with a touch of the middle ages about it.

This fine castle is a huge, massive building, flanked at the four corners by handsome towers, the high tapering roofs of which have been unfortunately done away with, and replaced by bulging tops of singular effect. However, on the whole, it has a very good aspect; and the bridge, by which alone the interior can be reached, adds to its quaint appearance. The building itself is not more than about 300 years old; but some other castle must have existed prior to this one, for Biljoen is one of the most ancient in the province. The oldest and finest charter among the archives of Guelderland is its constitution Act, signed by the Emperor Henry IV., of heretic memory, in the year 1076.

A few years ago, Biljoen possessed the charm, no longer in existence, of being enclosed by the most magnificent trees. It contained also many precious treasures, and was a central point of attraction for artists and lovers of the beautiful. Alas! all this has disappeared. Death knocked at the door.

> . . . Omne sacrum mors importuna profanat,
> Omnibus obscuras injicit illa manus . . .

His breath passed over Biljoen. The castle was
T

put up to auction. For a moment the hope sprang into existence that treasures, timbers, and castle would all be saved. The nobility of Guelderland regarded the manor as specially belonging to their province, and as such they agreed to purchase it. But a foreigner arrived on the scene—a German, devoid of any love of art, of country, or of nature. The precious treasures were dispersed to the four winds; trees, a century old, were cut down, the old manor converted into a common dwelling, and the forest became a desert.

'Only one of them came into the country, and yet you see everything is destroyed,' remarked M. Van T——, with whom we were lamenting this disaster. 'Imagine what would happen if our poor Guelderland were invaded by a number of them!'

'I am sure I should be the last one,' I replied, 'to wish you any such experience.'

CHAPTER XVIII.

ARNHEM—'VIR BONUS'—THE *ARNHEMSE FABRIQUE*—ST. EUSEBIUS AND ST. WALBURGUS—THE DEVIL'S HOUSE—CARNIVAL OF 1525—PLEASURES AND AMUSEMENTS—'*GELRE! GELRE!*'—THE RHINE AND THE WAAL.

F in olden times this town was called *Arnhem de lugtigste* (Arnhem the Joyous), what could it not be called now? For the last fifty years this handsome town has been growing handsomer every day. Its old ramparts have been transformed into magnificent boulevards, its military courtyards into bright flower-beds, and its ancient moats have been turned into a flowing river ornamented with tiny isles, and shaded by trees a century old. It is no longer a fair-sized town, 'chef de l'Estat and Seigneurie de Weluwe,' of Guicciardini's time, but the capital of the whole province; an aristocratic capital, too, abounding in pleasures and distractions of every kind.

Situated in the centre of a hilly country, washed by the calm majestic Rhine, well laid out, well built and with a salubrious air, Arnhem seems to have been predestined by nature and by man to be the *buen*

retiro of Holland; and indeed it is so. Fortunes are made in Amsterdam and Rotterdam, or better still in Java; but it is in Arnhem that they are spent and enjoyed, where well-earned repose and peace are the reward of years of toil.

Here the houses are as handsome as in Amsterdam, Leeuwarden, or Groningen, of elegant outline and carved ornament; yet, owing to their being constructed in brick, their aspect is severe; they have no pointed gables or sloping roofs reminding one of Norwegian winters; no narrow doors, no granite steps, no chains or boundaries giving the appearance of a rampart to each individual house, and preserving the privacy of *home* so dear to the Batavian race.

On the contrary, the various soft, tender shades of colour give to the houses a fresh gay appearance, and the terraced roofs, defying rain and storms, add to the spring-like aspect of the town. Windows are wide open, and terraces, verandahs, and gardens are as fully occupied as the interior of the habitations, enabling passers-by to gain an insight into the domestic life of the owners. Again, the presence in Arnhem of a large number of Indian families has given an exotic character to the recently-erected buildings, which is very marked. Some affect Italian style, others old Batavian; but all are decorated with rare shrubs, plants, and tropical flowers, which, tastefully arranged, give a very festive appearance to each and all of these habitations.

Pontanus, an old author, describes the people of

Arnhem as '*cives humani ac bonarum litterarum amantes.*' This is almost the '*vir bonus dicendi peritus*' so dear to the ancients. Now Pontanus was born at Arnhem, so he naturally was a partial writer; however he gives examples of his statement, and tells us of many persons occupied in literary works about his time. So we must accept his assertion and remember that scholars are no rarer at Arnhem now, than they were in his day.

'Their courage,' adds the old annalist, 'has been proved by their brave deeds.' And we have no reason to doubt that, when called upon, the Arnhemers would do their duty as bravely now, as ever.

However, notwithstanding its reputation for scholarship and bravery, this charming little city has never given birth[1] to any great genius, or scientific discoverer, or hero; and, with the exception of Wemmer Noott, a painter of very mediocre talent, cannot boast of any known artist. Even in the fifteenth century, when Arnhem was a ducal city, it was obliged to borrow its artists from the towns of Flanders and the Overyssel; hence its archives abound in curious revelations. There is one dated 1459, in which Clais Van Braband, a Brabant artist, figures as having painted a picture, to ornament the Town Hall, for the sum of five florins.

---

[1] Perhaps we ought to mention that the Emperor Henry III. was born at Oosterbeck in 1027. But Arnhem at that period was only a small village, and had no seigneurial right over the surrounding country.

Certainly the arts were not in a flourishing state in this town, for in 1522 the Duke of Saxony, wishing, in honour of his deceased wife, to give to the Brotherhood of St. Nicholas a mark of his favour, was forced to apply to a painter of Zwolle for a window, for which he paid the sum of thirty-six golden florins.[1]

Throughout the sixteenth century there is no mention of one celebrated worker in gold, or embroiderer, or cabinet-maker; in fact, to find one industrial art we must turn to the last century, and then we only have a manufactory of faience, the existence of which is still open to question. If this manufactory were to be re-established in Arnhem it would be a great ornament to its mural crown, for the specimens we obtained, as belonging to the town, were certainly very exquisite, being of beautiful enamel of pure cream-white, covered with delicate and chaste designs. They are all of the Louis XV. period, and the ornaments surrounding them are of rockwork, and also of elegant design. A few of them are marked with a cock. They had been attributed first to Delft, and then to Amsterdam, but without any special certainty. But a plate I saw one day at Brussels, at M. Evenepoel's the collector, representing a river with a manufactory in the background, put me on a new scent. The plate bore the inscription *Arnhemse Fabrique*, with a cock perched on a branch.

---

[1] Dame Christian, Duchess of Saxony, Queen of Saxony, Sweden, and Norway, who died in 1522, and was interred in the large church.

The style and ornaments made me certain of the period, and the words seemed to me to have been spelt by a French hand. A Dutchman would have written *Arnhemsche fabriek* or *fabrijk*; but a foreigner on the contrary, ignorant of the language, would write according to his own mode of spelling; so all that was left for me to do was to try and discover among the archives of 1740-75 if a manufactory of faience had ever existed in Arnhem. I interested two archivists, one for the country the other for the town, in my research, and very soon the truth was found out, and not only perhaps may M. Evenepoel's plate be attributed to the artistic activity of Arnhem, but also the coffee-pot of M. Van Romondt of Utrecht, the pretty dishes belonging to M. Fèlis of Brussels, the superb fountain of M. Paul Dalloz, and a hundred other celebrated specimens adorning collectors' cabinets.

Arnhem is not badly off as regards architecture; not that the town possesses a great number of remarkable monuments, but rather two or three well worthy the attention of archæologists and artists. The Church of St. Eusebius is the most important, the erection of which is relatively recent, the first stone having been laid in 1451, on the Cardinal Legate's visit to the town. The building must have been carried on with marvellous rapidity, for the following year there was question of the Duke of Guelderland visiting the Cathedral (*ad cathedram*), and the archives mention that on the 23rd September of that same year a canon of Leyden, Jean van Hanen, presented to St. Martin (the name the church then bore) a silver cup of great value. It is presumable also that in 1453 the immense building was completed, because the burgomasters judged the church in a fit state to receive the relics of St. Eusebius, which were transported thither in great pomp on the Wednesday following the Assumption, and from that time forward the church dropped its former name of St. Martin to assume that of the saint whose bones reposed within its precincts.

In spite of the rapidity of its erection, St. Eusebius is one of the largest and finest churches in Holland. At a time when Gothic architecture was not much in favour, Blaeu speaks of it as a magnificent work (*opere magnifico*), which is not saying too much, for it certainly is very grand in appearance and pure in taste, in spite of its having been erected so recently. It has a very high nave, and two aisles void of chapels. The choir is semi-hexagon, enclosed in a semi-decagon circuit, and presents the peculiarity of having been erected after the nave. The vaults of the nave and transept, constructed in brick and divided into very graceful caissons, are about five centuries old, whilst those of the choir are faulty, although they do not appear so. M. Eyck Van Zuylichem, who has minutely examined the building, says that he was unable to discern the slightest trace of injury outside; and what confirms this statement is the fact of there being no buttresses to the exterior of the choir, while the nave and the transept are both furnished with them. The interior of the church, unfortunately, is plastered throughout. Even its windows have been deprived of their very interesting stained panes. The only break to the colourless monotony everywhere around, consists in a few shields, formerly belonging to ancient corporations, suspended on the walls. Close to the entrance to the choir stands the mausoleum of Josse Sasbout, the first chancellor to whom Charles V. confided the government of his Duchy of Guelderland; he did not fill the honourable post long, however. I have referred in my other work[1] to the eloquent lines on his tomb, and never were lines more happily inspired. The sculptor proved himself worthy of his work, and the mausoleum is a *chef-d'œuvre* of taste and elegance. Impossible for the chisel to have more completely realised a dark philosophical thought, than is done here in this work of art.

Another monument of larger proportions, and much more interesting, stands in the centre of the choir. It is the tomb of Charles Egmont, the last Duke of Guelderland. In 1538, bowed down by old age, vanquished, humiliated, his last hope gone of reconquering the Duchy he had conquered, lost, and fought for during half a century, Charles Count Egmont found here that peace and repose he had never known during his life. His tomb consists of a vast pedestal of black marble, upon which he rests armed

---

[1] 'The Dead Cities of the Zuyder Zee,' p. 359.

to the teeth, with his hands clasped, and his eyes closed. Six lions holding the arms of his family surround him, and in sixteen niches in the sock of the pedestal stand as many statues representing the Apostles and Evangelists. Each one of these pieces of sculpture is beautifully executed, slightly heavy, perhaps, but eloquent of a grand epoch and grand style.

Another statue of the Count, also life size, but in a kneeling position, stands in the choir. Strangely enough it is placed in a kind of niche, one might almost call it a cage, about twenty feet from the ground. What the reason was for placing the Count in a kneeling attitude of defence, in such an isolated position so far from the ground, we were not told, and could not find out.

The pulpit is a charming specimen of architecture at its best epoch. It is octagonal in shape, with a fine *pseudo*-Corinthian column at the summit of each angle. The panels are covered with scrolls and designs of exquisite finish. Seats are dispersed around the pulpit with most studied care for the comfort of the worshippers, having small curtains hung round of woollen material to subdue strong light, and at the same time to prevent draughts and cold air from reaching the occupants.

The exterior of St. Eusebius is as elegant as its interior. It is constructed in brick and ornamented in sandstone, which sadly requires restoring. Its lateral *façades* front two large open spaces or squares, one of which, the market, would be remarkably picturesque if it were not hemmed in by pretentious-looking buildings, erected during the French occupation, in that heavy, severe style in vogue for official dwellings, at the commencement of this century.

The principal entrances to the church are in these squares; each has a fine portico, and stands at either end of the transept. A third door is to be found at the base of the tower; rarely used, however, as it leads on to a street of narrow proportions and ill fame; rather a peculiar surrounding for a church. The tower is handsome, but famous specially for its height.

The other old church, St. Walburgus, belongs to the Catholics. According to M. Eyck Van Zuylichem it was erected in 1328; according to other authorities in 1421.

Although from an architectural point of view the former date appears most probable, still, as I did not know the reasons for asserting this date as a fact, I thought I would hunt up for myself the documents relating to it. The only record I could discover is dated 1391; translated literally it is as follows:—
'Furnished to the Messieurs of St. Walburgus in town for constructing, fifty-two thousand bricks.' Hence, as that year (1391) the church was not completed, the latter date (1421) must be the correct one.

Be the date of its erection one or the other, St. Walburgus is a very interesting building in brick, and consequently simple in style. In form it is an oblong square, the size of which has been enlarged of late years, by a choir of polygon shape. In spite of the bareness of the interior, with its square pillars, it is not devoid of elegance. Unfortunately, in order to increase the number of seats, one portion of the aisle has been cut off, thus spoiling the general effect. When we visited the church the plasterers were busy in it (those people pursue me everywhere in Holland), consequently the pictures had been taken down, and we were enabled to gratify our curiosity by examining them. Among the number we made a charming discovery. It was two divisions of an ancient triptic, the work of one of those great Flemish artists who were the ignored disciples of Memling or Van Eyck, and for that very reason, perhaps, were faithful interpreters of the Christian faith. The panels were soiled and slightly scratched, but for all that very precious and very interesting. One of the plasterers cleaning the church, came over to us, and announced that the picture was going to be washed directly. We protested in strong terms against such a desecration, and tried to make him understand the enormity of the crime he was about to accomplish. He smiled incredulously; but, seeing our distress, he promised to respect the poor picture, and leave it as it was. We went away reassured; but it is doubtful if the man kept his word.

Besides these two churches, the only other ancient monument possessed by Arnhem, is the Town Hall. We went to see it, not because it is handsome, but because it is interesting. Exteriorly it has a singular and peculiar appearance, with which art has had little to do. It is called by the country people *Duivelshuis* (the devil's house), on account of certain caryatides of coarse aspect, representing satyrs, which figure on it. For my part, I should have thought it obtained this name in remembrance of Maarten Van Rossem, a stern general of Charles Egmont's, and a sort of brigand disguised as a soldier, fond of carnage and devastation, who once made it his favourite residence. One saying of his will show the man's character: 'As the *Magnificat* is the ornament of the vespers, so fire is the ornament of fields of battle.' He did not live much in his house at Arnhem, and did not even die there, for he expired at Antwerp in a most inglorious fashion, while gluttonously eating a pigeon with great enjoyment.

It is some time now since this house was used by the Municipality of Arnhem. About the beginning of this century the Town Hall stood on the *Grootemarkt*. In 1804 it was demolished to make room for a government house and a 'temple of justice,' both of which face the market with their pretentious appearance.

Unfortunately it was not a favourable time for restoring, and when the municipal body took possession of their new Town Hall, they spoilt the *façade* by destroying its character. The enormous roof was removed, and a storey added to the main building, which is surmounted by a kind of flat roof, and the *façade* was plastered in blue grey. The interior had been stripped of its ancient appurtenances, and we would not have passed over the threshold of the door, had it not been that we were obliged to do so in order to see the archives, museum, and library.

The latter is very extensive, containing about fifteen thousand volumes, most of which were inherited from Harderwyk, at we remarked when mentioning the library at Deventer. Unhappily, although the number of books is good, there are no rare ones amongst them, no precious incunabula, and very few manuscripts of any peculiar kind, except one, and that one deserves the attention of artists, for it is the great book of the monastery of Bethlehem. It dates from the thirteenth century, is magnificently bound, and comes from the famous abbey of Dœtinchem we have already referred to. The cover is ornamented in silver, with medallions and ornaments, inlaid in uncut jewels of rubies and rock-crystal. On the recto is a curious bas-relief in ivory. This beautifully bound manuscript—precious in so many points—ought not to be in the library, but rather in th museum, where so many other valuable objects are to be found.

First among these latter is a complete collection of goblets of the different guilds, of enormous size, most of which were exhibited at the Paris Exhibition of 1867. The one belonging to the vintners carries off the palm in point of ample dimensions. Side by side with these goblets are the different sceptres of the guilds, burgomasters, and municipal bodies, heads of drums, and various instruments of torture. Then come the seals of the abbeys, those of the town of different epochs, and those of the Duchy of Guelderland; and last, a small collection of various curious things, and old vases, among which are several Roman ones, discovered in the neighbourhood of Nymegen.

If it is to the convent of Bethlehem that the museum owes its finest attraction, it is to that also that it owes the most beautiful charters of the archives. I refer more especially to the archives of the province, because the town archives, on the contrary, were added to by the Harderwyk inheritance. M. Oosterbuk, who has succeeded M. Nyhoff in the office of archivist of Guelderland, showed us these paleographical treasures, which certainly deserved closer inspection than we had time to bestow on them at the moment.

They comprehend all the titles relative to the history of Guelderland from the twelfth century to the treaty of Venlo, the account books of the Dukes from 1329, fief books, law proceedings of the Landdag, and resolutions of the States provincial, &c., &c. The history of the country day by day could be ascertained by studying these records.

Added to these provincial archives are those from the abbey of Bethlehem, which consist of more than four hundred and fifty charters in fine writing ornamented with seals, of which one hundred and twelve date from the thirteenth century, and a hundred and fifty from the fourteenth. The most ancient one is dated 1200.[1]

The archives of the town are not so old, and are placed apart under the care of M. Sannes.

Although some say that the Arnhem of to-day was founded by the Romans, that it is in fact the *Arenacum* referred to by Tacitus, or the *Harenatum* of Antonin, in spite of Peutirges and the Theodosian table referring to it under the name of *Arenatum*, its antique splendour was not of very long duration. In the tenth century it was merely a small village of so little consequence that the Emperor Otho barely referred to it in his letters—and it was not till the 13th July, 1233, that Count Otho raised it to the dignity of a town, surrounded it with walls, and endowed it with certain privileges. This Act has an interesting clause—'*In morem cæterarum civitatum liberarum ac præsertim oppidi Zulphaniensis*'—showing that Arnhem had been preceded in titles, dignities, and privileges, by a good many neighbouring cities.

Besides this special record, the archives contain a mass of other documents of a most interesting nature, such as the Acts from 1423, the register book since 1435, that of sentences since the fourteenth century, and the rules regulating the Guilds and *Schrutterijen* since 1582, besides a hundred others.

We have no intention of giving the history of

---

[1] The charter dated 1076, relating to Biljoen, which is also among the archives of Guelderland, we have referred to before.

Arnhem drawn from these records—to do so we should have to relate the history of the whole of Guelderland, that is to say, recount all its wars, family contentions, and hand-to-hand fights for four centuries. We should also have to tell of the hatred between the Bronckhorst and the Heeckeren, of wives faithless to their husbands, of brothers slaying brothers, of Adolf of Egmont who dragged his father five German leagues, half naked in the cold, to fling him into a dungeon where no light of day could penetrate, except through a hole in the wall, and of those assassinations and pillagings which inspired Pasquil Merus with tardy lamentations, and the Guelderlanders with their sombre but amusing motto:—

>Hoog van Moed
>Klein van Goed
>Een Zwaard in de hand
>Is t'wapen van Gelderland.

>Much courage,
>Little money,
>A sword in the hand,
>Such are the arms of Guelderland.

Neither sorrow nor distress would prevent the Arnhemers from drinking and singing, as we may easily find out from old books and accounts of the town. They are always gay, and if there is no special love of the arts among them it is at least compensated for by their love of wine.

If we open old accounts of the year 1525 we shall see how the Duke and Duchess of Guelderland amused themselves during the carnival. 'On the

Monday evening our honoured Dame amused herself at the tavern with the Councillors of Arnhem, and their wives and daughters. The minstrel received one golden karolus for his music, the blacksmith one golden florin for dancing after the old fashion, a boy of the smithy seven sous, the clowns received one golden karolus for their performance on the Monday and their speechifying on the Tuesday, and the brewers had three herrings from Monseignor and Madame according to old custom, making in all five florins and six sous.'[1]

Shrove Tuesday was not spent in amusement of this kind, but casks of beer came into requisition with wine and sweet cakes (*Zuyckes-Koicken*).

At the present time, however, all these excesses have been regulated, and the carnival is passed at Arnhem as properly and decorously as elsewhere.

The inhabitants of Arnhem are thorough judges of good wine, and, if they do not indulge in the wild excesses of their ancestors, they take care to have the quality of their drink of the best. The Rhine furnishes them with the finest, besides sending them its clear or clouded waters accord-

---

[1] I conclude the people mentioned in this document are the Duke and Duchess, although they are called merely 'Mijn gen; Heer ind Vrouw.' This curious record was published, in 1790, in the *Kronijk van Arnhem*; written in old Flemish with such peculiar orthography that it is almost unintelligible, even to natives of the country. Hence many of the words I could only guess at; 'in t'wynhuis,' I only suppose to mean 'tavern.' It might be the municipal establishment called Wine House; but that I cannot say.

ing to the season. But water is not much drunk in Arnhem.

'I taste that water!' said one to me, whom I was congratulating on having such water. 'When I think that, may be, Germans have bathed in its coolness—pouah—it makes me sick.'

Arnhem has higher tastes than that of drinking. Few towns in Europe are so well provided with pleasures of various kinds. With the exception of one pretty little church in the new quarter, every edifice built within the last fifty years is devoted to amusement of some sort. There are about a dozen clubs and *societeiten*, the indispensable ornaments to every Dutch town.

But Arnhem possesses the rare advantage of a good theater, perfectly managed, and prettily decorated, while a public garden consecrated to the Muses, '*Musis sacrum*,' and exquisitely laid out, opens its concert-rooms and flower-beds every summer for the amusement of the highest society. Added to this, during excessively hot weather the ingenious Arnhemers have devised what they call a *Buitensocieteet*, a club outside the town. It stands on a hill overlooking the Rhine, commanding a splendid view of the country. A Dutch architect, M. Oudtshoorn, superintended its building, and made it most heavy in style; but its situation is so fine one forgets to find fault with the architecture. Thanks to the kindness of one of the Municipal Councillors, M. van T——, we were enabled to see, not only all the suburban and rural amusements, but those of town also, some of which are easier of access for foreigners, and very agreeable. Arnhem is one of the few Dutch towns where the public walks and boulevards are pleasant to the eye, the beauty of which is enhanced by the number of families who, as we have said, live chiefly in their gardens in the summer weather, and add colour and life to their lovely surroundings. Then, again, the extension of certain portions of the town towards Velp and Rosendaal, and the position of various Châteaux in the neighbourhood, render communication between the town and villages less difficult, and the constant passing to and fro of carriages on the highway enlivens the scene. When the time came for us to quit Arnhem, we were sorry to leave the gay little place to continue our route to Nymegen *viâ* the Rhine. However, we had to do it, and that too in weather which was anything but agreeable, for it rained and thundered and lightened very heavily. In the midst of this terrible storm, with the thunder rolling over our heads, and our eyes nearly blinded by the vivid flashes of lightning, we arrived at the mouth of the Yssel, avoiding as well as we could the huge masses of wood, the conductors of which had sought shelter from the inclement weather along the banks of the river. Then we continued our course between flat monotonous banks, for the Rhine on entering Holland leaves behind it its towering mountainous borders and fantastic castles, almost as if it understood that such feudal remains would have no value in the eyes of a country given to citizen independence and equality. The moment it passes the frontier it becomes genuinely Dutch, and Van Goyen might sign all the landscapes between Arnhem and Pannerden.

The tempest continued unceasingly. The black clouds above, clashed with deafening noise, and the darkness began to get so dense that, as I dimly perceived the scenery around me, I could not help thinking of that other dark legendary night to which Guelderland owes its name.

It was in the year 878, last of the reign of the Emperor and King of France, Charles the Bald. One evening in the month of January, there appeared in the middle of this verdant country a 'most horrible, savage, fearful beast, who devoured alike men and animals.' It had eyes 'fiery and sparkling like flames, and constantly uttered a terrible cry as if pronouncing the word *Gelre! Gelre!*' Very soon the country was abandoned, for all who could, hid themselves from the sight of this monster; and fields, houses, and castles were alike deserted. This terrible creature spared no one, and the seigneur had to suffer equally with his people. Now this seigneur had two sons, Wichard and Luppold, who begged their father's permission to go and fight the monster. The father consented, and blessed them, and they departed. The darkness grew thicker when they started, and a terrible tempest shook the whole country with the power of its fury. The two young men were not daunted, but, sword in hand, advanced on their road till they reached the den of the beast, whose glaring eyes betrayed him in the surrounding obscurity. The brothers kissed each other as a fresh incentive to fight bravely, attacked the creature in the name of God, and killed him. The people, overjoyed at the victory of the young men, offered them the sovereignty of the land, and they, in return, gave the name to the country which their terrible foe had pronounced with his dying breath : *Gelre.*

The storm over, we arrived safe at Pannerden, at the confluence of the Waal, where the Rhine divides into two large arms. We passed the fort of Schenck, long since abandoned, but which at one time was regarded as a stronghold of great importance. 'Nothing can pass either in or out of the two rivers without the cognizance of the governor of that castle,' said an author of the last century, ' which may be called the key or centre of communication between Germany and Holland.'

Although it was believed impregnable, it was taken no less than three times within forty years. First by the Spaniards in July, 1615; then the following year by Maurice after a siege of six months; and finally in 1672 by Turenne after only eight hours' fighting. The attack of the French army was so brilliant and rapid that the garrison took fright, and the gates were thrown open to the troops of the great king. Six days before (12th June, 1672), the governor of the fortress might have watched from the heights of the bastions, the famous passage of the Rhine, sung of by Boileau and painted by Parrocel and Van der Meulen.

This celebrated event took place at a spot called *Tolhuys*, but we did not visit it. We doubled Pannerden point, passed the fortress of that name, entered the Waal, and about an hour later perceived in the distance the outline of the town of Nymegen.

CHAPTER XIX.

NYMEGEN—THE VALCKHOF—CHARLEMAGNE'S CHAPEL — INSURRECTIONS —TOWN HALL AND MUSEUM — THE PEACE OF NYMEGEN — THE HOUTENROKKEN—ST. STEPHEN—'SIC VOS NON VOBIS.'

NYMEGEN is situated on the slope of a hill on the river Waal, which washes the lower town and separates it from Betaw, a flat piece of land forming an isle between the Waal and the Rhine. Formerly it was the spot inhabited by a people the Romans called Batavians, to whom they allied themselves when they subjugated the neighbouring inhabitants of Gaul and Germany. Betaw and Waal were the old German names changed by the Romans to *Batavia* and *Vahalis*. Betaw, in old German, signifies rich earth; in the same way as Velow, a large country covered with brushwood, on the other side of the Rhine, signifies barren ground. I cannot quite decide if Nymegen is derived from *Neomagus*, or *Neomagus* from Nymegen; but from certain indications of old ruins and the old castle still in existence, it appears that it was once a Roman colony. 'The town is in a salubrious situation, and surrounded on three sides by extensive dry heaths inhabited by good people.'

So wrote Sir William Temple of Schenne, ambassador at the Hague, in reference to Nymegen towards the end of the seventeenth century, when he had been sent by the King of England to negotiate at the great European Congress which met to sign one of the most famous treaties of modern times. The description is tolerably exact, only Sir William might have added that on arriving at the Waal, or on the great plains of Betaw, the most magnificent panorama stretches away to the horizon, that one could wish to see. The town is not low down and flat, scarcely rising above the plain itself, like those we had left behind us. On the contrary, Nymegen stands boldly out from the mountain side with its fine houses towering one above the other, their pretty gables and turrets and roofs forming irregular lines, at once pleasing to the eye and picturesque in appearance. Its bright colouring is enhanced by the green slope covered with large trees on one side, and on the other by the imposing and grand massive beauty of the Church of St. Stephen.

Sir William Temple had not much opportunity of contemplating the beautiful view, for he nearly lost his life when he arrived, owing to the burgomaster's desire to do honour to the great diplomatist. His equipage, with six horses attached, was being ferried across the Waal when the cannon boomed forth a salvo of honour. 'My horses,' wrote

Sir William, 'were so terrified at the noise and at the swaying of the boat under their feet, that I feared we should be turned over into the water. However, by the aid of my servants we safely reached the other side.'

This mark of honour was a very natural attention, on the part of the town, to such a great man. The congress meeting within its walls was an event of great importance to Nymegen. Other towns had claimed the honour, but Nymegen was chosen as a sort of compensation for the losses it had suffered during the war.

Saint Didier tells us that the French ambassadors arrived in the imperial city incognito, and without any retinue, although one might say that they had a public reception, owing to the concourse of people who turned out to see the arrival of 'the long-desired ambassadors.' To which we must add that although they arrived 'incognito and without retinue,' yet they were accompanied by such a large number of waggons loaded with baggage, that they extended from the gates of the town to the ambassadors' residences. No doubt, even now, such an incognito would make a strong impression on the population of Nymegen, and excite their curiosity to a large extent—fortunately for us, not being encumbered with so much baggage, we entered the town unnoticed.

Nymegen is divided through the centre by a broad street, from which all the smaller ones lead, on one side towards the Waal, on the other in the direction of the open country. It is here in this principal street that the chief public buildings are to be found, for it crosses the Grootemarkt, leads past St. Stephen's Church, skirts the University, and terminates at the beautiful park where a century ago the battlements of the ancient *Valckhof* stood towering above the ground.

This *Valckhof*, the name of which, according to Pontanus and Blaeu, is derived from Waelhof (residence or castle on the Waal), is incontestably the most ancient establishment of the country. It is to it that Nymegen owes its existence, and certainly it was the origin of civilisation in that part of the country.

According to tradition, it was occupied and fortified in turn by Celts, Teutons, and Gauls, and one of the kings of the country, called Magus, conceived the idea of adding a town to the citadel. Hence arose Maga, which was afterwards destroyed by the Celts when they invaded the country. Then a king named Baton restored, enlarged, and fortified it with three walls, and called it Novio-magus.

This name was not preserved by the Romans. Tacitus called it the fortress of the Batavians (*Batavorum oppidum*), a title it truly deserved, when Claudius Civilis turned it into the last ramparts of national independence. The place, to this day, is shown where the rebel general watched the defeat of his troops. It is a sort of belvidere, commanding a view of Betaw and the double course of the Waal, from whence the steeples of Arnhem can be seen in the distance. Ten towns and fifty villages are dotted on this fine peninsula, now become a rich fertile country.

The Castle, of which this belvidere was formerly one of the terraces, is entirely demolished, and a public promenade has been laid out on its site. Of the noble building where twenty emperors and their suites were lodged; of the grand vast halls where foreign ambassadors bowed their heads before the Christian successors of pagan Cæsars; of the luxurious chambers where Charlemagne, Louis le Debonnaire, Charles the Bald, Otho I., Conrad III., and the Emperors Sigismond and Albert slept; of the rich sumptuous walls wherein Henry VI. was born and wherein his first cry was heard; of ancient gates through which the paladins of old made their way to the Holy Land; where Renault III., Charles the Bold, Charles Egmont, Maximilian of Austria, Charles V., and Philip II. were complimented by the burgomasters of Nymegen—of all this grandeur there only remain now a couple of small simple vestiges, and even they were only preserved at the earnest entreaty of the antiquarian, M. In van Betouw, who by dint of prayers and supplications succeeded in saving them when the castle was destroyed in 1799.

The largest, but least perfect, of these remains is the vault of an ancient chapel, most likely contemporary with the restoration of the castle by Charlemagne's order in 774. Hemicycle in form, it is headed by a demi-cupola, the centre arch of which has defied alike the devastating hand of man and the inclemency of the weather. A vaulted crypt fully lighted by circular openings formerly extended beneath the choir, and fine narrow windows let in the thick walls dispersed a dim light over the altar. In front are two beautiful columns, in white marble, the Corinthian capitals of which would decide the antiquity of the chapel, if the hemispheric headings, analogous to those in Italian basilicæ, did not indicate its exact date.

The other fragment, in still better preservation, is a small octagonal building, already so well described by M. Oltmans[1] that I shall merely refer to its most curious points.

Form and ornaments are of charming simplicity. The interior has a double gallery, supported by carved arches for the lower, by double arches for the upper one; both galleries are vaulted, but many of the arches, and a certain number of exterior openings, were reconstructed at a later date, in the pointed arch style. This very peculiar little construction is called the Roman Chapel.

At a period when architectural science was not very extended, many scholars attributed the origin of this chapel to a very antique age, some even supposing it was an ancient pagan temple. Birchemius pretends that it was built in honour of Julius Pru-

---

[1] 'Description of the Carlovingian Chapel and Roman Chapel, formerly of the Castle of Nymegen,' by Alex. Oltmans, Amsterdam, 1847. In 1840 Mertens wrote a description of the Roman Chapel published in the 'Algemeine Bauzeitung' at Vienna.

dens, whose tomb stood close by. Paul Merula thought it was a sanctuary consecrated to Janus, and M. In van Betouw, the gentleman who saved it from destruction, believed it had been dedicated to the god Thor.

Others, again, say that it is not older than the eighth or ninth century. Certainly the form of the upper arches, with their peculiar cupolas, makes this statement appear very plausible. Supposing this version to be the correct one, it remains to be proved what was the original intention of this little sanctuary. It is generally thought to be the ancient Imperial Chapel where the Emperor went to hear mass, and even the place is pointed out where the illustrious monarch's throne stood. Now a little reflection will show that this could not have been the case, for many reasons. First, it only requires a little knowledge of those times to perceive that the surroundings of princes, the number of dignitaries, prelates, and knights, who accompanied the Emperor everywhere at that period, would make it an utter impossibility for him to have worshipped in such a narrow space.

Besides, the *Valckhof* was not a temporary resting-place, nor was Nymegen a chance residence. The old town had the title of second imperial city of Lower Germany; it was called the 'foot of the empire,' and in hierarchical order it was secondary only to Aix-la-Chapelle. In 829, when there was question of holding a diet to reinstate Louis le Debonnaire in his title of Emperor, Nymegen was chosen for the honour. Hence it was in a position to lodge three kings, an emperor, and their respective suites. The palace also was worthy of its guests. One author, H. Cannegieter, asserts that it derives its name from *Falckenhof* (palace of the hawks), in reference to those Louis le Debonnaire had bred there for the chase—proving that he was in the habit of staying at the castle and hawking in the neighbourhood. Eginhard,[1] the companion of Charlemagne and the historian of his life, tells us that the Emperor had two magnificent palaces built (*operis egregii*), one close to Mayence, the other at Nymegen, above the Waal. It is the same palace that the venerable Radevicus, 'chanoine' of Freisengen, calls '*nobile palatium opus fortissimum,*' and that Lambertus the monk, who inhabited the monastery of Hirschfeldt, spoke of as a 'royal residence of admirable and incomparable work' (*regiam domum miri et incomparabilis operis*); and when Charles the Bold seized Nymegen and the *Valckhof*, it is known that he gave special orders to his troops to respect this antique palace.

All this has not escaped M. Oltmans' notice, who seems not only to have studied the history of the construction of the castle, but also the manners of the times in which it was built; and he grows eloquent in imagination as he pictures to himself the pomp and grandeur of which this place was once the scene.

[1] Vita et gesta Caroli Magni.

'Imagine,' he cries, 'what this monument must have been like at the time of its inauguration, glittering with mosaic and frescoes, filled with the magnificent retinues of the peers and lords of the realm, surrounding the throne of Charles the Great, with richly robed prelates standing by, and the air resounding with the glorious music of canticle and hymn.' Certainly, I must acknowledge, a very inviting picture, but difficult to imagine in a small chapel about twenty-five feet in diameter.

Then again, another reason for objecting to this little chapel having been the scene of so much show and grandeur, is, that it is composed of materials of very inferior quality to those used for the large chapel, added to which it was detached from the main building in the old plan, whereas the larger one was enclosed in it. But if it was not a chapel, what was it? is a very natural question.

It was a baptistery. During the eighth and ninth centuries baptism was performed by immersion. The convert undressed, entered the enormous basin in a state of nature, and received his baptism, as Christ did at Jordan. And to prevent members of the Church from being forced to witness a ceremony which might shock their modesty, a small sanctuary was erected close by, where the service could be performed before a limited number of witnesses. Several of these baptisteries are still in existence, some even very celebrated, as, for example, the one of S. Giovanni Lateran in Rome, and those of Florence and of Pisa. All are constructed on a model almost identical with the octagon Chapel of Nymegen, only they are somewhat larger, and the architecture is more elegant and more ornamented, and the materials they are made of much richer.

The number of Churches of octagonal form is, on the contrary, very limited, there being only two in existence, Santa Vitale at Ravenna, and the little Church of Othmarsheim in Alsace. The nearest approach to this model is the dome of Aix-la-Chapelle Cathedral, which has sixteen sides. It is very likely that these Churches were originally intended for baptisteries also, for their dimensions are very limited, and scarcely harmonize with the title of Church, especially in the case of the *Dom Kirche* of Aix-la-Chapelle which is called a Cathedral.

Now when it is remembered that it was only a very short while after the arrival of Pope Leo III. in the country, that the octagon Chapel was erected,[1] and that Charlemagne often visited Nymegen to celebrate Easter there, during the years 804–808, and that he received a large number of Saxon chiefs baptised there each time, it must be acknowledged that our supposition has an air of truth about it. Besides, this supposition is confirmed by a tradition, to the effect that a *baptistery* in precious material was buried in the middle of this sanctuary. Only a few years ago the treasure was sought for, but of course nothing

[1] 'Noviomagi Annals.'

was found. Tradition has made a mistake, and confounded the contents with the case.

This tradition, which plays an important part in the history of the little Chapel, we heard from M. Pabst Van Bingerden, an archæologist of standing, who accompanied us on our visit to these curious ruins.

The interior, as also the exterior, of the octagon Chapel has been stripped of its ancient decorations, even to the stonework which once covered it. To give it an interest in the eyes of the public it has been converted into a museum containing a number of antiquities found in the neighbourhood. A small wooden flight of steps leads from the centre to the upper gallery,[1] which does not always see those come down who mount it. It is the flight of steps leading to the scaffold.

On quitting this venerable little building we could not help remarking how vividly the memory of Charlemagne is preserved, in every country he visited for any length of time. His memory seems to fill people's hearts, as his name does their ears. Certainly this is the case here, and the only reason for transforming this baptistery into a royal Chapel appears to be, that the people may have a pedestal on which to stand their venerated prince.

It is not, however, the only souvenir of the great

---

[1] Another point which confirms our supposition that this chapel was a baptistery is, that it has no staircase like S. Vitale of Ravenna and the Domkirche Aix-la-Chapelle. The upper gallery is reached by a ladder.

Emperor to be found in Nymegen. Every evening an enormous bell, which is nothing less than an old curfew-bell, rings out its droning noise, and for some reason, which I could not discover, is called 'Charlemagne's prayer.' A few years ago the burgomaster, like a sensible fellow, wished to abolish its use, thinking that by so doing he should please the whole town. Nothing of the sort—complaints arose in every direction, people objected in strong terms to abolishing the old custom, and 'Charlemagne's prayer' was re-established and again heard every evening.

Now it must not be imagined from the affection shown to these relics, that the inhabitants of the ancient town were submissive, peaceful subjects. Far from it. The hill on which Nymegen is built was continually swept by the breath of independence and rebellion. The town was always in a state of smouldering or open insubordination. Guicciardini says that 'In times past they cared for nothing but the handling of arms,' and Blaeu adds that the 'citizens being exempt from servile conditions' they were not constrained to submit to anything, and that they were remarkably tenacious of their rights and all that concerned the liberty of their city. Besides have they not inscribed on one of the gates of their town, '*Melius est Bellicosa libertas quam servitus pacifica.*'

Sometimes this spirit of rebellion led the population to commit acts which did not always redound to their credit, as for instance, when they assisted Count Adolf to rise against his old father the Duke of Guelderland, who on being taken, demanded as a grace and with the tears in his eyes, not to be taken to Nymegen, so much did he fear the 'populace and citizens.'

Another time these worthy sons of this war-loving town, which had shown a bold front to the Duke of Burgundy, and forced Charles the Bold to enter through a breach, resisted the troops occupying their town and dispersed them.

'In the year 1585,' says an old chronicler, 'the town of Nymegen was in a great commotion; the bourgeois took counsel together how they could get rid of the garrison from the town. Fifty men were found of the same mind, who seized the arsenal and the market-place on March 16, and imprisoned the soldiers, persuading their fellow townsmen that these men had determined to pillage the town.' Upon which news each citizen fled to his arms, they attacked the garrison, turned it out of the gates, and announced that for the future they could defend themselves and had no need of soldiers to help them.

The States on hearing this ordered Count de Meurs and Colonel Schenk to retake Nymegen. They, thinking they had to do with second-rate soldiers, tried a few stratagems but without much success, though one encounter with the rebels cost the poor colonel his life.

At the head of his company, he traversed the

Waal during the night, hoping to take the town by surprise while the inhabitants slept. His soldiers were noiselessly disembarking on the other side, and congratulating themselves upon the success of their stratagem, when suddenly a cry rent the air! In a house close to the water's edge a wedding was being celebrated. One of the dancers had gone outside to enjoy the cool when he perceived the boats loaded with soldiers, many of whom had already disembarked. Rushing back to the house he raised the alarm, and the friends, armed with anything they could seize hold of, attacked the soldiers at once. The tumult caused by this unexpected engagement attracted the attention of others; windows and doors opened, and men, women and children, threw themselves, armed as they best could, on the assailants. Furniture and crockery of every kind were hurled at the enemy, even young girls forgot their timidity, and ran down to the streets half dressed, to join in the commotion. One of them, a girl called Clara Wanray, seized a trumpet and blew a blast as loud as she could. The noise terrified the assailants, who meeting with so much resistance where they expected to find an easy victory, and thrown into disorder by the blows showered on them whichever way they turned, fled to the river side and scrambled into their boats. But the boats being over-loaded foundered, and the next morning a hundred corpses were seen floating in the water.

Among them was the body of Martin Schenk. The inhabitants, not content with knowing their enemy dead, revenged themselves for the night's unexpected attack by dividing the body into four portions and publicly exposing them till the governor of the town, the Marquis de Verambon, had them gathered together and placed in a tower.

Before the town would return to its submission to the States, Prince Maurice was obliged to besiege it in person. Even then the rebellious town held out for the space of three months, although it had no hope of success from any quarter, before it would consent to an honourable capitulation, which took place in October 1591.

Then again in 1672, when the French invaded the country, it was just the same. Nymegen was attacked among the first towns, but it did not surrender till forced, and even then its magistrates obtained every concession in its favour, possible to be granted.

Now it must not be imagined that these magistrates, who spoke with so much dignity when conversing with the enemy, who stipulated so firmly for honourable conditions, and who obliged the vanquishers to respect the vanquished, were always respected by the citizens of Nymegen.

In 1702, to quote only one instance, when the death of William III. was announced, the people demanded a change of magistrates and the municipal body. The result was a great tumult; the old body, backed up by the States, protested, but the populace seized them at the doors of the Town Hall, and publicly decapitated the burgomaster of highest rank, William Ronkens, and hung a few others on the windows of the *Stadhuis*.

This happened on the 7th and 8th August, 1705, and the place is still shown where these summary executions were carried out, for the *façade* of the Town Hall has not been altered since the building was first erected in 1554. As its date will indicate, its style is very simple, but very elegant and very characteristic. Besides Nymegen was rich enough in the sixteenth century to afford handsome edifices.

Three centuries earlier, William II., its sovereign, who was Count twenty years, and seven years king, had pledged the town for the enormous sum of 21,000 silver marks. In 1554, having again become an imperial town, belonging to the Hanseatic league, and 'given to commerce,' it could well afford to expend largely. Hence the Town Hall was erected in freestone, composed of a ground floor and one above, and with seven front windows to each story. Those on the ground floor were secured by formidable gratings of iron which still exist, though from the very first a needless precaution. They are surmounted by a graceful attic, above which is a head carved in high relief. The windows in the upper story are very simple in style and almost square, above which again is a large entablature, ornamented with a series of medallions representing the busts of those emperors who were benefactors to the town.

On entering, there is a large vestibule or hall, in

the form of a lengthened parallelogram, at the upper end of which are the seats of the ancient tribunal.

These seats, about three centuries old, are raised a few steps in order to permit the judges occupying them to command the rest of the hall. Below the steps is a balustrade, where the advocates plead. Above the presidential throne stands the figure of Justice, with the traditional attributes, and the inscription: UTRAMQUE PARTEM AUDITE at its feet. Three fine doors framed in beautiful carved woodwork complete the architectural decoration of this noble hall.

In this room there is also a very curious clock, a master-piece of mechanism besides being a very elegant looking object. It marks the years, months, days, hours, minutes, and seconds, and could for a very little, mark also the age of the magistrates, the number of inhabitants, and the total of deaths and marriages. It is decorated at the top with a miniature belfry, and in the centre with the signs of the zodiac, encircled with legends with indiscreet allusions, to which we must add a picture, bearing the peculiar title of 'The Nymegen Enigma,' representing a young girl who, by a series of matrimonial combinations, is found to be the mother, grandmother, daughter, aunt, and sister of her father's children. Words cannot adequately express the idea of the grand beauty of this vast hall.

Besides this vestibule, the ground floor contains a secretary's office, tapestried in Cordova leather, the burgomaster's room wainscoted all round in rich carving of a fine style, the marriage-hall, and the council-room. Although the latter were occupied at the moment of our visit with the municipal elections, the burgomaster kindly allowed us to enter and examine them. Both are hung with old tapestry of the most beautiful workmanship, and each contains one of those ancient monumental fireplaces, the mantelpiece of which is ornamented with allegorical paintings, and rests on two columns of black marble. Thus decorated these apartments have a rich municipal air, which I might almost call, august.

On the first floor is the museum, a collection of antiquities, carefully arranged in a well-lighted handsome room. It is approached by a long corridor, ornamented with Roman remains and fragments of inscriptions, let into the wall as in the lapidary gallery in the Vatican. The various objects composing the museum have been gathered together from the neighbourhood or from the town itself, hence they have a twofold interest. They have been catalogued with the greatest care. Commencing with the polished stone age, the collection continues through the bronze age, of which it has a few interesting specimens. Then comes a goodly array of Norman remains, cinerary urns, fine dishes, pretty cups, lamps, and bowls, and a curiosity of some note, consisting of a mask in whitish clay on the sides of which the holes intended to hold the strings are still visible. Of the group appertaining to bronze, we have rings, hooks, statuettes, emblematic animals, amulets, toys, pots, vases, covers and basins, which remind one of Pompeii and its inexhaustible treasures. Two of the basins are very beautiful, one being fluted, the other engraved, the frieze representing a curious incident in hunting. Then come bronze lamps, bells, mirrors, keys, a great many medallions, and arms which are very rare, also rings, seals, engraved stones, bored stones, and a mass of things in ivory, such as were always left behind after every Roman occupation.

A rather surprising fact is, that the mediæval age, the epoch of Nymegen's true grandeur, is poorly represented in this museum.

With the exception of a few *Iakohakannetjes*, a few arms covered with rust, seals, and some old charters, there is nothing to speak of, but an old embroidered banner or curtain of very remarkable workmanship.

The Renaissance period is more fruitful. First we have a series of sandstones of peculiar form and detail, and a few painted glasses; next the treasures of the Guilds, emblems, goblets, drinking horns covered with medals, presidential vestments heavy with embroidery, and standards, even books for mass and account books. Among the prayer books is one belonging to the bakers, a magnificent missal dated 1482, richly ornamented with beautiful miniatures, also an account book of the blacksmiths containing the very useful bit of advice, always to choose secretaries from those who could write a good hand.

The municipal treasures, kept in another case, include burgomaster's sceptres, a pelerine formed of pieces of money, the signification of which I have forgotten, halberds, the throne of William V., and two curious instruments called *Houtenrok*, which I will explain presently.

In a room on the upper floor we were shown a picture, attributed to Rubens, representing a king called David. We were also shown a view of Nymegen, and of the *Valckhof*, supposed to be by Van Goyen, but which I think is more likely to have been painted by one of his pupils; a portrait of William III., and two large allegories, one signed by Stevens-Palamedsz, the other by Rutger Van Langevelt (1670), who I confess I never heard of before as a painter; he was born in Nymegen, and died in Berlin in 1695, at sixty years of age.

The allegories represent the imperial city acquitting herself of her dues *vis-à-vis* to the empire. These dues consisted, according to Guicciardini, of a glove full of pepper, which had to be forwarded to Aix-la-Chapelle each year; but Frederic Sandius gives another explanation of these dues. He speaks not of a glove full of pepper, but of a pair of deerskin gloves, and two pounds of pepper, which the town was obliged to send each year, not to Aix-la-Chapelle, but to Liege to be free of 'toll' on the Meuse.

In this same room there are also portraits of some of the plenipotentiaries who signed the famous treaty of Nymegen, — Sir William Temple, d'Estrath, William Van Haren, Bevernink, Bevilaqua, and a person of unamiable mien, who, according to the inscription in the corner, was 'een der vier ambassadeurs van Spanje' (one of the four Spanish ambassadors), most probably John Baptiste Christyn, afterwards Chancellor of Brabant.

The portraits of the others are not very amiable looking, and a glance at them enables us to understand the etiquette and ceremonial complications which arose, and thereby lengthened the negotiations into two years' duration,—difficulties which Temple designated 'impertinences.'

In order to completely realise the absurdities and weaknesses of a body of clever men, each one more susceptible of his own dignity than the other, one must read the history of the diplomatic campaign from beginning to end, not forgetting that while the nice questions of etiquette were being decided in Nymegen war was ravaging the country, towns were being bombarded, villages pillaged, and blood flowing. But not even the roar of cannon, or the flames of conflagration were able to rouse these diplomatists from their cool serenity. No wonder Temple exclaimed that 'the interests of those who govern are always different to the interests of those who are governed!'

Our visit to the Town Hall over, we were taking leave of the burgomaster, when our *cicerone* called our attention to a large press on the ground floor, which we had not hitherto noticed. It contains the deeds of the town, and is an enormous wooden piece of furniture, lined with iron, and bristling with bars of steel, locks, and padlocks. It can only, it appears, be opened by a clever locksmith after many hours' labour. Formerly, when one of the documents it contains was needed for consultation, the municipal body met together, the garrison was called out, doors were closed, and artillerymen placed along the ramparts by the side of their pieces; because it contained the deeds and privileges of the ancient powerful city, of which the other towns were jealous, and which in themselves were likely to rouse their covetousness. First, there was the Grand Charter signed by Henry VII., August 31, 1230, conceding to Nymegen the same rights and privileges that Aix-la-Chapelle and those cities favoured by the empire had received from their predecessors, and the power to freely send forth their merchandise and goods, either by water or land to every part of the empire. Confirmed by Richard, King of the Romans, in 1257, it was added to by the Emperor Rodolph I., in 1282, who secured his dear inhabitants of Nymegen [1] from all molestations, arrestations, and armed attacks; and by Henry VII. also, who in 1316 accorded to them the right of pronouncing sentences without appeal.

But it would take us too long to enumerate all the emperors, kings, dukes and princes who conferred privileges on the town, and added to its grandeur and power—each one relaxing in its favour

---

[1] 'Delecti cives Nri Noviomagenses.'

their usual demands; even Turenne, who in the articles accorded to the burgomasters, magistrates, council, and citizens of the town of Nymegen, July 9, 1672, conceded to the inhabitants the power of 'remaining in town, to return or go out without molestation to their goods or their persons,' and decided that the 'artillery belonging to the town should remain to guard it, and should not be transported without the consent of the magistrates.'

And now for a word of explanation on the *houtenrokken* (wooden petticoats). These singular things are in the form of a barrel, narrower at the top than at the base, painted with every imaginable colour, and decorated with the arms of the town, also furnished with an iron collar and chains. They were taken to the market-place, where girls who had gone wrong were stripped and put into these 'petticoats,' and then marched round the town in the midst of a crowd of wags and noisy persons of all sorts. Bad women were treated much more severely, for they were stripped of their clothing, and placed in open barred cages and the populace were encouraged to pelt them with dirt and injurious expressions.

Now, however, these barbarous customs are no longer in existence, and Nymegen has become, on these special points, very much more civilised than it was formerly. We were anxious to know more on this head, but unfortunately we could find no one able to inform us on the subject.

The market-place where these punishments were

NIMWEGEN (THE GREAT MARKET-PLACE).

performed is called the *Groote markt*, and a very pretty, dainty place it is, with its bordering of old houses, and pointed gables. At one corner is the 'Weigh-house,' used now as a guard-room—a very handsome square building with an ornamented gable, dating from the beginning of the seventeenth century. Close by is a house divided at the base into two large bays, surmounted by a surbased arch, dating at latest from the fifteenth century. Above this portico is a building of about a hundred years later date, but graceful in outline, and interesting to study.

It was through this curious door that we reached the place where St. Stephen stands, a narrow pent-up place enclosed by a double row of houses all in a dilapidated condition, but very picturesque in appearance.

The one which attracted us most was the Grammar School. It is two stories high, and surmounted by a large roof. Each story has eleven windows, and each of the windows, bowed with a surbased arch, was formerly separated from the other by an elegant statue, standing on a wide console. These statues were placed there in 1544, and marked the completion of the building, but were destroyed, or rather mutilated, at the time of the Reformation. The consoles also are in a very sad state, as also the beautifully traced frieze forming a graceful finish to the *façade*.

This building is not the only one which has suffered from the lapse of time in this little corner of the town. Its neighbour, the large church of St. Stephen, has fallen a victim to the same cause, as its decaying walls, crumbling under the wind and worn away by the damp, amply prove. And I do not see how it could be otherwise, when one takes into consideration that the softness and want of consistence of the stone with which it was outwardly protected, was not of a nature to resist the influence of the weather; hence the reason for the holes caused by wind and rain being stopped up with brick walls.

According to old chronicles St. Stephen was built in the thirteenth century. William, King of the Romans, recognising that the parish situated outside the walls (no doubt the chapel of the castle) had grave drawbacks, resolved in 1254 to erect a church in the centre of the city, giving for the purpose the necessary piece of land—an ancient cemetery where Christians were buried, it is said, during the early days of Christianity. The sanctuary was erected in 1273, and on 7th September, Albert the Great, Bishop of Ratisbonne, consecrated it to the Virgin and to St. Stephen.

The greater part of the church as we now see it does not date earlier than the fifteenth or sixteenth century. It has very noble proportions on the whole, spoiled slightly by the timber roof which has replaced the former fine vaulting. It has an immense nave with large aisles, and the transept with its aisles terminates in a porch at the west end, formerly ornamented with carving, but which even now has a very bold and elegant appearance. The Chapels around the circumference are all of pentagon form. There is nothing left of the *façade* but the tower, and that, perhaps, is the only original portion of the church left. It stands on a small sloping hill, formerly a cemetery, where weeds and grass grow undisturbed now, and commands perpendicularly a small narrow street, where the houses seem to be inclining in front of the old church—as if on their knees, a situation which has an original and picturesque effect.

The interior of St. Stephen contains several ancient bas-reliefs, injured at the time of the Reformation, and daubed over with plaster, but for all that very graceful and fine; and several good carved wainscotings of the early part of the seventeenth century, as well as the vast mausoleum of Catherine of Bourbon, mother of the last Duke of Guelderland, and wife of that Adolf whose sad memory was so dear to the citizens of Nymegen.

This mausoleum is formed of an immense cube of black marble, very simply ornamented with a few mouldings, and decorated with engraved bronze plates. These plates, one on each of the four sides, represent saintly personages, interspersed with the arms of the powerful families of Valois, Bourbon, and of Egmont, Dukes of Guelderland. The upper slab holds the effigy of the sweet princess, who not being brought prominently forward in history, seemed to have passed unnoticed amongst all the terrible deeds accomplished around her.

It was at the Court of her brother-in-law, Charles the Bold, that she met young Count Egmont, who fell in love with her and married her. According to Philip de Comines it was 'Sunday, 18th December, 1463, that the town of Bruges witnessed at the hotel, at the expense of the Duke of Burgundy, the marriage of Monseigneur Adolphus, only son of Arnault, Duke of Guelderland, with Catherine, daughter of the Duchess of Bourbon. The Count of Charolois was at Rotterdam, and the Countess at the Hague, where she entertained this same Adolphus on the 25th December, who had gone to pay her a visit with his wife.' She was called the 'Young Madame of Guelderland.' For a long time she stayed at the Court of Burgundy, where she was tenderly loved. But when her husband was excommunicated by Paul II., put under the ban of the empire, and menaced by the Duke of Cleves and her own brother-in-law, Charles the Bold, she returned to his side to share his fate.

She died at Nymegen in 1469, and on 22nd May her body was laid in the church of St. Stephen.

But she was not allowed to remain undisturbed under the bronze cover, and the same fatality followed her in death which had weighed so heavily on her in life.

The mausoleum was opened a few years ago, when it was found that the remains of the poor princess had been enclosed in a box and put in a corner, to make room for a Duke of Saxony, dressed in full robes and lying in a large coffin.

One might almost say that it was for her Virgil wrote his famous '*sic vos non vobis*,' and Ovid the verse he addressed to the manes of Tibullus :—

> Ossa quieta, precor, tuta requiescite in urna.

CHAPTER XX.

GRAVE—DUKE ARNOLD—THE DEFENCE OF GRAVE BY CHAMILLY—CARNOT'S MAXIM—THE CHURCH OF ST. ELIZABETH—THE CHARNEL HOUSE.

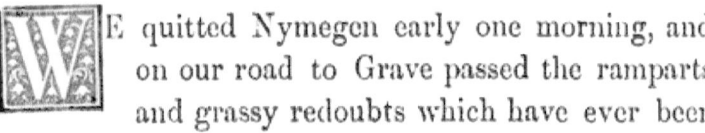E quitted Nymegen early one morning, and on our road to Grave passed the ramparts and grassy redoubts which have ever been the pride and glory of the town, and which extend for a considerable distance towards the plain.

The English Sévigné, Lady Mary Wortley Montague, while travelling in the country during the last century, had her attention first directed to these grand fortifications, and on her tablets she wrote concerning them: 'Those learned in the arts of war praise them highly.' A phrase which did not compromise her much.

Beyond the fortifications, the landscape has quite another aspect, and the moment one reaches it one feels one has entered another province. The country is more rugged, trees twist their gnarled branches, golden fields are interspersed with patches of heath, and broad clearings announce the presence of sandy soil, where harvests are only reaped after interminable labour.

If the aspect of the country is changed to a certain degree, the population seems transformed in the most absolute manner. Along the highway women are to be seen carrying panniers of vegetables, or baskets of fruit, which rest on a sort of pad attached to their waists—while they walk they talk, and while they talk they gesticulate, which gives them a very animated appearance. Their hair is darker than that of their neighbours, and their complexion is browner, and the expression in their faces more changeable, and the glance of their eye much brighter. An animation rarely seen in the women of Guelderland, or of the southern provinces, charms one here at every turn. The toilette, too, of this province differs in a very marked degree from that of the one we had just left. The gown is large, heavily plaited, and with puffed sleeves, as worn in Belgium; and the gilded casque with the cap and black headband have yielded to a large voluminous sort of cap, which is sometimes black and sometimes white, often trimmed with lace, but never very becoming or graceful in appearance.

A two hours' drive brought us to the Meuse—and Grave is situated on the opposite side. As we drew near we thought its aspect corresponded well with its past glorious history. High brick walls, topped with mounds of green, almost entirely conceal from view the roofs of the houses and a steeple in ruins, while right and left the bastions extend in formidable array. At their feet the Meuse rolls along in silvery beauty.

The river is traversed by means of a ferry-boat, as at Nymegen. When we took our places, in company with some of the neighbouring people going over to the market, we could not help thinking of the disguised soldiers who surprised Zutphen. 'Dressed as common peasants, they stood at break of day before the gate of the fortress, loaded with butter, eggs, and cheese, like ordinary countrymen, waiting for the opening of the gates to enter.'

Truly generations succeed each other, but habits and customs remain.

We disembarked at the foot of the ramparts, passed under a dark resounding arch; followed the winding of a little street, and then suddenly found ourselves in the heart of the little city, in the important part too, where the chief monuments are to be seen, or rather those which are still left:—the Town Hall, a 'respectable edifice' as it is described, and a large portion of the ancient St. Elizabeth.

Most of the houses are of modern construction, the oldest among them being scarcely a century in age; and yet Grave is by no means a modern town. It existed in the thirteenth century, and even at that time was a freehold of the family van Cuyck, one of the oldest in Brabant. In 1322, Otto, seigneur of Cuyck and Heverlee, presented it to John III., Duke of Brabant, who restored it to him the following year under form of a fief, that he might enjoy its privileges according to the custom of the Duchy.

Later on the Dukes of Guelderland laid claim to the sovereignty of Grave, and took possession of a castle in the town as their residence. This castle was a huge square building, surrounded by a ditch of deep water bordering a long wall flanked by four turrets. It was destroyed in the bombardment of 1674. Its exterior appearance had nothing very grand about it judging from old views of it, but the interior must have been richly decorated, for we hear at various times of illustrious visitors staying within its walls. In 1460 Mary, Queen of Scotland, paid the castle a visit, and was ill there, for a paper, found among the archives of Arnhem, informed us 'that in that year J. Adriaenss, the apothecary, was sent to Grave by order of the Duke, with medicines prescribed by M. Philips for the Queen of Scotland, who was ill.' No doubt both the doctor and apothecary were clever men, for the princess did not die till four years afterwards at Bruges, where the 'Duke of Burgundy assisted at the obsequies of the Queen of Scotland, in the church of Saint Donas.'

While the poor queen was dying at Bruges, a sad tragedy was being performed at the castle of Grave. The old Duke of Guelderland, her father, overcome with grief at his daughter's sad fate, retired to his favourite residence to indulge in his grief, where he was joined by his son, the ambitious Count Adolf, with whom he was on terms of estrangement, but who now sought a reconciliation.

The old Duke opened his heart and his house to his son. 'But this reconciliation,' says Comines, 'was only a pretence, for Prince Adolf, while pursuing his mother contrary to all filial feelings, endeavoured to apprehend his father, and to undertake the government.'

One evening, the Duke having finished his usual game of chess, his son proposed his having a dance with the ladies. But the old man refused, and expressed a wish to retire to his room. He did so, and then the ball began. Under cover of the noise of the music and dancing, accomplices were introduced within the castle, who hurried towards the Duke's chamber, where they knocked against the door as if they would break it in. The Duke cried out from his bed :—' Children, let me alone to sleep ; I cannot dance to-night, another time I will try.' Whereupon the men burst open the door, and with drawn swords ordered him to surrender himself prisoner. The Duke, seeing this, immediately asked for his son, for the poor man feared that harm had happened to him, and that the men were come to take them both. The prince appeared and said : ' My father, you must surrender yourself a prisoner—it must be done.' The old Duke looked at the prince with tears in his eyes, and replied : ' My son, what do you want ?' I have given this simple account as I found it, for few pages in history are more touching.

The old Duke did not return to the castle he loved so well, and from which he had been dragged so mercilessly, till nine years later, when he died. He was buried in the church, and a monument was raised to his memory, which is still to be seen there.

The next guest of note who visited the castle was Charles the Bold, who confirmed all the privileges hitherto enjoyed by the brave little town from his predecessors, which was a sensible mode of making himself agreeable to the inhabitants, for, an author of the last century tells us that, 'at that time, the burghers of Grave had so many privileges that a stranger esteemed it an honour to marry one of the maidens of the city, without any other dowry than the right to be enrolled himself among the burghers.'

This town, at the period we mention, was regarded as the key to the whole country, and the people of Brabant attached so much importance to its possession that their sovereign dukes were obliged to swear on their succession that they would never give up their pretentions to Grave. And, in spite of its annexation by Charles the Bold, the town with its domains returned to the Dukes of Brabant, from whom it passed into the hands of William III.; and, later on, was confiscated by the Duke of Alva, as an appanage of a rebel prince.

Retaken by the Earl of Leicester, and cowardly defended by the seigneur of Hémert,[1] who later on

---

[1] Hémert and two of his captains, Banck and Korf, were arrested in Utrecht, tried, and executed for the crime of cowardice.

paid dearly for his want of courage, the town fell back into the hands of the Spaniards, who kept it till 1604. That same year Prince Maurice besieged it in person, and after a siege of two months took possession of it, where he exhibited his customary skill, of which Blaeu, in one of his fine engravings, has preserved the history and the plans. In 1672 Turenne succeeded in taking the town after only a few days' assault. A part of the garrison had been ordered to assist Bois-le-Duc, which was supposed would be attacked. When they returned the place was invested, and they themselves were completely routed and cut to pieces.

The French troops did not occupy Grave for longer than two years, but when they quitted it the little town of only three thousand inhabitants had made itself signally famous by the heroic siege it had just undergone. The Marquis de Chamilly had been charged with the defence of the place, having command over 4,000 men and three hundred and twenty-five pieces of cannon. The troops of Louis XIV. by withdrawing had left the town undefended, and Rabenhaupt, the victor of Koevorden, besieged it in the early part of July.

By the kind intervention of a Flemish literary man, we were enabled to walk along the ramparts, and retrace for ourselves the history, day by day, of that splendid defence, which Napoleon considered one of the finest feats of arms of modern times, and to read over again on the bastions themselves the correspondence carried on between the hostile generals.

This correspondence was begun in the most courteous manner, after the fashion of Fontenoy. 'It will not be my fault,' wrote Rabenhaupt, on the 23rd July, 'if we do not conduct well the business we have in hand.' To which Chamilly replied on the same day: 'I would rather have to do with you than another, for I hope I shall have it in my power to gain the esteem of so gallant a man as yourself.'

But amiabilities of this kind do not last long. The siege continued for a month, and then seeing that the troops could not approach the place, and that the soldiers were disheartened by the vigorous defence of the garrison, the Dutch general counselled his adversary to capitulate: 'If you do, matters will be more advantageously arranged now than at a future time. Consider this, and that I should be grieved if harm befell such a brave man as you.' To which Chamilly indignantly replied: 'It is exactly for that very reason that I counsel you with all respect to be off at once instead of later, and by no means to await unhappy extremities.'

Rabenhaupt lost his patience, and bombarded Grave. The castle was destroyed, the church fell in, and the houses were burnt; and then Chamilly, overcome by a touch of humanity, did his best to save the women and children by demanding for them to be allowed to pass out of the town. Rabenhaupt refused in arrogant terms, and finished his letter with the remark: 'You should avoid offending the States General.' To which the Governor replied by a witty jest: 'I had allowed the women who wished to withdraw to pass out; you have sent them back, and I received them willingly, wanting for nothing to subsist them and ourselves; besides which we have gallantry enough for both, and we are not therefore surprised that, at your age, you have been unwilling to receive them.'

The bombardment not having the desired effect of making the town capitulate, Rabenhaupt tried another plan. He softened his tone, and transmitted to the governor the alarming news that several French troops were in possession of the neighbouring country. 'You have done all that a brave governor could do,' said he, 'and you have been splendidly supported by your garrison. I am ready to acknowledge this publicly, for you deserve all the praise you can get.' But this mode of proceeding had no more effect than the former. Chamilly replied that he had not yet done enough to merit the esteem of his adversary, expressed a doubt about the news he had had transmitted to him, and finished by begging to have the *Holland Gazette* sent him: 'I don't suppose,' he added, 'you doubt it yourself.' On the 9th October Rabenhaupt wrote again, but this time exasperated beyond measure: 'The intentions of the High and Powerful States General are such, that you had better try and merit some quarter at their hands. For my part, I tell you plainly that your obstinacy will prevent my asking anything for you.' To which the Governor replied with indignant haughtiness: 'I will accept quarter from neither them nor you. I shall await you at the passage of our outer trench; there, you and I will know what to do.'

This noble energetic provocation closed the correspondence.

Chamilly received one more letter, not from the enemy's camp, but from Louis XIV. It was a formal order to capitulate.

'Monsieur de Chamilly,' wrote the king, 'the stout resistance you, and the officers of my troops of the garrison of Grave, have hitherto offered to the enemy, gives me the greatest satisfaction; but I have resolved not to lose so many of my brave soldiers, preferring their lives to any advantage to be gained from a longer resistance.' Then followed the conditions of the surrender, and the letter finished: 'Understanding that if these conditions are not granted, you will defend the town to the best of your ability, and carry matters on to the very extreme you judge it right to do.'

For a moment Chamilly hoped the conditions would be rejected. But exacting as the demands were, they were not refused. The siege had already cost the besiegers sixteen thousand men, without their being in a position to lay claim to the least advantage, and the Prince of Orange was forced to be present in person. 'But for the ardour of the Prince, who led on the assault and encouraged the men by his presence when they were unsteady,' the soldiers would have refused to move.

When he knew for certain that the conditions had been accepted the poor Governor was in despair. 'What!' he cried, 'give up a place to the enemy, when they have not even gained one advantage over us.' Nevertheless the capitulation was of the most honourable kind. In fact it was a sort of homage rendered to both men and chief. The first article was to the effect: 'That the garrison should march out with arms, horses, and baggage, drums beating and colours flying;' and the rest was in keeping. The besiegers sent up carriages for the sick and wounded, conveyed the artillery as far as Charleroi, furnished an escort to the garrison, distributed rations on the road at the expense of the States, gave up the prisoners without any ransom, and granted a general amnesty to the whole of the inhabitants.

Thus Chamilly justified the military maxim which Carnot formulated a hundred years later: 'In the defence of strong places, valour and industry cannot dispense the one with the other; united they can accomplish everything.'

St. Simon has given us a description of Chamilly as 'a large tall man, the best, the bravest, the most honourable, but so stupid and so dull, that one can scarcely understand he had any talent for war;' which testimony is a little open to doubt, for Chamilly said twenty witty things, and performed striking actions during the memorable siege, which placed him in the front rank of the most brilliant officers.

One day whilst dining, he was informed that the enemy had seized a trench, but not one of much importance. Chamilly rose immediately, asked for his sword, and said to his officers : ' Up, gentlemen, we will go and dislodge the enemy and then return here for dessert.' He went out and chose five hundred picked men, ordered the gates to be thrown open, and precipitated himself like an avalanche on Rabenhaupt's soldiers, routed them, dislodged them from the trenches, killed half of them, and drove the rest, sword in hand, as far as the outworks of the States' army. An hour later he returned, and finished his dinner as if nothing had happened.

Another time, about seven o'clock in the evening, the Prince of Orange had headed in person an attack on one of the outposts, which he took. The outpost had been bravely and energetically defended, and two Captains, de Morinval and Gonthier, of the Normandy regiment, were killed in the work itself. The news was carried to Chamilly, and the officer he was conversing with at the moment, seeing him turn suddenly pale, observed : ' But will you not lose something, sir, after three months of trenches ? ' ' No,' he replied, ' I shall dislodge them presently.' And dislodge them he did.

On his return to France he was received by the king, who complimented him upon his brilliant doings, and requested him to demand a favour. Chamilly might have obtained a title, rank, or wealth; but he contented himself with begging for the release of his old Colonel, at that time a prisoner in the Bastile. He knew that his request would irritate the king and retard his own advancement, but he did not mind that; he listened only to the dictates of his kind heart, and pressed his demand to be granted. The consequence was, he was not made Marshal till 1703, when ten others had the same honour conferred on them,—' in the fear of omitting him,' as Saint Simon remarks.

The next siege of the citadel of Grave was in 1794. But this time the rôle was changed, it being the Dutch who occupied the town, and the French who besieged it. On the 13th October the enemy invested it; on the 7th November the garrison was called upon to surrender. To which General van Bons replied as became a loyal soldier: ' The place confided to me is in a good state, the garrison is full of ardour and bravery, and I hope to prove myself worthy of its command.' The siege was carried on with redoubled vigour. December 7th there was a fresh summons to surrender, and a fresh refusal; on the 10th the bombardment commenced. The 20th December the inhabitants besought the governor to capitulate, he refused stoutly; on the 23rd some French soldiers picked up five or six bottles, which had been thrown into the Meuse, each containing the following touching appeal: ' We, the burghers and citizens of Grave, entreat that a trumpeter may be sent to us. We assure you the town will be surrendered on his arrival; otherwise we shall all be reduced to the most extreme poverty. *Signed:* The citizens of Grave.' The following day, the 24th, van Bons hoisted the white flag.

Hence it can well be understood that the town of Grave cannot be very rich in old monuments and ancient houses. The most ancient building of all is the church of St. Elizabeth, which bears traces of the heroic struggles we have just been recounting. Commenced in 1290, it has had a most checkered architectural existence, for so early as the fifteenth century the choir had to be reconstructed, owing to its destruction by fire. In 1674 the roof of the nave fell in, during the bombardment of the town by Rabenhaupt. The nave was never rebuilt, and the opening to the transept was closed in by a straight wall, thus separating the choir from the tower as at Utrecht. In 1794 the church was slightly injured in the bombardment by the French, but no extensive damage was done, beyond splitting the walls and spoiling the mausoleum of old Duke Arnold. At last, in September 1874, a fire broke out in the steeple, which finished the destruction the bombardments had begun. Now it is a grand venerable pile of ruins, the majestic appearance of which, seems to relate from a distance, the sad series of disasters which have reduced it to its present state.

The interior of St. Elizabeth still contains several good pieces of carving. The pulpit, although designed in the affected style of Bernini, is very beautiful. The altar belongs to that pompous style in vogue during the latter half of the eighteenth century, of which the church *dei Gesuiti* in Rome is the finished prototype. But the splendour here is illusive, for the marbles are painted wood, and the gold is in leather. Everything is a copy, even to the picture above the principal altar, which is said to be by Van Dyck.

With the exception of a small Flemish painting dated 1528, and a memorial panel of a certain Jacob van Haen, all the paintings, seemed to us, to be very mediocre indeed.

The mausoleum of old Duke Arnold of Guelderland is worse however. It was built in 1493, destroyed in 1794, and then rebuilt in 1802 in the 'troubadour' style of that time. The pyramid itself, with the casques, swords, and flags which decorate it, seems still more ridiculous when one thinks of the 'poor old man in tears' who reposes beneath this pompous show of arms.

On the exterior Saint Elizabeth is enclosed by the walls of an ancient monastery, the ruins of which have been converted into a kind of *Campo Santo*. Here vegetation has grown abundantly, creeping plants twine along the crumbling walls, and cling to the jutting arches and antique consoles which formerly supported the shafts of the vaults. Peeping out from beneath the plants one perceives several large memorial slabs in blue stone, with either figures or arms on them, sculptured in bas-relief, and in a corner of this enclosure there is a ridiculous phantasmagorical imitation of purgatory in earthenware, which has been turned into a regular charnel house. There the refuse, if one may so term it, of the cemetery is collected, till it is almost full of human remains—blanched skulls, arm and leg bones are all thrown in there indiscriminately, the mass perhaps representing about ten generations; sex and age have no distinction in that terrible receptacle, and if Chamilly and the brave van Bons could return to this earth, they would certainly not be able to distinguish their own soldiers, or know one from another.

CHAPTER XXI.

THE MOOKERHEIDE — VENLO — ST. MARTIN — VANITAS VANITATUM — AN AMBITIOUS INSCRIPTION — THE CELEBRATED SONS OF VENLO.

N quitting Grave, we went up the Meuse towards Venlo. The passage is rather pleasant, though a little long perhaps, especially as there was nothing interesting about it; still one can always find something worth seeing or knowing when one is determined so to do. The passage is made on one of those small steamers going from Rotterdam to Maëstricht, taking from two to three days to accomplish the journey. The society on board was somewhat limited, and amusements were *nil*; but then, on the other hand, the windings of the river and its verdure-clad banks occupied one's attention entirely.

Grave, in fact, is surrounded by far stretching meadows interspersed with shady walks and bordered by grand old trees. These rich pasture lands, which Blaeu celebrated for their fertility and verdure, are found more on the left than on the right side of the river. On the opposite bank, just after passing the first bend of the Meuse, and beyond the pretty village of Mook, are perceived those arid eminences covered with wild heath, which bear the sinister name of Mookerheide, a name very lugubrious in Dutch ears, for it reminds them of a terrible defeat, and of the death of three brave noble men.

It was on this very heath that Counts Louis and Henry of Nassau, and Prince Christopher, the son of the Elector Palatinate, were surprised by the Spaniards and massacred, without the cause, for this terrible misfortune, ever becoming known. There is no hope now of elucidating the mystery, for the historians of the time could not agree on the subject, and those who have followed have differed just as widely from each other, although they have had at their command every document that has been written about it.

Rheidanus thinks that, deceived by the spies and not knowing that the enemy had crossed the Meuse at Grave, the Count was surprised in an unfavourable position.

Grotius attributes his defeat to the mutiny of his troops, who, in face of the enemy, clamoured for their pay. According to Meteren, the Count had scattered his soldiers too much; the different corps being so far apart he could not concentrate them in time. But one and all, even the Spanish historians Bentivoglio and Strada, agree that the bravery and courage of the chiefs was irreproachable. All mourned these three noble men, who fought to the death, and were so confounded in the mêlée with their brave soldiers, that their bodies could not be found afterwards.

After passing Mookerheide, the banks of the two rivers regain their smiling aspect, among meadows, fields and clumps of trees; then come the villages Middelaar, Oeffelt, Heijen, Afferden, and Bergen, with their pointed steeples; from time to time a ruin is passed, and then we see a convent with nuns, which indicates to us in a moment how very much we have changed in latitude, that we are, in fact, in Catholic Guelderland. As we advance, the difference becomes more marked, until at last Venlo appears in the distance concealed behind her huge half-demolished bastions, and with the remains of her old walls and a few new houses extending along the river side.

One cannot call Venlo a handsome town; it has no fine squares or beautiful promenades, or excellent boulevards; its streets have no buildings of any note, neither are they very broad or well-arranged, but such as it is, this kindly little town possesses a special interest for the archæologist, inasmuch as it marks a very sudden transition line. To pass beyond her walls is to enter quite a new region; the province of Limbourg is the only one which does not, as it were, form a part of the whole, for it has neither the same religion nor the same traditions, and we can add, neither the same manners, nor the same language as the sister provinces. It is Netherland at heart quite as much as the others, but it has the appearance of forming the rear guard to this generous country in a special, peculiar, and original manner, and to have placed itself there with its extenuating differences to round off the sharp edge of transition. One finds again and again among the populations of these frontier towns the grand qualities inherent in the Batavian race; and while they repudiate most energetically all Germanic characteristics, they have not hesitated to adopt many manners and customs from the neighbouring provinces, who, up to the end of last century, were under the Austrian sceptre, although they bore the name of the Low Countries.

Venlo is by no means an ancient town, in spite of some saying that it was founded in the year 95 by a noble, rich and powerful seigneur named Valuas; the truth is that the first mention made of the town was not till the year 900, when it figured among the deeds of Wichard de Pont, attorney of Guelderland. Then its archives, although complete and in perfect order, and quite at our disposal in our researches, make no mention of it till the year 1272, when we found out that it was in possession of a judge (*rechter*), magistrates, and burghers. Another document, dated August 18, 1339, makes mention of its burgomasters and magistrates, and of its council. But Venlo was then only a village (*dorp*), and it was not till September, 1343, that it attained to the dignity of a town, by the grace of Duke Renault, third of his name, who enclosed it with walls and endowed it with privileges.

As regards its name, the linguists of the country

affirm that it is derived, not from the doubtful Valuas, but from a Dutch word—*veen*, signifying marsh, and from *lo* which in olden times signified wood or forests, as for example in a distich of Walther van Vogelweide's of the thirteenth century:—

> Sumer mache uns aber fro
> Du zieriest auzer un lo.[1]

Incorporated into the Duchy of Guelderland, Venlo remained faithful to its suzerains, even in time of sorrow. It was besieged by Margaret, aunt of Charles V., and heroically resisted the imperial troops. In 1543, it was united to the crown of Spain, and fell a victim to the fate attending all the towns belonging to that country, of being taken and retaken, occupied now by the troops of the States and then by those of Austria, until the year 1715, when by the Barrier Treaty it was definitely added to the United Provinces.

Thus, subjected to so many assaults, to which we must add one more—the siege of 1794, it is not difficult to imagine that Venlo possesses few uninjured monuments. The large church, the most ancient and venerable building of the town, has suffered perhaps more than many of the smaller edifices. It would be hard to tell now what its plan was

---

[1] 'Summer make us happy:
Thou beautifyest the field and wood.'
In the sixteenth century Folcuin, Prior of Lobbes (Lobach), made use of the same word to explain the etymology of his abbey, which word 'lo,' passed into the Latin tongue became 'laia,' which, translated into French, becomes 'laye.' 'Saint-Germain en Laye' might be translated into 'Saint Germain en forêt' with very plausible reason.

originally. Inaugurated in 1458, by a son of Venlo, William, bishop of Nicopolis and archdeacon of Brünn, it was enrolled under the name of Saint Martin. In the present day it is a large temple with three naves of equal height, surmounted by beautiful arched vaults. The windows are fine, but furnished with modern panes of an agreeable tint. The pulpit is cleverly carved, but in the Louis XV. style; the carved wainscoting around the baptistery belongs to the early years of the seventeenth century; the baptistery itself is of the same period, and is composed of a magnificent piece of bronze in the form of a cup, mounted on a projecting foot and ornamented with heads of angels. The lid is round, surmounted by a group of pinnacles connected by arches intermixed with foliage, forming an arbour, under which Jesus receives from John the Baptist the first holy rite. Above, God the Father appears, pronouncing the words in holy writ, 'This is my Son.'

Saint Martin contains several interesting pictures, but we will speak of them presently.

Close to the church stand a certain number of old houses with very curious *façades*. Like many of the Dutch houses, their gables jut out on the street; sometimes the edge of the gable, instead of being smooth and straight, is curved into very singular form. One *façade* of this kind, dated 1588, with its windows cut under a surbased arch, and with arms and grotesque heads carved in stone, and let into the brick wall, seemed to us to be well worthy of the attention of archæologists. But of perpendicular gabled houses there are very few, most of the buildings being much less pointed in the roof than is generally to be seen in the northern provinces. On the other hand, they are much broader and stand on a larger base. As a rule they are whitewashed or plastered in light colours, and often have in front, either a court-yard, or a small structure with an enormous gateway.

A large number of these porticoes lead down side streets to defaced shaky houses, the ruined walls of which would make the fortune of artists in water-colour. Others lead to ancient places of worship, for Venlo abounds in old churches or chapels; at every step one comes across these consecrated buildings, some transformed into barracks and others into shops. In our anxiety to miss nothing and see all we could, we paid a visit to one of these old chapels converted into a depôt for guano and manure from private dwellings. Need I enlarge on the fearful odour which has replaced the perfume of incense, or on the coarse language of the men resounding through the vaulted chamber, where formerly rich sonorous chants filled the air with harmony? Truly here one can say: 'Vanitas vanitatum.'

While wandering about the town we watched the inhabitants with no little curiosity. As a rule they are pleasant and amiable-looking, with smiling faces and agreeable manners, which disconcerted our preconceived impressions of them, for history has given them a somewhat alarming reputation. We are told that they were fierce and warlike and impatient of the least control, and that when they were not fighting their enemies, they sought subjects for dispute among the garrison, who rarely had the last word. 'These people of Venloo,' writes Francois le Petit, a conscientious chronicler of the sixteenth century, 'are always fighting and irritating soldiers, no matter to which party they belong. I have seen them no less than three times change their garrison, one party just as well as another.' According to whether they belonged to one camp or the other, it was the Italians, Spaniards, English, or Germans whom they attacked. In 1586,[1] the Duke of Parma took the town and placed there a strong garrison, but in 1590 these troops were expelled by the inhabitants, who, 'not content with getting rid of them, heaped abuse of every objectionable kind upon them.' The same thing had occurred ten years before. One ought to read the authors of the time to gain an insight into the doings of the turbulent energetic population, who in more than one way resembled the intractable Nymegeners. The amusements they indulged in will sufficiently indicate their spirit. In 1588 one kind of recreation was the invention of bomb-shells. The people were delighted with a sight of such

[1] In the royal library at the Hague there is an excessively rare engraving giving an account of this siege. It was published in Antwerp in 1586, the same year that Venlo was captured, under the title of 'Beschrijuinghe der Stadt van Venloo.' Under the title is a small vignette, representing the Duke in front of the ramparts of the town.

projectiles bursting in the air, and on each fête-day a large number of them were sold, till it was found out, by half the town being on fire, that such dangerous weapons might be used much more advantageously than as popular amusements.

The inhabitants are not so fierce and war-loving now; on the contrary they are on very good terms with the Dutch army, who possess a school for cavalry in the town. It is also very likely that if the garrison were removed from Venlo many faces would grow sad, and many tears flow.

Towards night we found out a very good reason for this remarkable change in the manners and disposition of the population. We had eaten a detestable dinner, and retired to our rooms to enjoy the rest we merited after our exertions all day, when suddenly we were disturbed by a violent vibration of the windows. Loud sounds of harmony soon reached us, making the walls and ceilings shake; a trombone was rending the air, other brass instruments were resounding with deafening noise, and an ophicleide was bellowing forth its notes in a fashion to drive a musical person mad. We hurried to the window to see what it all meant. The street was narrow, and on the opposite side a company of amateurs, belonging to a philharmonic society, were exercising their lungs to the best of their power, each on his own instrument. Evidently they dispensed by this means of their superfluous warlike propensities, and although there was very little harmony in this music, it nevertheless softened their manners and calmed down their ardour. The concert lasted till midnight. A goodly number of persons had gathered together under the windows, and from time to time proved that they had more correct ears than the would-be musicians, by the remarks they unhesitatingly made use of in loud tones.

The next morning we continued our inspection of the town, still rather tired from the effects of the disturbance of the previous evening. We only had the Town Hall to visit, so we directed our steps thitherward at once. The *stadhuis* of Venlo is built on one side of a square or place very clean and tidily kept, but shockingly paved. This place is enclosed by very simple, but elegant houses, coloured in light yellow or mouse or grey. The municipal building itself has not escaped the process of plastering; but its two octagon turrets and its double flight of stone steps prevent the yellow covering from spoiling it; in fact, on the whole it has a very picturesque appearance. Constructed in 1595, it once formed the residence of Archduke Albert, who left nothing behind him, as a memento of his presence in the house, but a pretentious inscription which proves very forcibly that shyness is not always the most prominent virtue in princes :—

IVSTVS SVBJECTIS, PRVDENS MIHI, FORTIS IN HOSTES
 IMPERO, CONSVLO, STO, LEGIBVS, ORE, MANV.
CLARVS AVO, ALBERTVS, PATRE FRATRE QVE, CÆSARE,
 REGE.
SVM PATRE, REGINA MATRE, ISABELLA SA. T. A.

The interior of this Town Hall was restored in 1609, and then again in the eighteenth century when Venlo was definitely yielded to the United Provinces. It contains only one room of much interest, and that is the *raadzaal* or council chamber, which might with more truth perhaps, be called the hall of the capitulations, for no less than four have been signed within its walls. It is entirely hung in Cordova leather embossed with gold, and decorated with a monumental chimney-piece and several good pictures.

Among the latter, is one representing the last judgment, placed above the entrance, which might very well be attributed to Rubens, and certainly is by one of his pupils. Then comes a portrait of Christ, followed by one of the Virgin belonging to the Florentine School, good well-painted pictures, but unfortunately hung against the light. Then again, there are two curious monuments, of the end of the sixteenth century, or the beginning of the next, which stand in the opposite corner of the chamber. They are enormous scrolls of good design and elegant form, one containing a complicated timepiece which marks everything but the exact hour, the other an allegorical painting, representing Justice and Peace clasping hands. Then, to complete the decoration of the hall, the magistrates of Venlo, like true and faithful citizens, have hung up the portraits of certain celebrated men, born in the town.

First we have Michel Mercator, who I confess I

never heard of, though I have no doubt he was a relative of the famous geographer of that name, buried at Duesbourg. Then comes Hubert Goltzius, a Latin and Greek scholar, who must not be confounded with Hendrik Goltzius the painter, and lastly Ericius Putenaus (or, if one likes, Hendrik Van de Putten, or Henri du Puy), whose works are known to all scholars.

His works on the Ambrosian library of Milan, and on the invasion of the barbarians in Italy, alone would have entitled him to a just amount of fame, if his pamphlet on the royal crown (*Isaaci Casauboni Corona regia*), by bringing upon him the enmity of King James,[1] had not sealed his reputation. So true is it, that a little persecution is a great impetus to becoming famous.

There are two other sons of Venlo whose portraits I should have liked to see hanging in this municipal hall. One is the painter Jan Van Cleef, who ought at least, to have one of his pictures placed against these walls; the other is Foder, the founder of the museum in Amsterdam, bearing his name. Foder was an amateur collector of antiques, and quite widely known enough in the artistic world to have been admitted here on canvas. Although Van Cleef's

---

[1] The angry monarch did not hesitate to claim from his cousin, the Archduke Albert, 'justice and reparation against Iricius Putenaus, professor of the University of Louvain, for the defamatory libel he has dared to write and publish against us, by which he has maliciously damaged our reputation.' Fortunately these demands were not accorded, and Putenaus retained his chair at the University.

portrait does not hang in the Town Hall, and not one of his pictures, he is well represented in the large Church, where two or three of the latter, the 'Annunciation' and 'St. George,' are well placed. As to M. Foder, his native town perhaps is a little jealous, that he should have enriched Amsterdam with a collection which ought to have been handed over to his birth-place, which by the way, is singularly in need of a collection of the kind.

CHAPTER XXII.

ROERMOND—FLEMISH CATHOLICISM—SMALL CHAPELS—A WORK OF INGENUITY AND PATIENCE—THE MUNSTER—SAINT CHRISTOPHER—PATRIOTIC POETRY—INTRODUCTION OF THE PIPE.

IF Venlo surprises the traveller coming from the northern provinces, by revealing to him a world of new customs and manners, on reaching Roermond his impressions are confirmed with double force.

No one could imagine, on finding himself in Roermond, that he was visiting a town of old Guelderland, a neighbour of Arnhem and Zutphen, the special quality of which rhymed with that of Nymegen.[1] Policy, in withdrawing Roermond from the old province and uniting it to Limbourg, followed the dictates of geography and ethnography. In Guelderland it was an alien, but in Limbourg it returns to the bosom of its family, if I may so express it, morally, intellectually, and religiously.

[1] See page 224.

Roermond is essentially a Catholic and Episcopal town, not after the Italian or French manner of indifference or even scepticism, with a large amount of indulgence for the priesthood and toleration on all sides, but according to the Flemish manner, that is to say strict, watchful, intolerant, and severe. It would almost appear as if Calvinism had cast its shadows over Catholicism in this Flemish country, so sombre and taciturn has the latter become. It has none of the bright pleasing adjuncts to be found connected with it in the South of Europe. Regarding the nearness of the 'enemy' as a continual menace, feeling controlled and watched by the Protestants around them, and believing themselves and their actions misunderstood, the priests have adopted an austere and reserved manner, that people are not accustomed to in France or elsewhere. Instead of being pacifiers or preachers of peace, they have become pugnacious Christians urging to a crusade. The priest here gathers his vestments about him for fear of being contaminated, and in order to establish more firmly his power over men's minds, dictates and rules where he ought to act or not interfere at all. In this small town of Roermond the bishop has been known to preside at municipal elections, and from the height of his pulpit issue decrees against liberal candidates; and his subordinates, following in his steps, throw themselves bravely into the battle without taking heed to the chance that they might incur defeat. The result of these ignoble encounters, where divine interests are too intimately mixed with earthly interests, is to increase the austere reserve of the priests. Aware that at any moment they may be called upon to fight both for spiritual and temporal benefit, they show themselves genuine soldiers above all, and not knowing who may be an adversary on the morrow, they avoid mixing too eagerly in a society which suspects them at every turn.

No one sees here, as in Italy, ecclesiastics loitering about the cafés or visiting the theatres, for that would create frightful scandal; but they do not even visit the families of their parishioners on the friendly terms usual in France. They exist, on the contrary, within themselves; their faith becomes exalted, they turn to works as the expression of their religious sentiment, and do their best to increase the number of their sanctuaries.

Around Roermond the latter are to be found on every side. All along the high road, about every hundred steps, little chapels are erected, containing lamps, waxen figures, and artificial flowers. Some few of these Madonnas perform miracles—when this is known a church is built on the spot, and in course of time a superb convent.

We paid a visit to the most celebrated of these miraculous Virgins in the neighbourhood. About three centuries ago she was found in a well. The shepherd who drew her out fastened her to a tree. At the close of the sixteenth century this rustic shelter was exchanged for a simple little chapel, which has now been converted into a small, pretty church, in the Roman-Byzantine style. It is visited as a place of pilgrimage for twenty leagues around, and when we were there a commodious religious residence had just been installed.

We had the curiosity to examine very closely this statue of the Virgin. We found it was a small wooden carved figure of good workmanship of about the seventeenth century, very elegant and very graceful. Unfortunately one cannot say the same of every statue to be met with on the road. The gigantic crucifixes in the streets of Roermond are also far from perfect.

In fact their workmanship is most coarsely finished, and the taste of their design most abominable; added to which the appearance of these rudely painted wooden figures is in itself scandalous, when one considers that the town, for many long years, has been able to furnish the churches and chapels, within a radius of a hundred leagues, with holy objects, statues, altars, shrines, &c. There are several fabrics in the town where these things are manufactured: the native sculptors and painters are widely known for their talents. Some among them are really very remarkable artists. We visited the studio of one of them, M. de Leeuw, who was just finishing a masterpiece of patience and manual dexterity. It is a portrait of the Queen of the Low Countries in carved wood, surrounded by a framework of graceful nymphs, fat cupids, and garlands of flowers. The whole does not measure more than a foot in length, and is beautifully and delicately carved. The nymphs are not more than a couple of inches high, and yet one can distinctly count the dimples in each cheek and the nails on each hand. The cameos of their jewellery can be recognised as portraits, and with a magnifying glass we discovered flies settling on the roses, which could not be seen by the naked eye, all beautifully carved. I am not quite sure that by the aid of a microscope we should not have found parasites on the flies, for nothing appears to be forgotten.

But we must return to our description of the town. Although Roermond is a pretty, well laid out city, there is nothing about it to warrant its being called 'very large,' as affirmed by the old Guelderlander couplet. It must either have strangely decreased in size since that time, or the others must have been considerably enlarged, for Roermond is now by far the smallest of the four. Guicciardini relates that in his time it was a 'city well peopled, rich and abounding in fine buildings.' Pontanus depicts it as an 'agreeable town, rich, spacious, and abounding in religious and civil buildings, both public and private.' An opinion which might still be quoted of it, if war, and above all fire, had not despoiled it of its monumental beauty.

The most disastrous of these conflagrations was the one of May, 1665, caused by an act of imprudence. During a procession which took place on the anniversary of the dedication of the town, the armed burghers, following the holy cortége, fired off their guns as a token of rejoicing, and accidentally set fire to a thatched roof. In a moment the flames spread with most frightful rapidity, burning down to the ground a large number of houses, churches, convents, and the episcopal palace. A little more and the town would have been entirely destroyed and reduced to a state of cinders, and Roermond would have finished as it began—that is, if it had perished by means of a religious festival, it was to a religious establishment it owed its existence.

At the commencement of the thirteenth century, on the site it occupies now, there was only a castle, or rather a simple place of meeting for the hunt; just at this spot a little river called Roer empties itself into the Meuse, so the place was named Roermond—mouth of the Roer. In 1218 Gérard III., Count of Guelderland, at the instigation of Richard of Brabant, his mother, who was to be the first abbess, supplemented the château by a fine convent. This convent was granted to the noble ladies of the Cistercian order. To cultivate their land these noble dames required a goodly number of servitors, to accommodate whom houses were constructed around the convent. 'In a few years,' says Pontanus, 'this little colony grew so rapidly that it may be regarded as the true origin of the town, besides being the cause of its celebrity.'

This magnificent abbey, the cradle of the present city, was unfortunately partly destroyed by fire in

1665, and completely demolished in 1797. Although the cloisters and its dependencies have almost entirely disappeared, the church remains, and constitutes one of the most curious monuments of the present day; we might add, indeed, the rarest, for with the exception of the Church of the Apostles at Cologne, there is not, perhaps, in Europe another basilica where the Roman-Byzantine style of the borders of the Rhine mingles, as in this case, with that of the Transition. But my own personal opinion is that monuments built in this Transition period are neither so fine nor so imposing as those of the great epochs. Architecture ought to be the expression of ideas, thoughts; that is its purpose—and those ideas are far more striking when their means of expression are pure and according to rule—a compromise may be more agreeable to the eye, but is nearly always wanting in force, and oftener than not in clearness. With this reserve in view, I do not hesitate to acknowledge the *Munster* of Roermond as a first-class archæological curiosity, meriting the attention of those learned in the subject.

Like most abbey chapels, the *Munster* is of mediocre size. Its primitive form, that of a Roman cross, is admirably preserved. Its other architectural arrangements are similar to those of the basilicæ of the eleventh and twelfth centuries. Two aisles complete the nave, and above is a gallery, which terminates at the transept with a wall. This wall contains a niche, which no doubt was formerly used for small altars. The body of the church is built in a half-circular style with the exception of the vault of the choir and those terminating the arms of the transept, which are pentagon-shaped instead of in hemispheric form, which is never seen in the basilicæ of the eleventh and twelfth centuries, and not even in the Church of the Apostles at Cologne. At the point where the nave and transept meet, the decoration of this part of the edifice is completed by an octagon cupola. Then, at the western end, there is a structure in ogive style with long arched windows, which indicate having been built at some previous epoch. This structure, which is connected with the interior galleries, forms a kind of *jubé*, which was formerly underneath the principal entrance to the church, but is walled up now, no doubt to prevent the sinking, of which this special part is beginning to show signs.

Marvellously preserved in the interior, Our Lady of the *Munster* is unfortunately not so well off as regards the exterior. The vaulting has not suffered much, and its elegant cupola, canted by two towers, is almost intact. But then, the western part no longer bears any trace of its original formation, from it having been demolished and then reconstructed at a later date, so that the repairs going on at the present time are guided by pure conjecture. Fortunately they have been put in the hands of an architect of considerable talent, who has had some experience in this sort of work, but whose projects are controlled by a scholar who has made these subjects his special study; and it was with a great deal of pleasure that we glanced over M. Cuyper's plans endorsed by M. Viollet-le-Duc. Hence no fault can be found with the way the work is being carried on, or with the zeal employed in executing it. Indeed, it would perhaps be as well if this ardour were slightly moderated as regards the embellishment of the old church. Examining minutely the capitals of the columns lately repaired, those I mean surrounding the altar, we discovered small heads of modern date, with whiskers and spectacles, mingling with the other ornaments, which in such a place had a very ridiculous effect. These portraits may be very good in themselves, but the taste which placed them here is open to question, and it would be well if they could be removed, to avoid the famous saying *Nomina Stultorum* being applied in a manner, not difficult to guess.

Fortunately the Munster contains other monuments of more value. First there is the magnificent tomb of the founder of the church, Gérard III., Count of Guelderland and Zutphen, and his wife Margaret of Brabant.

The two slab figures reclining on the vast mausoleum are a couple of precious specimens of the sculpture of the thirteenth century. They are very simple both in design and workmanship. The Count and Countess repose side by side on a slab of black marble supported by twelve small columns with gilded capitals; their heads rest on a gilded cushion, their eyes are half closed, their features calm, the expression on each face kind-hearted and amiable ; the upper lip of the Count's mouth slightly pressing the lower, and the dimple in his chin give an air of truth to his portrait, and at the same time suggest a smile as if the good seigneur had gone to sleep in a merry mood when he closed his eyes for ever. He is habited in a long blue plaited robe, with a green mantle thrown back, and instead of a sword at his side he has his purse, which is better for those who build churches. The Countess is robed in white with a golden mantle, on her head a cap fastened under her chin, and on her face the placid quiet expression of one who has passed a saintly existence. Both have their left hand resting on their heart, both have their hair gilded, and both wear a huge medallion suspended from their neck.

The epitaph above the Count sets forth in glowing detailed terms the origin and foundation of the convent.

Not far off is another fine piece of work—a magnificent altar-piece. The centre part, divided into six compartments, is full of scenes carved and painted representing the principal episodes of the Passion ; the doors are covered with excellent paintings, one of which, the Garden of Olives, recalls to one's mind the well-known engraving by Goltzius; the portrait of St. Peter is striking in its resemblance. According to the archæologists of the country, the church of the *Munster* possessed at one time many other monuments of precious value which must have been parted with by the priests either from ignorance, or indifference, or perhaps from avarice. This fine altar-piece would have shared the same fate, if it had not been in such a dilapidated state. We cannot but say that 'to some things misfortune is good,' for one of the elders of the town asserts that not so long ago, when this work ' was put aside as rubbish in the grille of the church, people thoughtlessly detached many of the little figures and carried them away.'

The tomb and this altar-piece, both restored as cleverly as possible, are the only objects of any value left in the *Munster*. I say the only ones, because it is scarcely worth while mentioning a picture of moderate quality, divided into sixteen compartments, representing various scenes of the Passion, and a portrait of a bishop, which I merely refer to on account of an inscription, which might possibly interest some of my readers, inscribed on the lower border of the frame, which I copy according to the text:—

PATRON CONTRE LA PIERRE ET LA GRAVELLE.

The name of the saint I could not find out, though I have no doubt it would be easy enough to obtain if applied for at the sacristan's.

This curious and very interesting church, the *Munster*, is not as might be supposed the Cathedral of Roermond; but a simple chapel of ease. At the time of the institution of the bishopric, it belonged to the order of the Cistercians, so the bishop installed his chapter in another church, situated in the market-place, and dedicated to the 'Blessed Holy Ghost,' then the parish church of the town. The antiquity of this parish procured it the honour conferred on it by William Lindan, 'a very learned and honourable prelate,' says Guicciardini, 'who has written many good books for the profit and edification of his own generation and of those who followed.' This last-mentioned church is referred to in a charter of 1279, hence its construction is contemporaneous with that of the *Munster*. In 1659 it threatened to fall into ruins. Architects were consulted, but they pronounced it too far gone to restore and repair, and it being thus condemned as useless, the Chapter abandoned it on Maundy Thursday, and transferred themselves to the church of St. Christopher, where they still reside.

St. Christopher is a much more modern building, dating from the beginning of the fifteenth century, and of Gothic style. It presents the peculiarity of a nave, with double aisles, enriched with lateral chapels reaching as far as the transept, from which point the aisles are converted into three naves of equal height without circumference. Two of the latter terminate in three sides of the octagon, while the third, the one on the right, is intersected by a dome with a huge window. The whole building is of brick, hence both the interior and exterior are exceedingly simple in style. Several fine confessionals, a pulpit dating from the seventeenth century —and very remarkable too—and many paintings, notably one belonging to the Rubens school, are still preserved in the interior. Lately, beautiful modern panes of glass have been added to the windows, a tribute which the town owed to itself, as its name has figured somewhat prominently in the history of painting on glass.[1]

The principal entrance to the church is under a kind of porch at the end of the south transept. At the west end there is a high square tower of the same date as the church. This tower is flanked at the top by four turrets, over which, in the centre, is a tall tower of very singular form—all of which give a very picturesque appearance to the church.

On the north side of St. Christopher there is an ancient burying-ground, which formerly extended close to the ramparts. A grand noble old tower in brick, with thick walls, without any openings, and with formidable machicoulis of severe aspect, still stands, and is the only remaining portion of the ancient ramparts. Originally it formed a part of the second enclosure of the town, the one which supported a dozen sieges and four or five assaults. In fact Roermond had more demands made on its prowess than any other city of Guelderland, for it was not only attacked by the enemies of its suzerains, but by

---

[1] See 'Notices on the Stained Glass of Belgium,' by M. O. Kelly, of Galway.

its suzerains also, because it remained true and faithful to its legitimate rulers. For example, Adolf of Guelderland never forgave the city for being faithful to his miserable father, and to avenge this noble fidelity, he made continued incursions on his territory, laying waste by fire and sword all before him.

At seven different times, in 1572, 1577, 1632, 1637, 1702, 1795, and 1797, Roermond was besieged and taken. One of the most disastrous of these sieges was in 1572, when the town was pillaged. In 1632, although the garrison consisted of only three hundred men, the attack through an open breach continued during four days, and cost Ernest Casimir of Nassau his life. At last, in 1637, Roermond was 'reduced to obedience, after having been furiously attacked during five days at four different points, and pressed by a general assault which it could not resist.'

The occupations, on the other hand, which seem to have left least disastrous effects behind them were those of 1672 and 1795. During the latter, the revolutionary idea imported by the French troops seems to have been particularly to the taste of the Roermonders. Everywhere, clubs, in imitation of those of Paris, were installed, the 'Patriots' under the presidency of Judge Schommers, and the 'Jacobins' at the Recollets. One can easily imagine the avidity with which these discourses were listened to when one remembers the profound hatred against the 'Imperialists' as they were then called. One example will give an idea of the terribly excited state things were in:—' An old man called Maertins was all but massacred because he was suspected of having hidden some Austrian flags in his house.'

Thanks to a triple chronicle recently discovered, we can follow, almost day by day, the history of this interesting epoch.[1] One might relate days of touching episode, and retrace at the same time patriotic ceremonies. The last of these chronicles relates to the planting of the tree of liberty on the 2nd 'Pluvoise.' An embryo poet, inspired by democratic enthusiasm, wrote a doggrel, the virtue of which lay only in intention, and attached it to the tree. Translated it is as follows:—

> Traveller, who see'st me in this happy place,
> Learn how I came by this most lucky grace;
> Bless my foundation, the day that gave me birth,
> And swear to have no master here on earth.

When the French regiment in garrison at Roermond started for Italy, the same poet attached to the same tree another verse :—

> Cherished tree of liberty,
> Here the French have planted thee.
> To Tiber's banks they go, to teach
> Freedom to all in acts and speech.

The population—not satisfied with simply utter-

[1] This triple chronicle was discovered a few years ago by M. Charles Guillers, a notary of Roermond. It is the diary of three persons, who, without being personally known to each other, took the trouble to relate the events passing around them. They were the Demoiselle van Elsachen (whose diary dates from 1769 to 1819), Pieter Hendrick Scheurs (1794 to 1799), and Ramoekers (1781 to 1802).

ing their farewells in this poetical way—accompanied the troops some distance, crying out '*au revoir, au revoir!*' Even the priests joined in the marks of sympathy, for they had been on good terms with the republican army during the occupation of the town. Hoche when staying in the country had been the guest of the curé of Maëstricht. Vandamme had lodged with an ecclesiastic during his stay at Roermond, and the troops had received strict orders to respect every thing in connection with church worship; the least dereliction of discipline on this head was most promptly and severely punished.

One day, a few soldiers, during the absence of their officers, broke the large crucifix of Merum. The peasants of the village, indignant beyond measure, attacked the culprits; they killed one and captured another, whom they pinioned and conducted to Roermond, where they presented themselves with their prisoner before the general. The latter went out, assembled his soldiers in the Rue Basse, and there, before the troops, first had the sacrilegious offender's hair shaved and then turned him out of the army, to the intense gratification of the crowd around.

In 1673, the same pleasant understanding existed between the priests of Roermond and the French army. This time the soldiers introduced into the country the use of the pipe,[1] instead of revolutionary

---

[1] M. Louis Figuier mentions the fact that it was during the siege of Maëstricht, 1672, that the use of the pipe became general in the French army. Up to that time it had been the fashion to take snuff.

ideas. In their intercourse with their new friends, the ecclesiastics took so kindly to smoking, that a few years later, in 1677, Bishop Reginald Cools issued a mandate to forbid the priests of Roermond the immoderate use of tobacco, alleging that it was more a military habit : '*tabaci more militari immodicum usum.*'

It would be somewhat difficult to foretell the sort of reception French troops would receive now if they had to return to this country ; and after all it does not matter, considering there is no chance of their doing so. But one thing I must affirm before closing my remarks on Roermond, and that is, that the inhabitants of this town receive most kindly and hospitably all foreigners and strangers who knock at their gates in a peaceful spirit. Indeed their hospitality is most cordial to every one, and I for my part shall never forget the many charming hours I passed with a young magistrate of the kindly city, nor the many pleasant excursions we enjoyed in his society round about the town, and in its environs.

CHAPTER XXIII.

MAËSTRICHT—ANCIENT SOUVENIRS—THE OUTSKIRTS OF WIJCK—HISTORY OF A CHAPEL-MASTER—THE GATE OF HELL—NOTRE DAME—SAINT SERVAIS—THE CHAPEL OF CHARLEMAGNE—THE FAIR OF RELICS—THE TREASURY AND THE ARCHIVES—PURGATORY—THE MIRACULOUS STONE.

N leaving Roermond, we were singularly near the end of our journey. Maëstricht was within a few leagues, and we could go no further without quitting Holland, that old Gallo-Roman city being in truth at the extreme limit of the kingdom. East, west, and south it is surrounded by foreign lands, and to the north a narrow strip of territory alone attaches it to the northern country. To describe Maëstricht faithfully would need at least a volume, or even more, for many volumes have been devoted to its history without exhausting it. Every step in its street calls up a flood of memories; there is not a place nor monument which has not a tale to tell or the memory of some glorious hero to recall; at every stroke of the pick in the ground faces are revived which have disappeared beneath it. People who have cultivated, inhabited, embellished it, and

MAESTRICHT (ANCIENT RAMPARTS).

covered it with monuments, or generations which have watered it with their blood, and died in its defence, are resuscitated.

At the place of debarkation, on the spot where the railway buildings are now in course of erection, Roman remains were found; three large red earthen jars and a glass barrel in addition, prove the presence of the old remains in this locality. In the whole country round eloquent proofs of their sojourn abound. There are ruins of villas, funereal urns, and half-destroyed monuments, to perpetuate the memory of those illustrious conquerors.

Long before them again, in the times which history has been unable to reconstruct, the country was well peopled, and the flint implements frequently found in Saint Peter's Hill attest the presence of primitive races and those wandering tribes who had dwelt in this favourite resort.

On approaching the town, proud bastions invoke recent recollections. The ramparts of Wijck, the outskirt of Maëstricht, are the portions of the city situated on the right bank of the Meuse. Their designation—the refuge—has an eloquence of its own. It seems to have been acquired by the fact that when the town was lost, the citizens felt sure of an asylum there.

A few years since Wijck possessed another enclosure much more ancient and curious. It was that against which the Spaniards spent their strength in vain, that of which Strada had seen the ditches filled with the blood of the besiegers. It surrounded the whole town, and every stone had its deed of heroism to tell; for not only did the citizens defend their soil foot by foot, but the women, brave as their valiant husbands, shared in the defence. In 1632, and before that, in 1579, the intrepid women of Maëstricht, organised in battalions, underwent the severest hardships. They were mustered by beat of drum, and shouldering their picks and shovels, marched with colours flying, to repair the breaches caused by the enemy's fire.

Such an example electrified the men. To mention only the siege of 1579, the Spaniards had been so often driven away from the ramparts, that they did not venture an assault. The besieged, as Strada narrates, 'did not despair even with the enemy upon their walls,' and so not being able to reduce it by force, the Duke of Parma resorted to stratagem; he opened negotiations with the besieged, and taking advantage of the reliance placed on his parole by the citizens, who neglected all precautions, he introduced some of his soldiers by night, surprised the town, and carried it by assault.

Exasperated by the heroic resistance of the besieged, his troops behaved like wild beasts, killing every man and woman, young and old, whom they met for three mortal hours, until the Prince ordered the butchery to cease, and those who were afterwards taken to be ransomed. It was one of those victories in which the vanquished wept, and of which the victors are ashamed to boast, says old William Bandart, an author who cannot be charged with over-sensibility.

This was not, however, the only occasion on which Maëstricht underwent a similar disaster. Three years earlier, a like resistance was followed by a parallel assault and devastation. An old engraving has preserved a detail of this horrible slaughter, and the Latin notice accompanying it is full of painful revelations.

Happily all the sieges to which Maëstricht has been subjected did not end so ill. Five times, from 1284 to 1408, the valiant city repelled her invaders. The sieges of 1284, 1304, 1334, and twice in 1408 were ignominiously raised, and the attacking armies pursued by the victorious burghers. Even had these creditable feats of arms not been accomplished, the defence of 1676 would have rendered the town illustrious.

In the month of July of that year, while negotiations were going on at Nymegen, the Prince of Orange besieged Maëstricht, hoping to derive advantage from the absence of the governor of the town, Marshal d'Estrades, who was away as plenipotentiary at the Congress. But he reckoned without his host, as the second in command, the brave Chevalier Calvo, a sturdy Catalan, resolved to carry matters to the last extremity. 'I know nothing about the defence of a place,' he said to the engineers, 'but I do know that I will not surrender.'

The Prince of Orange commenced his investment near the end of July, pushed on the siege with much vigour, and delivered such severe assaults that heavy odds were taken at Nymegen that Maëstricht would be captured in a certain time. We do not know whether Marshal d'Estrades bet the contrary, or whether he knew that the place would be so well defended; but, in spite of the terrible assaults, Maëstricht held her own. The assailants, always and everywhere repulsed, began to refuse to approach the ramparts. The prince soon paid tribute in his own person, for, on one of the days of attack, when his soldiers were being dispersed by the besieged, he attempted to rally them with signal valour, and sword in hand drove our people back to the very gates, says Temple. He was wounded in the arm, and said to those who had done so ill :—' This, gentlemen, is how you should act ; you are the cause of my wound, regarding which you profess so much concern.' But all those gallant efforts were vain and fruitless. Marshal Schomberg drew near; they did not dare to do battle with him, and the siege was raised precipitately, the besiegers withdrawing with the loss of all their war material.

At the French Court there was much misgiving about Maëstricht, and so, when its deliverance was known, there was corresponding joy. Madame de Sévigné, in her letter of the 2nd of September, 1676, records how ' Monsieur de Louvois ran to give the good news to the king, with whom the Abbé Calvo chanced to be. The king embraced him warmly, gave him an abbey with a rental of twelve thousand francs, and bestowed on his brother a pension of twenty thousand livres, with the government of Arie, and thousands of thanks which were thought most of all. Louis XIV., indeed, attached supreme importance to the preservation of Maëstricht; for, beyond the value of the place to his army, he retained very pleasant recollections of his triumphal visit there years before. His victorious entry in 1673 had been celebrated in every way, and caused rhyme to run as freely as tears to flow. Scarcely had he made his first appearance, when a singular poem, written in the district dialect by the Jesuit Jean Berthet, was presented to him. The poet was a learned critic, an astronomer, a professor at times, and always a courtier. It was a very short and simple poem, yet it pleased the king. It ran thus:—'Saint Peter, with shaven crown, said before Maëstricht the other day to Saint Paul, to fight to-day lend me your sword, to enter to-morrow I'll lend you my key.'

A number of poems, addresses, and petitions were presented to the king when he passed through; but there was one, composed on that very day, which no one had been bold enough to submit. It was a song in dialogue, in which poor Maëstricht, knowing not His Majesty, complained bitterly of the rigours of war. It is too long to reproduce, and whether the king heard it or not, he could not understand it, for it was written in Dutch, and the royal ear was filled with the music of the grand *Te Deum* sung at Saint Servais.

At one time, however, it was feared that this pompous ceremony would be shorn of its customary splendours. For a whole month the Director of the Chapel Royal, a Liégois named Dumont, had disappeared, and been sought for in vain. He was found at Maëstricht, where he had ventured to make love to a pretty damsel of the town, had been shut up by the investment, and had to remain during the whole of the siege. The king spied him out in the crowd assembled to receive him. 'What! is that you, Dumont,' said he in an angry voice; 'what business had you in the middle of enemies while I was laying siege to this town?'

'Sire,' replied the ready master of the Chapel, 'I was composing a *Te Deum* for the success of your Majesty's arms.'

The king smiled and passed on. This Dumont was not the only artist who entered Maëstricht with the French army on the day of the king's entry. Some actors pitched a tent in the market-place, and commenced their representations, which was the first playing of comedy in the town, and an entire novelty. The inhabitants received them kindly, and the French reciprocated their friendliness. Louis XIV. visited the temporary theatre twice, and so the good folks prospered in their adventure.

The tent remained for five years in the great market, and created so great a taste for the histrionic art, that a room in the old Town Hall was turned into a theatre, in which the performance continued.

This soon became too small, so when in 1748 the French, under Marshal Saxe, again occupied the town, as they brought a fresh host of spectators, a call came for a bigger place to play in. A great riding establishment was converted into a theatre, and remained true to its destiny until 1786, when the States gave to the town the Church of the Jesuits, which had been confiscated with the rest of their property in 1638. This in turn was transformed into a play-house, and in it representations are still given.

But we have unconsciously wandered to the centre of the town, and so must retrace our steps along a road paved with memoirs of the past. And first, to go from Wijck into Maëstricht, the famous bridge to which the city owes its existence must be traversed. The view from it merits a passing pause, for the panorama from this side is most charming and richly coloured. The old houses, the ancient monuments, the ramparts, and the churches commingle their picturesque outlines, their hard and elegant forms, their bright and gay colours, their bricks and their stones. It is a charming disorder, in which neither large trees, green swards, high belfries, majestic towers, with ancient profiles in walls embowered by age, are wanting. They seem to watch over the busy city as elder brothers do over younger ones.

All is animation everywhere, a busy hive of life and general rejoicing, in which the ancient river rolling its silver ripples under foot appears to participate. She bears lightly the burthen of stones which has traversed her for so many ages, and her waves bury themselves under the broad arches with a strange whistling which resembles a kiss, for the town loves the river, and the river loves the town. This, in fact, is the spot where Maëstricht originally began, for it was a fortified Roman *tête-de-pont*, as the old road from Turgau to Cologne attests, as well as the underground structures of the ancient villas. Tradition affirms that it was where Wijck now stands that the Batavians, led by Claudius Civilis, exterminated the legions of Vespasian in the fourth century.[1] The *tête-de-pont* soon became a fortified town, to which Saint Servais, feeling incensed at Turgau, transferred the seat of his episcopacy for security against the Saxons and Huns, who were always rapidly approaching the Rhine. The presence of the holy prelate seems to have brought luck to his new living, for from this time it began to increase and prosper. Its splendid position is universally recognised. Blaeu has painted it as 'a convenient and well planned city;' which other authorities have endorsed. Its bridge was in truth of too great importance, for in consequence of its rich revenue all the authorities of the banks of the Meuse only sought to seize and to hold it.

---

[1] This has been contested by a Belgian archæologist, M. Caumartin, on the ground mentioned by Tacitus, that the troops of Sabrinus fought in a defile; and where can such a place be found in a plain as flat as the palm of the hand?

This bridge, however, is not altogether unknown to us. It has a civil history, which is unfortunately incomplete, from the frequent dispersion of the archives of Maëstricht and of her churches. But we know that in 1139 the Emperor Conrad II. presented it to the Chapter of Saint Servais, 'for their use and its advantage to maintain it, and to divide the revenue not absorbed in such maintenance into two parts, the one for the provost of the town, the other for the Chapter.' It was a wooden bridge, and the Chapter acquitted itself so ill of the first part of the pact, that in 1275, worm-eaten and rotten, it fell during the procession of Notre Dame, and killed more than five hundred persons.

It was reconstructed in wood on the spot which it now occupies, and later on (1581 to 1585) it was rebuilt in stone. This is the bridge which is now seen, but renewed more than once, arch by arch, and bit by bit. To tell of all the important events associated with this bridge would be to recount the history of Maëstricht—bombardments, butcheries, massacres, triumphal entries, religious festivals, ceremonies and rejoicings of all sorts. One of the most brilliant of the latter was the nautical fête given by the town to the Czar Peter the Great.

This fête was held on the 28th of July, 1717. The Czar had entered the town at five o'clock on the previous evening, and on the same day had visited the fort of Saint Peter, as well as the ramparts; and supped with the magistrates at the Town Hall. The next day there was an attack of the fort on the Meuse. This fort was a sort of square tower built on a pivot in the centre of the river; several boats filled with boatmen attacked it simultaneously, and endeavoured to carry it by escalade. But two men in the interior of the fort defended it with muskets and hand grenades; and, by turning it on its pivots, tumbled over the ladders and the boatmen carrying them. This play lasted a couple of hours, to the great amusement of the Czar, after which he left the town to dine at the Château of Canne, from whence he immediately departed for Holland.

The bridge which has detained us so long, interesting as it is, is neither the most curious construction nor the oldest building possessed by Maëstricht. That which is considered the most ancient is certainly the *Helpoort*, or Hell-gate. I said considered the most ancient, because the archæologists of the country have been exercised considerably concerning it. One party, headed by M. Alexander Shaepkens, thought they had discovered in it a Roman fortress; others, with M. Schayes, relying upon more or less doubtful tests, wish to find in it a fragment of the enclosure reconstructed in the thirteenth century. To our perception this *Helpoort* deserves neither 'much praise nor much abuse,' for it seems to belong to the commencement of the Roman architecture of the country, that is to say, the ninth or tenth century. It is, however, more interesting than beautiful, consisting of a lofty masonry basement, flanked by two towers, round externally and square within, surmounted by small pointed roofs. This basement is preceded by a large vaulted arch, and at its summit by three windows now blocked up. The indifferent masonry has not resisted the ravages of time, which has accomplished its usual work of eating away the stone and mortar, until this noble structure is covered with myosites, giving it a rustic but picturesque and repellent look.

As to the terrible name of Hell-gate, it originated in a sign which formerly ornamented the little street on which the gate abutted.

Not far from the Hell-gate was an ancient and much renowned sanctuary, the church of Notre Dame. According to M. Eug. Gens, who has studied and described it with much care, Notre Dame dates from the fifth century, when it must have been built in the shape of a parallelogram by Saint Monulf. Subsequently, in the ninth century, it was enlarged and modified, to be again touched up and finished in the pointed arch epoch. Unfortunately the nave was so horribly restored in 1764, that it is nearly impossible to trace out the original building, which is the more to be regretted as the choir, nearly intact, is a perfect gem.

As to itself, there can be no mistake that it belongs to the eleventh century, the period of perfection of the Roman style, and of its best models. The choir is composed of a semicircle, with two superposed ranges of arcades supported by thirty-two pillars most beautifully carved, and with extremely rich capitals. They are adorned with twenty subjects from the Old and New Testament, of exquisite workmanship, and delicious simplicity.

The *Last Supper*, *Jacob's Ladder*, *His Struggle with the Angel*, *The Sacrifice of Abraham*, and *Joseph Sold by his Brethren* are masterpieces of delicate and fine sculpture. The other capitals represent fantastic interlacements of extraordinary animals, and hyperbolical vegetables of most graceful design—than which it would be impossible to dream a more elegant phantasmagoria.

Upon one of them, M. Franquinet, the learned keeper of the Limbourg records, who accompanied us in our visit, devoted our attention to a little bas-relief on which was an inscription. This bas-relief represents a personage offering what looks like a Savoy cake to a lady. The Limbourg archæologists fancy that they find in this the architect offering his work to the Virgin, and in the second part of the inscription—S. MARIA J. EMO—the name of the artist. It needs a genuine archæologist to accept this plausible explanation. We regretted it, because in the eleventh century architects were of less account than are builders of our time, and it would have been the height of presumption, in a man of mere science, to venture to dedicate to the Virgin a building which he had only designed and constructed. This was the privilege of the Duke of Brabant, protector of the church; of the Bishop of Liége, its spiritual chief; of the dean, or of some wealthy donor; but the architect, who cares for a poor devil of a mechanic? **As for** the inscription, the following is our **unhesitating** translation, SANTA MARIA IN EXCELSIS JESUS MATER OPTIMA. The reader may take his choice of two explanations, both of which are more or less conjectural.

The choir of Notre Dame, where this controversy occurred, is placed in an interesting crypt. It has a ridged, vaulted arch **supported by divers ranges of** extremely simple cylindrical columns, **and with** the exception **of a Christ on the Cross in the style of** Van Dyck, there was nothing more worthy **of notice. With** the exterior it is happily otherwise. Besides **the apse,** which has preserved the form and primitive decoration of the best Roman style, Notre Dame **has a** Western *façade,* which is one of the strangest and most unusual to be met with anywhere. It is an enormous square tower, heavy, massive, ungraceful, flanked by two small round turrets, **lanceolated, painted, spare, with no other openings than a few** attic windows. **This gives a correct idea** of this singular and repulsive **structure, which is** more like a fortified tower than an ecclesiastical belfry.

There are only two other known *façades* like it: one at the Bonn Cathedral, the other at Saint Denis, in Liége. That now under consideration is the **most** ornate of the three, for it has sham arcades at its summit, which the others are without.

Notre Dame possesses in addition a prettily finished arched cloister, a treasury, and a treasure room, which claim a few words. The cloister is good Gothic, in elegant style and perfect preservation. Its galleries are backed at the sides by a square court-yard with a central garden. There are few more agreeable walks, where philosophic reading or calm contemplation can be more completely enjoyed.

The treasury is simply what the word means. Formerly, according to ancient collegiate catalogues, it was one of the last founded of the diocese of Liége —but in 1798 the most precious of its treasures had disappeared. Some, like the bust of Saint Barthelemy, and several other silver statues were melted down for their metal. Others, to escape the revolutionary requisitions, were confided to Canons, who proved untrustworthy depositaries, as witness the Byzantine cross, brought by Philip of Swabia from Constantinople in 1204. The Abbé Willemsem describes it as unequalled in richness, and M. Shaepkens has written its sad odyssey.

Why the treasury of Notre Dame is so poor is explained by these spoliations—yet, it still has some precious objects. Among them a Greek reliquary in silver of the eleventh century, with carved and enamelled figures, is most noteworthy. Another in rock-crystal in the form of a shrine of the thirteenth century, and a third in silver, turret-shaped, dating from the fourteenth century. There are also several purses of relics of the fourteenth and fifteenth centuries elegantly embroidered, and an ivory horn with an oriental mounting worth recording.

The archives have been as sorely tried as the treasury. But jewels quite as precious, from their small apparent value and more difficult disposal, travelled less far, and returned home willingly to their nest. Nevertheless, an index of documents recently recovered, and containing a summary of the privileges, bulls, and donations which formed its archives at the end of the last century (an index of two thick volumes) indicates the exact and irreparable nature of its losses.

There remain in the archives 411 documents, the most ancient of which, running back to 1312, is a diploma from the Emperor Lothaire, attesting the high antiquity of the College of Saint Servais.

The church of this latter, to which we must now come, is the most remarkable, the most ancient, the most complete, and the most famous of the buildings of Maëstricht. Archæologists are unable to agree as to the probable period of its construction. First of all there is the legend assigning it to the time of Charlemagne, and associating the shade of a great emperor with the fame of a great saint: but little account has been taken of this legend. Without admitting with the meritorious archæologist, M. Eug. Gens, that it is so ancient, there is little doubt that Maëstricht possessed a Church of Saint Servais in the ninth century, as attested by venerable and tolerably positive tests. The Bollandistes affirm that Charlemagne performed his Easter devotions there. It existed then, certainly not as it now is; but is it absurd to suppose that the crypt so stupidly destroyed in 1806, and the great flat dome of which the substructures were then discovered, dated from that time? And so it is for that species of *narthex*, which is by turns called the Virgin's Chapel, Charlemagne's Chapel, and the New Church (Nieuwekerk). It has evidently been frequently restored—but it is safe to date its massive masonry from the ninth century.

The rest of the building is doubtless of later date, as revealed by the old chronicle of Arras and Cambray, of which, in my judgment, sufficient account has not been taken. ' In the month of August, 1039,' writes the contemporaneous author of this chronicle, ' Bishop Gerard of Cambray accompanied King Henry to Maëstricht, and at the request of Bishop Nithard exhumed the bodies of the holy confessors Gondulf and Monulfe, from which he took relics. Then also the Church was dedicated to Saint Servais.'

Now this first dedication must have had some signification, and what more likely than that the church had been rebuilt? If it has no other merit, the principal archæologists who have investigated Saint Servais, are satisfied with it, viz.: Champeauville, who thinks the church was probably built in 1015; M. Schayes, who believes in the probability of the end of the tenth or beginning of the eleventh centuries; and MM. Eyck Van Zuylichem and C. Schnaase, who agree with him.

It seems then to be fairly made out that Saint Servais was built in the ninth, and almost reconstructed in the tenth century. As for M. Eug. Gens, who assigns the whole to the time of Charlemagne, it is enough to tell him that the only religious edifice which is acknowledged to be really contemporaneous with the great Emperor is the Church of Aix-la-Chapelle. Now, this building is entirely ornamented with Italian columns, which seems to show that stone carving was nearly unknown on the banks of the Rhine, whilst the capitals of Saint Servais are of an elegance and finish indicating the presence of skilled workmen and accomplished artists.

Agreed as to this, we will, if you like, try back to times anterior to the Church as it is. The origin of this sanctuary is too intimately connected with that of the city to be devoid of interest. It was, in truth, the translation by Saint Servais from the seat of his bishopric to the town of Maëstricht, which gives the earliest certain date of its history; and Maëstricht, grateful from the first, vowed to its holy prelate boundless affection.

The adopted him as her patron saint and protector. He became the joy of 'its heart and the light of its eyes,' says the old Dutch poet, Heijndrijck Van Velden. The translation sounds like a biblical episode, and the legend relates that the 'angels of heaven honoured it with melodious chants.' Later on, in the tenth century, when Mathilde, wife of a king and mother of an emperor, attempted, by an abuse of power, to transfer the relics of Saint Servais to the Monastery of Quedlimbourg, the inhabitants of Maëstricht stole into the holy monastery at night, cut the cords of the bells, emptied the case in which were the precious bones, and carried their pious larceny back to their own town, where for ages they celebrated the return of 'the grand Seigneur of Maëstricht' to his home.

Saint Servais, on his part, was not ungrateful. On the morrow of his death he began to perform miracles, which acquired such fame that Saint Gregory of Tours thought them deserving of detailed record. One of the most remarkable was that the tombstone of the saint could not be wetted, rain, hail and snow appearing to respect it. This property inspired Saint Domitian with the pious thought of covering it with a wooden shed.

The incredulous considered it a useless precaution, and the wind seemed to be of the same mind, for it blew down the shed. But Saint Ronulfe would not have it; and so he built the basilica to replace the shed, and this rebuilt, enlarged, and transformed, is the magnificent church which we now admire.

During this time, the reputation of Saint Servais increased daily. Pilgrims flocked to the sanctuary, and the tomb of the venerable prelate became so lavish of prodigies that on January 15, 1147, the great miracle-monger, Saint Bernard, did not dare to heal the sick there, lest he should offend Saint Servais. It was even necessary to free his hands to get him to cure a cripple.

The speciality, however, of Saint Servais, which Saint Bernard knew well, was less devoted to healing, than to casting out *Putduivels, Boschduivels*,[1] and evil spirits—in fact, every thing in olden Flanders which was more feared than a club foot or the loss of an eye. In this respect the old saint feared no rival, and so precious a power was rich in results. He governed the Chapter, for all its neighbouring princes went to do honour to the relics, from Charlemagne who performed his Easter devotions at Saint Servais, to Louis XI. who endowed it with a chapel, to Maximilian and Charles I., who assisted at the opening of the casket in ecclesiastical costume. At length its popularity robbed the saint of his jaw bones, of which one was taken by the Emperor Henry III., and the other purchased by Charles IV. of Luxembourg. At last the popularity of the good man established a *Kermis*.

This Kermis, which was called the 'fair of relics,' was held every seven years, and was a source of wealth to the city. Whenever it drew near, provision was made on all hands to feed and lodge a large number of pilgrims, who brought grist to the mill, and left the greater part of their pelf in Maëstricht.

In the beginning of the thirteenth century, so great was the influx of pilgrims, that precautions against disorder were taken by the magistrates. In the eighteenth century they began a standing order, which was enforced at the beginning of each *Kermis*.

---

[1] *Putduivels*—the devils which inhabit wells; *Boschduivels*—those which roam about woods.

The ordinance of 1440 has been preserved, and it contains some provisions worthy of reproduction, and good to observe at all times. The first was a prohibition against selling unwholesome meat; the second, to have a barrel of water in the house as a protection against fire; the fourth, to be honest and decent by day and by night; the sixth, to keep the house clean; the seventh, to sell at fair prices to the pilgrims; the eighth, to use correct weights and measures, and so on.

It was in the *Vrijthof*, at the very feet of Saint Servais, that the fair was held and the relics shown, but now-a-days neither exists. The church only remains, to the splendour of which they contribute so much. From the place where the pilgrims crowded formerly, the grand outline of the apse may now be seen, delineating its dark mass in the clear blue sky, and exhibiting one of the beautiful vestiges of the Roman style. It is semicircular, adorned with two rows of closed arcades, of which the lower stones rest on cylindrical columns with ornamental capitals, and by an open gateway forming a series of little-arched arcades under the roof. Right and left two large towers, similarly ornamented, complete this very imposing architectural picture. This superb apse is not to archæologists the most interesting part of this beautiful structure. It is the fore-building, the *narthex* called the chapel of Charlemagne, which first attracts attention. It would make Saint Servais an unique monument of its kind if the Churches of Saint Bartholomew and Saint Servais at Liége in Belgium, did not possess the same peculiarity.

Of these three fore-buildings, the only ones known, Saint Servais is incontestably the most beautiful and the best preserved. Its frontage has not altogether escaped injury from age. It has stood the assaults of the weather, and, eaten into for centuries, it has glorious scars. It would seem also that immediately after its erection the walls must have lost their equilibrium, for they are supported by two enormous buttresses, resembling bridges in their massiveness and solidity.

The masonry of the buttresses appears to be of the same date as the walls supported by them, and its massiveness produces a singular effect. In disregard of the general lines of architecture, it considerably heightens the strange aspect of this sombre, bare and handsome *façade*.

Within, irrespective of this curious *narthex*, Saint Servais consists of a vast nave, with two low sides as far as the transept, and of a hemispherical choir surmounted by a demi-cupola. This forms a noble whole, the more suggestive as the old wooden ceiling of the ancient basilica was replaced by handsome pointed-arched vaults in the thirteenth or fourteenth centuries.

This is not the only addition with which that graceful epoch adorned the sturdy old church. A grand and well-proportioned cloister has been added, of which the vaulted roof is supported by a frieze of delicate columns, on which rest beautiful pointed arches, elegantly bayed, finely carved, and delicately ornamented with trefoil and quatrefoil.

All archæologists and architects do full justice to it. 'It is not only,' truly says M. Schayes, 'the most remarkable monument of the kind raised in Belgium in the middle ages, for such an eulogy would not express its real beauty; the porch of Saint Servais compares favourably with the most beautiful porches of the cathedrals of France, so richly endowed in this respect.'

For some years the internal and external restoration of this old basilica has been in hand; and those who have undertaken the heavy task are much to be commended, for they are executing it admirably. Saint Servais has the good fortune to be governed by a dean, who is as learned and artistic as he is kind and courteous. Calling to his aid the most skilled and enlightened agents, this worthy churchman has contrived to interest a host of rich and benevolent people in his much-loved basilica.

Money pours in from all sides, and the judicious use made of it attracts new gifts and givers.

In this restoration nothing is left to chance. Externally no column is recarved, no stone replaced, not a single stroke of the hammer struck, except under the advice of artists and archæologists to guide the hands of the skilled artizans engaged in this interesting restoration. Within, chapels are dressed in new altars, altars are re-covered with magnificent screens, and the marble pulpit, elegantly renewed, has returned to its proper place in the centre of the nave. Unhappily all these decorations, grand as they are, have in my eyes the defect of being modern. How much we would have preferred to them the old richness heaped up in this beautiful nave, of which, alas! there remains only the superb statue of Saint Servais, dating from the thirteenth century, and a few good paintings, two of which bear the name of Crayer, and a third is correctly attributed to Van Dyck!

To compensate a little for this, the treasury of the church is better furnished; its keeper, a learned priest, has taken pains to describe it with much knowledge and art; and his description, full of interesting facts, forms a thick volume of four hundred pages.

Of the precious objects preserved there, the post of honour properly belongs to the shrine containing the relics of Saint Servais, as it is the first object seen on entering the elegant chapel which contains the treasury. It is a pretty monument of copper, gilded, and chased, and adorned with a number of raised enamels and precious stones.

Its upper walls are covered with medallions full of curious figures, and on the sides are twelve semi-circular niches, separated by pilasters, and containing the twelve Apostles. The drawing of the figures, the character and nature of the ornamentation, and the shape of the capitals, show that this beautiful work was done in the twelfth century. Another cabinet presented by Charles Martel preceded this one, but no one knows what has become of it.

This precious piece of the goldsmith's art is not the only jewel secured to Saint Servais.

The key of the holy prelate, his cup, his pastoral crook, his crosier, his priestly vestments, and the portable altar on which he celebrated mass, must also be mentioned. In those distant times churches were few and far between, and no pastor went on a tour without carrying a consecrated stone on which to celebrate the Holy Communion.

All these objects are doubly precious, by the memoirs attached to them, as well as by the beauty of the work and the distant epoch to which they carry us back. But it must be confessed that their authenticity is open to question, when, in turning back to this distant period, we consider of what small importance the Bishopric of Maëstricht really was, and how very modest and simple was its pastor. Would they have buried in the grave of this venerable prelate such costly treasures, under a tomb covered with planks? Is it not more likely that these jewels are golden caskets, subsequently fashioned and fabricated to contain the whole or parts of these primitive objects? It is impossible to doubt the antiquity of the works, and they may be admitted to date back to Saint Hubert, the last Bishop of Maëstricht, or probably even to Saint Ronulf; but greater age than that is questionable. The work itself is there, to tell by its perfect style and finish the relatively recent time of its execution.

We have, moreover, an example of these later

enshrinements in a cup of Saint Servais, which was broken in the fifteenth or sixteenth century, and enclosed at that time in a goblet shaped like a pineapple. The cup was of glass, very simple and ordinary both as to form and workmanship. It was nevertheless (it is M. Willemsen who tells it) the work of God, for it was brought to the prelate by an angel.

If, at that time, divine work was so ordinary, is it not somewhat sacrilegious to attribute the workmanship of jewels so perfect as the key of the confessional, and the crozier to the hand of man?

In addition to the objects relating to Saint Servais are many other priceless curiosities. Among them is a golden cross with an ivory Saviour, enriched with precious stones, and dating from the tenth century; a curious shrine with an enamel cross of the twelfth century; relic tablets younger by a century; the bust of Saint John in silver, a very fine and interesting work; the ornament of Saint Agnes, a pretty silver-gilt jewel of the fourteenth century, enclosing the hair of the Virgin; a monstrance of the fifteenth century, in silver-gilt, elaborately foliated and beautiful in design; and four shrines in the shape of domes; but there would be no end to it if we were to describe all. But this treasury is far from complete, and we now only see a small part of what it contained in the last century.

When the revolutionary storm passed over the country, these treasures were scattered for the time;

but it would be wrong to attribute all that is missing to the revolution. To prevent their falling into the hands of the republican armies, they were divided among the canons, and it is no fault of the revolution if they or their heirs did not render a strict account of their trust. To form an idea of the rapacity of some of them, it is only necessary to remember the detainer of the relics of Saint Manilfe and Sandulf, who restored the despoiled Saints, but had melted and sold the leaden coffins which had contained them.

This sarcophagus, although of little saleable value, had a reputation for miracles which ought to have restrained the hand of the profaner. It was found that the Saints had emerged to assist at the dedication of the cathedral of Aix-la-Chapelle, when Charlemagne wanted 365 bishops for the ceremony, and the Pope could only supply 363. God, to please the glorious emperor, permitted the two venerable prelates to undertake this posthumous journey!

It was not in the last century alone that the treasury of Saint Servais was roughly attacked. In 1843 the church still possessed, besides the shrine of the saint himself, four other shrines, which, placed on the side altars of the choir, completed its ornamentation. In that year a broker tried to obtain them. They asked what they thought an exorbitant and prohibitory price, the dealer gave it, and so by this illegal sale these four precious shrines passed into the collection of Prince Soltykoff.

If the treasury has been treated with scanty respect, the archives have not fared better. Fragments of a goodly number of them are found in public collections, in the national library of Paris, that of the Dukes of Burgundy at Brussels, and in ten other places. Saint Servais does not even possess the oldest of its own diplomas relative to its Chapter. The most ancient mentioned in the chronological inventory of the charters and documents of the Church of Saint Servais dates no farther back than the year 1087, whereas in the archives of the State at Coblentz there are charters as old as 889, 898, 919, 994. Moreover, it is not long since an archæologist, M. C. de Borman, discovered in charters preserved in Paris, and which came from the old basilica, 'that the Chapter of Saint Servais had very long since lost all their title deeds anterior to the eleventh century.'

From what remains, after such dispersion and destruction, a good idea can be formed of the ancient wealth of this majestic sanctuary. Alongside of such sumptuous riches and luxuries of every kind all other churches fade, and one has scarcely the courage to glance at them. Yet there is close to Saint Servais a pretty Gothic chapel, which has been turned into a Calvinist church. In any other situation it would be most interesting, but here its great neighbour kills it, as it is only separated from the old basilica by a narrow street, dubbed Purgatory. Who is to determine on which side are the blessed?

The Church of the Dominicans, also formerly

celebrated, would in any other city have been of some repute. Within, it is of a fine Gothic form, in which are seen fragments of mural pictures. But after Saint Servais it is a mere debt of conscience to visit it, and not to regret that it has become an ordinary shop.

The Jesuits' church is a theatre, Saint Bartholomew's, and we should not dare to mention Saint Matthew's but for the great Christ in wood which is over the door, and has its legend.

Formerly it adorned the Convent of the White Ladies, and large as it is, is fabled to have come out of a walnut. This walnut had been brought from the Holy Land by a victorious Maëstrichter, who, during his pilgrimage, had picked it up on Calvary. The son of this man, on his return, asked him for a souvenir of his pious voyage, and he gave him this nut, which the child received with confidence. Later on he planted it, and, instead of a walnut tree, a crucifix grew up. The author of this anecdote declined to be responsible for the truth of the tradition —and I think it is advisable to share his prudence.

CHAPTER XXIV.

MAËSTRICHT (CONCLUSION)—THE TOWN HALL—THE LIBRARY—THE PROMENADES—*PIETERSBURG* AND THE BOHEMIANS.

HAVING described the religious monuments, we must now turn our attention to the civil buildings. Those which are of any archæological interest are few in number, and with the exception of a charming little dwelling of the sixteenth century in the Rue du Pont, which possesses some curious classical features ; of the *façade* of the old hotel de ville, and some pretty little gable houses in the *Brugstraat* and the *Neerstraat*, there is only the Town Hall worthy of a visit. Its noble proportions and the beautiful things contained in it will, however, detain us awhile.

It is situated in the middle of the grand market, which is a vast place, very regular, well built, and full of animation. It is at once an elegant and majestic structure, forming a massive pile nearly square, with four *façades*. Each of these frontages is two storied, ornamented with palisades, and resting on a dwarf ground floor. A great roof, cut on each face by a large attic, covers the building, and is surmounted by an elegant belfry, which replaces gracefully the old bell tower. A double staircase, ending in a large landing, leads to the vestibule. The double stair formerly was significant of its use. The town was under the double government of the bishops and of the Dukes of Brabant. The latter were the suzerains, and the former, as heirs of the rights and privileges of the Maëstricht bishops, of whom they were the successors, claimed the right to administer justice and levy taxes on the old town of Saint Servais. Finally, after much contention, they divided the objects of strife and the town into two parts. Every new dweller on his arrival had to declare which jurisdiction he elected; every old inhabitant followed that of his mother. The son of a Liégeoise belonged to the bishop's party, and those were held to be Brabanters whose mother was a dependent of the Duke of Brabant.

When the States took possession of Maëstricht, they simply claimed the rights of the duke, and the town remained divided as it was before, with the exception that the difference of origin then became the difference of religion.

Each of the two powers nominating their delegates, mounted the side of the staircase assigned to it, and both only met in the vestibule. This vestibule occupied the whole height of the building, and although a little heavy and massive, was not deficient in a certain dignity. It led to the principal rooms of the *Stadhuis*. There are on the ground floor the burgomaster's office, with beautiful coloured Chinese designs on gilt Cordova leather; the antechamber of the council, hung with superb Gobelin tapestry, representing the history of Moses; the council chamber, furnished in Flemish green, with a pretty ceiling painted by a talented native artist named Coelers, and lastly, the secretary's office furnished in a similar manner. All these rooms had majestic chimney-pieces, covered with allegorical pictures, which added to their imposing appearance. The greater part of these paintings partook of the strange character of the municipal power, which was formerly the 'particular sign' of the brave city.

On the first floor is the library, charmingly placed, and well cared for, but in too narrow a room. Besides a respectable collection of books, it contains a fine bust of Napoleon by Canova, a compulsory purchase when it was the chief place of the department of the Lower Meuse. Yet it was not a bad bargain, for it is the most artistic object contained in this sanctuary of thought. The library is not rich in rarities. With the exception of a few good manuscripts and a unique copy of Terence, it contains nothing out of the way. Two plates printed between 1470 and 1480, shown to us by M. Franquinet, formerly were especially interesting to Maëstricht. They are two little works by Matthew Herben, a native of the country, who when living, was rector of

D D

the schools of the Chapter of Saint Servais. The one is a scholastic work, the other a collection of three letters, which are still considered unique, and before its discovery these two copies were always thought to have been unpublished. These plates were not printed at Maëstricht, for printing was not introduced until long afterwards into the kindly city. It was only in 1552 that Jacques Bathen printed the first little work in a Maëstricht press, and the only copy which has survived was bought in 1846 for the royal library in Brussels.

Considering how many of the neighbouring towns were precocious in the matter, it is astonishing how stubborn Maëstricht was in the introduction of printing—between her and Louvain there is a century of distance. This tardiness is the more inexplicable that the gentle Brabantic city always contained a number of learned enquirers. She was likewise not always indifferent to the plastic arts; we have seen at Saint Servais and at Notre Dame what her sculptors could do. She possessed besides, in the thirteenth and fourteenth centuries, a school of painting, of which unhappily not a trace now remains, but which aided in the development of the schools on the banks of the Rhine. Half-way, however, between her and Roermond, is Maaseijk, the renowned birthplace of Hubert and Jan Van Eyck, the immortal predecessors of the great Dutch and Flemish masters. It has also at all times had poets, and if their reputation was not European, it was not that they were deficient in ability, but that they wrote in a language little understood beyond their town.

Maëstricht, indeed, has a peculiar dialect with a grammar and a syntax of its own, in which even now amusing dialogues and pretty comic operas are written. The people use no other idiom, and in their everyday discourse employ poetical terms and expressions, indicative of their love for their proper tongue, some of which when done into French lose neither their wit nor their sense. Thus they say of a lady favoured by nature that she has ' un beau gilet.' A woman of the lower classes will not threaten to box another woman's ears, but tell her to beware of the ' star ' of Maëstricht, a star which in the arms of the town has five points, resembling a 'five-leaved clove,' an expression still used in some remote corners of old France. In high society French is spoken, but no one is unacquainted with the vulgar tongue, which becomes more chaste and delicate when spoken by gentlefolks, yet is largely used. The Netherlanders complain because they do not understand a word of it, and it is amusing to hear them protest against this peculiarity.

'Maëstricht,' says one of them, 'is not yet a Dutch town. They have in the first place a special language in which books are written, next they speak French, and lastly they talk partly Dutch. They pay in Belgian francs and centimes; their cigars are five or ten centimes each. The people no longer go abroad in woollen coats, but in blouses; the women have ceased to wear caps or capes with metal fronting, but tie kerchiefs deftly round their heads.'

I have quoted this passage because it is typical and true to nature. What the author however does not tell us is that this population, proud in their ways, sympathetic and amiable, has a real regard for us. Nowhere have our misfortunes met with more sympathy than in and around Maëstricht. A striking instance of this is related. 'In 1871,' said a learned functionary to me, 'as soon as we heard of the capitulation of Paris, as I was a corresponding member of your Society of Agriculture, I raised 20,000 francs in a few days to supply seeds to your poor cultivators —each little hamlet sending its mite. But the subscription was stopped by a peremptory order from above, lest it should give offence over the border.'

On the other hand everything German is repelled. The Prussians, so insinuating and intrusive everywhere, have not overcome the antipathy of the Maëstrichtians, whose good-natured town has resisted their invasion. These feelings are intelligible enough. Maëstricht, in giving us her sympathy, is only repaying a pious debt, for during the last five centuries France has done her best to keep her honest citizens in good humour. Our Burgundy vineyards have always sent her the best of our produce, for if Arnhem is the Netherland town where the best Rhine wine is drunk, the best vintages of the Côte-d'Or find their way to Maëstricht. It may be that to this marvellous elixir the pretty Maëstrichtians owe their sprightly manner and their rosy complexions. They have only to be seen in the park, at the *Vrijthof*, the *Groote-market*, or in the streets for the great difference between them and their compatriots in the north to be seen. Everywhere are amiable smiles, lively talk, a gushing manner, and a light quick elastic step, somewhat at variance with the staid demeanour of the Dutch and even the Guelderland ladies. And so the public promenades are more gay and animated.

The most important of these promenades is on the bank of the Meuse. It is a kind of English garden, well designed, shady, and gaily bedded-out with beautiful flowers. Another much frequented promenade, a fine large place on which the military band plays, is called the *Vrijthof*, a 'Free Court,' which has been translated into 'parade ground' for some unknown reason, for at Maëstricht the names of streets are written in two languages, Dutch and French. On band days and summer evenings the *Vrijthof* is very lively. The shopkeepers and even the artizans put in an appearance, for there are several paper and porcelain works in the town.

But even were there not this large concourse of visitors, the *Vrijthof* would be the gayest place in the town, for it has on one of its sides the *Society of Momus*, and the *Courier of the Meuse*, where from all times the pretty Maëstrichtians have enjoyed their fun.

The *Society of Momus* is a club to be remembered.

All kinds of follies, masquerades, and queer notions are there organised. As for the *Courier of the Meuse*, it is a source of quiet gaiety and fun. An intolerant and fanatical paper, it plays the part of a pious Punch, and in Frenchified language indulges in amusing lectures, which are intended to be very serious. Its smallest descriptions are in dithyrambics. Everybody remembers its imaginative style: 'Clouds of crape making way for a sunny robe;' 'white roads transformed into rivers of men and women;' 'those byeways whence came hundreds of curious heads— women of fashion and women of lowly state, lawyers, and peasants '—all intended to announce the simple fact that the weather was fine, and the streets crowded.

But alas! everything degenerates, and the *Society* and the *Courier* are no longer what they were. The one having become reasonable and almost serious, organises patriotic cavalcades scientifically, and employs a learned archæologist to write the *libretto*. The other has ceased to indulge in preposterous hyperbole, and abandoned the Phrygian fashion to talk like the rest of the world. From time to time there is a slight relapse, but they have lost the sharpness of their ancient state.

Besides these inner promenades, Maëstricht has a hundred picnic places of excursion in its vicinity, some more picturesque than others. Of the number the most interesting is Saint Peter's Mount, called in the country the *Pietersberg*. It is there the famous quarries called, why I know not, the crypts of Maëstricht, are found. It is reached by a pretty road along the Meuse, or by a steep, lively path up the side of the mountain. These enormous quarries have six entrances. The quarry is usually entered by an anfractuosity of the mountain, which commands a little elevation surmounted by an ancient fort.

This construction is named the Mountain of Light (*Lichtenberg*), and it is conjectured that it was originally a Roman lighthouse. It is simply a feudal dwelling and nothing more; the vulture's nest of one of those ancient 'seigneurs' who profited by the quarrels of the Bishops of Liége with their subjects to ransom travellers and plunder villages. To enter the caves a torch and a guide are needed. These quarries, of which the plan was drawn up by the order of Napoleon I. in 1804, contain not less than 100,016 streets, and 11,332 great thoroughfares. Individuals without guides have frequently wandered about them and perished. The place is shown where, after many years, the corpses of three reformed ecclesiastics of the Order of Saint Francis were found. They were provided with a cord, which was fastened outside, but by rubbing against a flint stone it was cut, and the unhappy men wandering about in this sombre retreat, penetrated deeper and deeper into the galleries, where they died of inanition. In 1795, M. Faujas de St. Fond, who visited these galleries with Generals Daboult and Bolemont, found a workman who had perished from starvation many years before. An uncomfortable feeling is unavoidable in these interminable windings when one reflects on the prolonged and terrible agony which these victims must have undergone. This subterranean walk is, in truth, a somewhat melancholy affair; the tangled thread of never-ending ways crossing and recrossing forms an inextricable web of which the eye in vain essays to fathom the depths. And yet these apparently impenetrable highways have been often a refuge against persecutions and pursuits. For many times when armies ravaged the surrounding country, the peasantry found shelter and security in the quarries. In the sixteenth and seventeenth centuries, troops of gipsies took up their abode in them, and it needed the intervention of the Bishop of Liége to dislodge the 'Egyptians from the subterranean holes between Castert and Lichtenborch,' where they squatted down.

The quarries have held whole towns, and for thousands of years successive generations have found in them means of defence against their enemies. There are some galleries in the upper parts which must have been worked in the time of the Romans. In these galleries are seen, about five yards above the ground, the grooves formed by the rubbing of the chariot wheels against the walls, and the pillars are ornamented with heavy cornices. These cornices are not the only artistic remains found in the *Pietersberg*; there are likewise some coarse, rudimentary wall pictures, representing religious subjects, such as

Paradise and Hell. Other compositions are Pagan, and reproduce the deities of Olympus. In the depths naturalists have found the remains of antediluvian monsters, trees, and a natural fountain. Paleographers, again, may exercise their patience and ingenuity in deciphering millions of names inscribed by ancient and modern visitors, some of them of very remote date. Among them, a *Bregmatée* of 1039, a *Batibas* of 1229, a *Petre Nobbe* of 1408 : these are the oldest and are placed highest up. Beneath them are many others very illustrious, but of doubtful authenticity. Among the latter is that of Napoleon I., which has nearly disappeared by being hacked about. Half a century ago, Coustens, the grandfather of our guide, was forcibly held by two Prussian officers, while a third hacked at the name of the Emperor. His descendant still shed bitter tears in telling of his grandsire's rage and impotence to prevent the sacrilege. It was in truth a silly and unworthy act.

After having done the interior of the *Pietersberg*, which has been immortalised in song by Francis Halma, a Friesland poet, we visited the summit of the hill where there were said to be some Celtic monuments. Guided by an amiable engineer of the public works, we set out to discover them by a little slippery path, encumbered with brambles and stray branches, riddled with boggy places, cut into ravines by the rains, tacked on to the side of the hill, and overhanging a precipice 160 feet in depth. At every step the ravine expanded before us, and the magnificent panorama unfolded, alone made us oblivious of the perpetual danger of this giddy height.

At length, after a perilous journey in this tangled path, in which we lost and found our ravine a dozen times ; after braving the branches which struck our faces, and the thistles which impeded our feet, we found our way down to Belgian territory. There we came upon a good inn, kept by good people, and had a good bottle of sherry wine. Of Druidical monument we saw not a trace.

Having rested, there was nothing for it but to retrace our steps to Maëstricht by an easier way, and to end our journey by going quickly home, which we did. In the evening we dined for the last time in this charming town, and on the morrow set out for the Hague, wondering, with good reason, why so pretty a town, so well placed and so hospitable, with magnificent environs, picturesque landscapes, and a fine river, was so little frequented by the Netherlanders. They might find there all they seek for elsewhere ; fine sites, interesting promenades, superb monuments, an amiable people, excellent hotels, and cheap living . . . . but perhaps it is necessary to cross frontiers, and spend largely for true enjoyment ? We leave the solution of this question to others.

CHAPTER XXV.

CONCLUSION.

ON arriving at the Hague we could say: *Inveni portum* : our voyage was at an end. We had now only to return to our respective hearths, and to forget our fatigues in well-earned repose; but some friends, anxious to fête our return, had determined otherwise.

Warned of our arrival, they had organised a dinner in the best club at the Hague, the *Witte Societeit*, and there, in the evening we found ourselves for the last time, glass in hand, surrounded by loyal hearts and true friends.

The feast was sumptuously served, and above all, seasoned by the heartfelt joy, ever experienced after long absence on finding oneself in the midst of those dear to us. Nature herself seemed to share our lightness of heart, and to fête us. The last rays of the setting sun gilded the substantial dwellings of the *Plein*, a genial breeze trembled in the tops of the great trees, and the silence was only broken by distant songs, lost in the depths of the *Voorhout*.

We were silent for a moment. A cheery voice proposed our healths, and champagne cups were filled and emptied in our honour.

In response to this kindly toast, I, the sole Frenchman there, rose, and drank to the Netherlands.

According to the Dutch custom of saying a few words, I endeavoured to recount the object of our journey and its results, and to condense in a few sentences the impressions it had taken months to form.

Spontaneous expressions are always the best, for they have a stamp of sincerity, absent otherwise. On my return at night I took note of my short improvisation, and here it is, as far as I could remember it:

'My friends, I drink to your country! to the Netherlands! To that generous country, so industrious, so honest, so hospitable, and above all so thorough in its love of independence!

'I drink to the glorious past and to the future of the Netherlands.

'We have traversed that generous land, and from one end to the other, from Groningen to Maëstricht we have witnessed the modest expansion of those high qualities of the people, that substantial probity, that unchangeable pursuance of good, that thorough love of country, which still distinguish the old Batavian race.

'Assuredly, in that extent of country, we have met and measured many different shades.

'The soil, the types of men, the costumes, the

manners, the religion, all undergo constant change and modification—but what of that? Does the head resemble the foot, and is the stomach like any other organ? And yet, varied as they may be, they constitute but one body, warmed by the same blood, and moved by the same head!

'So, you may take my word for it, the old Batavian blood is in full flow on your blessed soil, and the good heart of the country beats in unison with those of all her children!

'And yet the individuality of this heroic corner of the world is disputed. Men have said in print that it was part of a great whole, without reflecting that it was itself complete, an indivisible unity twice conquered by your ancestors, first from the elements and then from foreign domination.

'But what would become of this land if it were wrested from the hands of the descendants of those who have built it up, watered it with their blood, and fertilised it with their genius? And where would justice be if a capricious stroke of the pen, wielded by a fanatic savant, or if an unscrupulous political reign, could extinguish the sacrifices and holy immolations of ages.

'Do we live in an age when numbers efface genius? Are figures our only factors? No. Numbers are nothing. Reconstruct without shame the map of Europe, effacing frontiers which are in their way, and disposing of people without their consent. All the steps of the operation have been conducted under your eyes, and supported by impartial proofs, not open to suspicion, for the documents produced date before the debate.

'I have been so scrupulous as even to withhold my impressions, omitting in my recital all that could recall the objects of our voyage, letting the facts speak for themselves.

'Can MM. Daniel and Kischhoff discover in this work anything in support of their strange annexations? I ask, what reasons can they assign?

'Are they based on manners, usage, ethnical characters? Remember Delfzijl and Nieuw-Beerta.

'Is it sympathy? Recollect Almelo, Oldenzaal and Maëstricht.

'What more? language, history—but where have we heard German spoken? Dutch is ever in possession of the field, and the language of Vondel alone is used. One province is perhaps an exception—Limbourg; but French and not German is the language of society there.

'As for history, what countries, say our geographers, with small exceptions, belonged to the German Empire, and, in fact, until 1866 to the Germanic Confederation?

'It is light, it is heat which illumine and warm the world. Who would have remembered the armies of Darius if they had not basked in the sun of Marathon?

'History is shown to protest with indignation against these theories of invasion, and the luminous track which your glorious history has left on the annals of Europe is too dazzling to allow of this grand fact to be effaced by fantastic policy or geographical illusions.

'The future is in your hands, for you have preserved the great qualities of your ancient race! But, come what will, the whole world owes to your country too many shining lights, ever to forget the debt of gratitude contracted by all mankind to the united provinces. My friends, To the Netherlands!'

These words, read again eight months afterwards, are an exact reproduction of impressions gathered in this long and painstaking journey. It is for you, dear reader, to decide which is right—the conscientious traveller who has completely traversed the country, the scrupulous archæologist who has visited its monuments, ransacked its archives, and restored to life its history, or fanciful philosophers, who from the depths of things devise a strange pretext for the annexation of a kingdom, that a slice of its territory was for thirty years nominally united to the Confederation! A strange pretension thus to trace back beyond the rule of the House of Burgundy in order to revive rights in abeyance for four centuries.

And these rights, so loftily proclaimed, what is their importance?

Of two hundred Dutch towns, four only ever directly belonged to the Emperor, and three of these— Zwoll, Deventer, and Kampen, were only in his possession for a few years. They were surrendered to him to furbish up his nearly tarnished glory, and to enable him to put on a good face. But as soon as they were able to break the chain, they repudiated the repugnant dependence.

One city alone remained to him for some time, Nymegen, the indomitable city, never subjected, rebelling against all masters, and having for its motto 'MELIUS EST BELLICOSA LIBERTAS QUAM PACIFICA SERVITAS.'

And this noble maxim would be endorsed by the whole of Holland, if a people were to leave the regions of Utopian geography, to enter those of violent annexations, a nation of invaders unmindful of the respect due from humanity to a generous nation which has always preserved its dignity and its sense of duty.

www.ingramcontent.com/pod-product-compliance
Lightning Source LLC
Chambersburg PA
CBHW020525300426
44111CB00008B/552